WHAT CAREER ~~RESULTS~~ YOUR
ASTROLOGICA~~L~~

WHAT SIGNS ~~MAKE~~ ~~THE BEST~~
BOSSES... A~~ND THE MOST~~
PRODUCTIV~~E EMPLOYEES?~~

CAN FIRE AND WATER
MIX IN THE WORKPLACE?

THE
SUN
SIGN
CAREER
GUIDE

can give you an important leg up on the corporate ladder!
Now you can choose the perfect career and ideal working
environment—simply by recognizing when the signs are
right...and when they're very wrong!

ROBERT G. WALKER (Taurus) is a trained Drama and
Movement therapist. In addition to his work in the thera-
peutic community, he also teaches at the Centre for Psychological Astrology in London.

HOWARD SASPORTAS (Aries), author, psychologist
and lecturer, is recognized as one of the world's leading
consultant astrologers—a recipient of the Gold Medal for
the Faculty of Astrological Studies Diploma Exam and a
co-founder of The Centre for Psychological Astrology.

They are both the resident astrologers for *SELF* Magazine.

THE SUN SIGN CAREER GUIDE

**ROBERT G. WALKER &
HOWARD SASPORTAS**

AVON BOOKS ◆ NEW YORK

AVON BOOKS
A division of
The Hearst Corporation
1350 Avenue of the Americas
New York, New York 10019

First Avon Books Printing: September 1991

Contents

Introduction

> Man's main task in life is to give birth to himself,
> to become what he potentially is.
>
> *Erich Fromm*

Our lives aren't always simple and clear cut. In this uncertain and fast-changing world, people have to ask themselves some pretty difficult questions:

- How can I make enough money to live?
- Will I ever find a relationship that works?
- I want to start a family, but I don't want to give up my career. Can I manage both?
- Should I put everything into this relationship, or keep my freedom?
- Could I make it as an actress?
- Should I give up my secure nine-to-five day and try working for myself?
- WHAT SHOULD I DO WITH MY LIFE?

It isn't easy finding answers, especially when the decisions we make affect other people's lives as well as our own. So how can we be *sure* we're doing the right thing?

Every year more and more people are turning to astrology to help them make the right choices. And they're discovering, often to their surprise, that this very ancient art is a sound basis for decision-making in the modern world. This book opens up the wisdom of astrology to offer you practical advice and creative guidance on your career, one of life's most important and pressing concerns.

7

If you're young and just starting your working life, you're probably asking yourself what kind of career would give you the most satisfaction. If you're a little older, you may have reached a point when you're questioning the career you've always known—is there another line of work that would be more creative, or offer you greater security and peace of mind? At any age, finding the right career presents a challenge, so where do you start looking? It would be far easier to figure out which direction to take if you could look at yourself from a new perspective and get a clearer idea of your true potentials and what it is you really need to be happy and fulfilled.

That's where this book will help you. Astrology can point you in the right direction by equipping you with a map you should never go anywhere without—a map of yourself. In the past, sceptics have laughed and asked what connection there could be between the month you were born in and your future career. Well, now the sceptics can laugh on the other side of their faces, especially since recent studies demonstrate the strong connections between astrology and career. In the 1950s, Michel Gauquelin, a French psychologist, initiated a massive statistical survey, with the intention of disproving astrology once and for all. He gathered together the horoscopes of many thousands of people working in different fields to see if there was any relationship between their charts and their professions. To his surprise (and dismay) he was forced to conclude that the positions of the planets at a person's time of birth have a marked effect on his or her eventual choice of work. Then in 1984, Professor Alan Smithers of Manchester University collected the birthdates of nearly two and a half million people, and examined their careers in relation to their month of birth. The result was once again an indication of obvious links between the times of year when people are born and the careers they choose. Of course, the facts startled the logic of scientists and statisticians, but they came as no surprise to practising astrologers.

For example, the majority of the artists studied in the Smithers survey had birthdays in late April and May, in the sign of Taurus—a sign ruled by Venus, the goddess of beauty. The majority of secretaries were born in late June and July under the sign of Cancer, traditionally known for its ability to serve the needs of others. And late March to late April turned out to be when most show business entertainers made their entrances, the period governed by the extraverted, dramatic sign of Aries. Gauquelin's research and the Smithers study are just two of many statistical surveys which have shown the same results: the time of year you are born gives a good indication of your innate skills and talents. And when you know what you're good at, you've taken a big step along the road to success.

At this point, maybe you're a little worried. If you're a Taurus but you're not an artist, does that mean you've made a mess of your career chances? That isn't necessarily the case, so relax. Obviously not all Bulls go charging into painting, and not all secretaries are Crabs (although there are bosses who would argue with that one). Artists are also known to pop out in Pisces during late February and March; and you could be a Lion (late July and August) and be a roaring success as a secretary. Just because you're an Aries Ram, it doesn't mean you're only suited to a career on stage—there are many other fields besides show business which you could happily dominate with your usual flair. Keep reading. In the next chapter, we'll explain this more fully, and explore astrology itself in greater detail.

How Astrology Can Help You

A lot of people think astrology is a joke—and who can blame them? When you sneak a peak at your horoscope in the newspaper—just to see if today's the day when you'll finally make your fortune or meet a tall, dark stranger—you can't help noticing that the astrology column is often on the same page as the strip cartoons. If astrology seems like a giggle, a bit of fun, a trick to sell more newspapers and nothing more, it only goes to show that you shouldn't judge by appearances. Astrology is a subject that has been taken very seriously by wise and learned people since the earliest days of recorded history.

Our earliest ancestors didn't have a sun sign column advising them what to do, but they were always on the lookout for clues. We know that as long ago as 15000 BC, people were carving notches on animal bones as a way of recording the movements of the sun and moon. That was only the beginning. By 3000 BC in ancient Babylonia, the early astrologer–astronomers (in those days it was all one subject) were watching the heavens and carefully recording all their observations. For instance, they saw that when the constellation of Aries was overhead, it was a time of fertility and new life. They also noticed that plant growth corresponded with the phases of the moon, and it didn't take them long to catch on to the idea that certain times of the month were favourable for planting, and other times were not.

These early astrologers were priests, men of high rank in their countries at a time when astrology figured prominently in the running of national affairs. A ruling monarch wouldn't dream of making a major decision on a matter of state without first asking his astrologers whether the day was auspicious. From its beginnings in Babylonia, astrology found its way over to Egypt, where it figured in the building of the Great Pyramid at Giza. As the New Testament tells us, the Hebrews were next to take up astrology—and they in turn taught it to the Greeks and Romans. In the second century AD, the great astrologer-astronomer Ptolemy gathered together all the astrological knowledge of his time in the earliest surviving astrological textbook, which is still in print and collecting royalties today!

When Christianity came in, astrology went out of fashion and favour in the West. But it thrived in the East, and thanks to the mathematical genius of the Arabs, it was in better shape than ever when it made its European comeback at the end of the eighth century. By the Renaissance in the fifteenth century it was flourishing. Great families of the period, like the Medicis in Florence, consulted astrologers on everything—marriages, deaths, political intrigues, even the erecting of a new statue or monument to see whether or not the signs were favourable. Tycho Brahe, Kepler, Galileo and Newton—prominent scientists of their time—all studied astrology. The first Queen Elizabeth employed John Dee as her personal stargazer. Before she even got on to the English throne, she needed all the help astrology could give her to keep up with her sister, Bloody Mary, who always had an astrologer on hand. But even when their predictions were spot on, astrologers didn't always get the appreciation they deserved. Poor William Lilly, the great English astrologer, accurately foretold both the Great Plague in 1665 and the Great Fire of London in 1666, and then got blamed for starting them! And before that, he had the unenviable task of advising both Oliver Cromwell and King Charles I (which was pretty tricky considering they were at war with each other at the time!).

For reasons hard to explain (but probably related to the rise of Calvinism, rationalism and capitalism) astrology all but disappeared again for two hundred years. But now in the twentieth century it is steadily regaining credibility, due mainly to the recognition it received in the work of the eminent Swiss psychologist Jung, and more recently as a result of the remarkable Gauquelin studies. Nowadays astrology turns up in the most unexpected places. It has been used by the American and Israeli governments (and probably others that we don't know about). Psychologists and psychiatrists are turning to astrology to gain deeper insight into their patients. In industry and commerce, personnel managers and business executives are using astrology to give them greater understanding of how other people work. And now, with this book, *you* can use astrology as well to help understand yourself better and sort out your career and work prospects.

As Above, So Below

Johannes Kepler, the famous German astronomer, once wrote that 'nothing exists nor happens in the visible sky that is not sensed in some manner by the faculties of earth and nature'. Which is a fancy way of saying there is a connection between what goes on up there and what happens down here on earth. You're probably aware that the tides are affected by the moon, but did you know that things as different as oysters, potatoes and rats are influenced by its changing phases as well? In one experiment, rats were locked up in a windowless room for a number of months. They didn't have a clue whether it was day or night, and yet their peaks of activity correlated with the moon's position in the sky. Our human bodies are seventy per cent water, so no wonder we feel the moon's influence as well. Surgical patients bleed more at the time of the full moon, and studies done by different scientists indicate marked changes in the electrical emissions of the body which coincide both with the seasons and the moon's cycles.

Admit it, don't you sometimes feel more stirred up than usual when the moon is full? The Philadelphia Police Department published a report called *The Effect of Full Moon on Human Behaviour*, which confirmed an old wives' tale that people have more trouble controlling themselves when the moon is at its peak. And if you think the moon is the only culprit, you should look into a study done by a Japanese scientist Maki Takata, demonstrating the direct effects of periodic sunspot activity on the properties of human blood.

These studies are all very interesting and important in their own way, but the purpose of this book is not to prove to you the scientific validity of astrology. So let's get down to business and look more closely at what a horoscope is, and in particular, how your sun sign is a clue to your career potentials.

The Big Picture

Your sun sign is the sign the sun was in when you were born. But there's so much more to a full birthchart (which is another word for horoscope) than just your sun. A complete birthchart is a map or picture of what the heavens looked like at the time and place of your birth–it doesn't just tell you where the sun was, it shows the positions of the moon, Mercury, Venus, Mars and the other planets as well. To explain this a bit more clearly, we need to define some of the terms astrology uses.

As far as astrology is concerned, the sun is moving in a circular path around the earth. Of course we *know* that it's really the other way round, that the earth moves around the sun, but astrology is based on how things *look* to us on earth. The sun's apparent circular path is called the **ecliptic**, more commonly known as the **zodiac**. The circle of the zodiac is divided into twelve **signs** of equal size, starting with Aries, then Taurus, then Gemini, and so on until the last sign of Pisces. Each of these twelve separate signs represent different styles of behaving in life. For instance, the sign of Aries is impulsive, energetic, and loves the excitement of getting something new started. The sign of Taurus displays persistence and stamina—the ability to stay with something once it's started. Gemini is changeable and adaptable, alternating back and forth from one thing to another; and the sign of Cancer behaves in an emotional and feeling way. In the course of this book, we'll be discussing the qualities of every sign much more fully.

The word planet comes from the Greek word meaning wanderer, which is precisely what the planets do—they travel through the different signs of the zodiac. (Remember, in astrology the sun and moon are called planets as well.) Your birthchart shows what signs the sun, moon and other planets happened to be moving through when you were born. So if you were born on 24 April, we know for certain that your sun is in Taurus, but your moon could be in Cancer, your Venus in another sign like Pisces, and your Mars might be round in Virgo, all depending on the year you were born. Astrologers have a book called an ephemeris listing the placements of the planets for every day of every year.

Every planet represents one of the basic drives or urges that exist in you. The drive of the planet will be expressed in the style of the sign it was in when you were born. For instance, the planet Venus symbolizes your urge to relate to other people, and how you behave in relationships. So if you were born with the *planet* Venus in the *sign* of Aries, your drive to relate (Venus) is strongly influenced by the sign of Aries—which means you have an innate tendency to leap impetuously into new partnerships. But if your Venus is placed in the more cautious sign of Taurus, you'll be more slow and steady in matters of the heart—you'll take your time before committing yourself to a new relationship, but chances are you'll stay in it for as long as possible when you do. Are you starting to get the picture? Each planet describes a type of activity or drive. The sign a planet is in at birth depicts how that activity or drive is executed or carried out. In other words, you could say that planets are *verbs*, and the sign placement of the planet is like an *adverb* which describes how the planet is expressed. Take the example of Mars in Cancer. Mars asserts itself wherever it is. In the sign of Cancer it does it in an emotional way.

In addition to the planet-sign combinations that were happening in the heavens when you were born, there are a few other factors in your full astrological chart which enable an astrologer to get a complete picture of your true nature. The most important of these is your **ascendant**, which is the sign that was coming over the eastern horizon at the time and place of your birth. The ascendant or **rising sign** describes how you meet the world, and how you approach everything in life—for example, whether you're direct and assertive (an Aries or Sagittarius ascendant), shy and reserved (a Cancer or Pisces ascendant) or wary and cautious of things around you (a Virgo or Capricorn ascendant). Once the ascendant sign is determined, the astrologer can then calculate the twelve areas of the chart known as the **houses**—departments of life where various kinds of activities take place: one house has to do with how you deal with money, another house is concerned with what happens to you on long journeys, another describes how you interact with your mother, and so on. In addition to houses, your full birthchart also shows your planetary **aspects**—the angular relationship between the different planets at the time of your birth. If you're curious what your complete chart looks like, you'll need to contact a trained astrologer. Based on your date, place and time of birth, the astrologer will be able to tell you the sign placements of all your planets, what your ascending sign is, and what the houses and aspects look like in your personal chart.

We're focusing in this book on the sign the sun was in at your birth, (If you're uncertain of your sun sign, please refer to the table on page 18.) Every planet-sign combination in your horoscope 'says' something about you, but your sun sign is the most important sign in your chart—the one which most accurately describes what you're like underneath it all. So let's look at that a little more closely right now.

Your Sun Sign

Most astrologers consider the sign your sun is in as the special key to unlock your deepest potentials. Your sun sign reveals those qualities, capabilities and strengths which, when you've developed them, give you the feeling you have discovered who you truly are. *If you can find positive ways to express the nature of your sun sign, you'll be happier and more fulfilled in life.* Of course, the work you do isn't the only way to give expression to your sun sign, but when you consider how much of your life is taken up with work and earning a living, it makes sense to be in a job that offers you the chance to make the most constructive use of your sun sign. This book highlights the careers best suited to your sun sign and points the way to the right occupation for you.

Trying to twist your body into an awkward shape is very uncomfortable. Likewise, trying to fit into a way of life that isn't *you* will only make you miserable. People born with the sun in Taurus, for example, don't like a lot of change, but they possess an innate ability to stick with one task and see it through to the end, no matter how long that takes. In contrast, people born with the sun in Gemini aren't at their best in routine sedentary work, where they're doing the same thing in the same place day after day—they need a lively job which gives them the chance to move around and use their quick, versatile minds and natural communication abilities. So what's the point of Geminis forcing themselves to do the kind of work that suits Taurus people better, and why should Taurus people be put through the agony of having to do a job which takes them all over the place when they really aren't good at adjusting and adapting quickly to new environments?

Of course, people with the sun in Taurus are sometimes born with their ascendant or a few planets in the sign of Gemini. If that's the case, they'll have some of the restlessness and the quick adaptability that you'd associate with Gemini, but their deepest nature will always be most closely aligned with the sign of Taurus. As they discover and develop themselves more fully, their Taurus qualities will shine through more clearly. Your sun sign is the heart of your horoscope. If you neglect your sun sign traits, no matter how many other signs are emphasized in your chart, you aren't being true to who you really are.

Plant an apple seed, water it and care for it in the right way, and you won't be surprised when it grows steadily into an apple tree. You'd be shocked if it turned out to be a pear tree, or a koala bear, or an office block. Apple seeds make apple trees—that's their nature. Astrology is a reminder that you too are a seed with the potential to grow into what you are meant to become. Your astrological chart, and in particular your sun sign, reveals the nature of your seed. Feeling guilty about what you aren't naturally good at will get you nowhere, but concentrating on developing your innate aptitudes, strengths and talents will open the door to greater fulfilment and success.

Aries	21 March–20 April
Taurus	21 April–21 May
Gemini	22 May–21 June
Cancer	22 June–22 July
Leo	23 July–23 August
Virgo	24 August–22 September
Libra	23 September–23 October
Scorpio	24 October–22 November
Sagittarius	23 November–21 December
Capricorn	22 December–20 January
Aquårius	21 January–18 February
Pisces	19 February–20 March

Each year the sun moves into and out of the signs at a different time, and sometimes on slightly different dates. Which is why if you were born on 22 December, let's say, you could find yourself called a Sagittarius in some books and a Capricorn in others. If you are born on or very near to one of the changeover dates, you'll have to check in the ephemeris for your year of birth or consult an astrologer who will tell you which sun sign you are.

Things You'll Need to Know

We'll be devoting a chapter to each sign, beginning with Aries and finishing up with Pisces. These chapters are divided into several different parts, each with its own subheading. To get the most from this book, you'll need to know a little more about the kind of information you'll find under each section.

The Four Elements

In astrology, the twelve signs of the zodiac are grouped under the four elements—fire, earth, air and water. The three signs belonging to each element differ in many respects from one another, but they share an approach to life that reflects the element category they're in.

The Fire Signs *(Aries, Leo, Sagittarius)* Fire represents pure spirit. All fire signs radiate a great deal of energy—they're warm, active, enthusiastic, and usually like a good dose of adventure and excitement in their lives. The worst thing you can do to any of the fire signs is to trap them or tie them down—they need plenty of room to explore their full potentials, even if they do occasionally fly a bit too high for their own good and wind up falling flat on their faces. They like being in charge—try telling them what to do and how to do it and you're liable to get your whiskers singed. If you know fire sign people who always look hangdog and depressed, it's probably because they haven't yet found the right outlet for their powerful drive, creative imagination and abundant energy.

The Earth Signs *(Taurus, Virgo, Capricorn)* Earth signs are just what their name implies, down-to-earth. They're in their element when they have their feet well and truly planted on the ground. They're cautious, sensible, and less spontaneous than other signs in the zodiac. Fire signs see the future possibilities in something, but earth signs see what's right there in front of their noses. What's been tried and tested is good enough for them, and they aren't always out looking for new ways of doing things. As workers they're usually diligent and dependable, and they like to see concrete and tangible results for all their efforts. If earth signs don't appear to have these qualities, it probably means that they have other signs strong in their chart which modify the typical earth sign nature.

The Air Signs *(Gemini, Libra, Aquarius)* Air signs are the 'thinkers' of the zodiac, who prefer to stand back and look at life objectively. They value reason and fairness—in fact, the thing that upsets them most is injustice. In their efforts to live up to their high ideals and principles, they sometimes lose touch with their gut reactions and true feelings, which is probably why it's so hard for them to understand anybody who is more emotional by nature. Like the fire signs, they need a lot of space and freedom to explore life. They love to exchange ideas and relate to other people, but when you try to fence in an air sign, they run a mile. Gemini and Libra are the most fickle, changeable and indecisive of the three; Aquarians are steadier in their thinking and beliefs, but every once in a while they'll shock you by doing a complete turnaround.

The Water Signs *(Cancer, Scorpio, Pisces)* Water signs are feeling types which means they're pretty emotional and incredibly sensitive to any environment they're around. They pick up hidden undercurrents in the atmosphere and all the subtle things most other signs wouldn't even notice. Sometimes they hide their vulnerable and sensitive side beneath a tough outer shell, but underneath they're quite easily hurt and offended. Periodically, all water sign people need time alone. However, when they care for you, there's really nothing they wouldn't do. Cancer and Pisces people are usually quite shy and reticent, while Scorpio is the most naturally dynamic and powerful of the three. All water signs are strongly swayed by their moods, so you may never really know what to expect from day to day . . . or hour to hour!

The symbol associated with each sign

Besides a ruling planet, every sign has a symbol. You're probably familiar with them already—Aries the Ram, Taurus the Bull, Gemini the Twins, and so on. It's amazing how much you can learn about a sign by just reflecting on its symbol, so you'll find a few pages in each chapter to get you started. Cancers, to take an easy example, really can be a bit crab-like at times (not to mention crabby); some Leos even *look* a bit like Lions. Of course, not all Virgos look like Virgins . . . but that's another story, and you can read about it when you come to that sign. Sometimes, just for the sake of a little variety, we refer to a sign by its symbol, so don't be surprised (or insulted) if every now and then we refer to Aries people as Rams, Virgos as Virgins, Capricorns as Goats, Pisces people as Fish, etc.

The ruling planet of a sign

Every sign has a 'ruling planet'—a planet whose natural qualities resonate with the style of the sign. Understanding the ruling planet of a sign gives you more insight into how the sign operates. For instance, people born in Aries are ruled by Mars, the god of war, which explains why they sometimes get a little overexcited or even quite warlike. Geminis are ruled by the changeable Mercury, and 'mercurial' is often an apt description for their up-and-down behaviour.

You'll notice that some planets rule two signs. For instance, Venus is ruler of both Taurus *and* Libra; Mercury governs Gemini *and* Virgo—but don't worry, this will all be explained when you read about those signs. Also, certain signs have two rulers—for instance, Scorpio is ruled by Mars *and* by Pluto; Uranus governs Aquarius along with Saturn; and Pisces is associated with both Jupiter and Neptune. There's a good reason why some signs ended up with two rulers. At the time rulership was first determined, only seven planets—the Sun, Moon, Mercury, Venus, Mars, Jupiter and Saturn—were known. When Uranus was discovered, astrologers observed its nature and realized that there was an important dimension to the sign of Aquarius which Saturn alone didn't explain. Likewise, Neptune's watery qualities fitted perfectly with Pisces even though the sign already had Jupiter as its ruler; and while Scorpio has an aggressive and Mars-like side, it's generally agreed that Pluto more accurately describes the depth and intensity Scorpions are famous for.

Temperament and types

A portion of each chapter is devoted to examining the sign's basic temperament. This will help you understand the overall style and attitude each birth sign exhibits. Please bear in mind that nobody has all their ten planets in Aries—or any other sign, come to that. Nobody is just an Aries, just a Taurus, or just a Fish. If you have a lot of planets in a sign other than your sun sign, you won't behave all the time like a typical example of that sun sign. (This can also be the case if your ascendant or rising sign is very different in nature from your sun sign.) Which is why all the people born under any one sun sign aren't carbon copies of each other, although they'll have many things in common. But as we said in the last chapter, *the sun sign is still the most important sign in your chart, and unless you develop its qualities, talents and aptitudes you'll never feel entirely fulfilled.*

The sun takes roughly thirty days to move through a sign, and in the section after temperament you'll find a short section which says a little more about the people born specifically in the first ten days of the sign, the middle ten days, and the last ten days of the sign. These divisions are called decanates, and they stem from an old astrological tradition.

The signs and work

There's a famous story told by Sir Christopher Wren, the architect of St Paul's. One day he was walking around the site of the cathedral as it was being built, and he observed the labourers at their work. Noticing three masons all involved in more or less the same tasks, he became curious to know how each man saw the job he was doing.

The first man told him: 'I'm laying bricks.'
The second man answered: 'I'm earning a few bob.'
The third man replied: 'I'm helping to build a great cathedral.'

As this anecdote illustrates, work means different things to different individuals. In each chapter on the signs, we've included a section analysing how people born under that sign approach the whole issue of work. There's also an exercise to help you sort out the kinds of problems which your sign commonly encounters in this area of life.

Your sun sign career guide

In the career guide, you'll find a colourful survey of the kinds of occupations which would offer you a chance to express and develop the aptitude naturally associated with your sign. To make it more interesting, we've included examples of successful and famous personalities—everybody from Mae West to Mussolini, from Mata Hari to Harry Houdini, from Joan Collins to Joan of Arc—who have brought a strong flavour of their particular sun signs to their chosen line of work.

But supposing you're a Cancer who wants to be an airline pilot, and you see that our list of suggested careers for Cancer doesn't include pilots. Does this mean you're destined to fail or doomed to crash? That isn't how it works. Each sign has something unique to offer in any chosen career. Although flying around the world isn't the first thing that comes to mind when we think of a Crab, Cancer's sensitivity and charm could produce the type of pilot who is able to reassure first-time flyers that everything is secure and well taken care of. Everybody would feel at home with a Cancer in the cockpit! Even a hundred miles above water, the Crab would still be doing its thing.

Which brings us to an important point—in the end it isn't so much what you do, but *how* and *why* you do it. Two people can be doing the same job, but they'll bring the particular qualities of their respective sun signs into it. You can see this most clearly in the styles and achievements of writers, musicians, painters, actors and other artists born in different signs. For this reason, we have listed creative careers under every one of the sun signs. What's more, different signs go into the same profession, but for quite different reasons. A Leo might choose flying for the glamour and prestige of the job; a Sagittarius would like the idea of travel and adventure; and some Taurus people might even consider flying just to get their hands on all those duty-free goods! So no matter what you do, pay heed to the nature of your sign and its basic needs. Fulfilling what your sun sign asks of you points the way forward to satisfaction not only in work, but in your whole life as well.

Bosses, employees, colleagues and compatibilities

Queen Elizabeth, the Queen Mother, once remarked, 'Work is the rent we pay for life'. More than that, it's one of the ways we share ourselves with the world. Our place of work can be a place to prove our worth and make money, but it's also a place to find friends, create enemies or meet lifelong partners. No matter what career we choose, its's hard to get away from other people. Our interactions with customers, bosses, employees and colleagues form a major part of our working lives. Even those of us who aren't very social and who truly prefer our own company to anyone else's, nonetheless benefit at times from another person's support, advice, encouragement and appreciation. In any case, we can learn a lot from other people's differences—even if they do annoy us. To help you make the most of your working relationships, we've included a section on how your sun sign gets on with all the other signs. And in each of the chapters on the signs, you'll also find a description of what people born under that sign are like as bosses, employees and colleagues. If you have a better understanding of the people you work with, your chances of working together peacefully and productively are greatly improved.

All the astrological signs put together form a circle, a whole. Like the different instruments in an orchestra, each sign plays its own part in the overall composition. In a world which sometimes seems fragmented and where our individual lives often feel incomplete, it's important to remember that each of us has something special to offer. Read on, and you'll discover what that is.

Aries

Element: Fire
Symbol: The Ram
Ruler: Mars

The Sign of the Ram

The fact that Aries is the first sign says quite a lot about Aries people: they like to come first, they want to be Number One. You won't find many sheepish, average or woolly characters born in the sign of the Ram. Every Aries woman and man feels unique and needs to be noticed.

Sheep aren't famous for their individuality. When you've seen one you've seen them all. They tend to follow each other blindly, and they don't seem to mind much where they're going. Not so the ram! An elderly Sussex farmer who has worked with sheep for over half a century scratched his forehead and laughted wryly when we asked him to tell us all about rams:

Well, I'll tell you one thing, you'll have to look a long way before you'll see an animal that's as cussed and awkward as some of the rams I've had to deal with in my time!

When a frisky ram isn't out in front being the big shot, he's charging off somewhere *he* wants to go—and don't let anybody try to stop him! The farmer proudly exhibited a broad-browed young male tethered in his front garden:

Better than a guard dog, he is. He'll belt into anything or anybody that tries to get past the gate. He doesn't stop to ask questions!

Like the ram, you Aries people always want to make an impact or impression. It just isn't your style to leave things the way they are. If you ignore something, it means you don't think it's worth bothering with. What you don't knock down, you straighten up or move around—we're talking about anything from the office furniture to somebody else's private life. You have something to say, you go ahead and say it. You see what needs doing, you do it. Simple. Or is it?

Rams know better than most that the quickest distance between two points is a straight line. More than any other sign, you're able to set unimportant considerations aside and get on with the job in hand. Your direct, confident approach usually wins you attention and admiration, but have you ever noticed that sometimes you seem to irritate other people? It's one of those unfortunate facts of life that some observers will see you acting in your typical straightforward and no-nonsense way, and criticize it as arrogant and insensitive. Have you ever stopped to wonder why?

The truth is you really are a bit like a battering ram at times. You get carried away in the heat of the moment and forget to take other people into account. Certainly you don't mean to do it, but you're so busy asserting yourself there's no time to be receptive to everything that's going on around you! It's not your intention to hurt or walk over anybody, so naturally you get upset when you're accused of being selfish and inconsiderate. Still, you can't deny that if someone's in the mood for a fight, you'd be more than happy to oblige them.

Mars, the god of war

Mars wasn't only the god of war. In ancient times, he was associated with agriculture and fertility. When the sun enters the sign of Aries in the northern hemisphere, new life is just beginning: we see it in plants and animals around us, we feel it inside. The influence of Mars makes Aries energy creative and forceful, fresh and exciting—like the sensation you get when you come out into the sun after a long time indoors.

But of course Mars is best remembered for his warlike nature. War was something the Romans did very well and they were proud of the fact. Statues of Mars were placed everywhere and treated with the greatest respect. The Roman army was huge—in the course of its history it conquered just about everything there was to conquer. In their own view the Romans weren't just in the war business for the sake of a good fight. They had developed an advanced civilization—the best thing until sliced bread—and, with typical Aries bravado, they were intent on exporting their learning systems, legal systems and sewage systems, by force if necessary. Force certainly was necessary, and an awful lot of blood was spilled as the Roman armies marched on to triumph after triumph. The rest, of course, is history—our history.

Aside from all their gods (Mars, Jupiter, and so on) what inspired the Romans was their deep-rooted sense of purpose. The same goes for Aries. If you live or work with Aries people you'll know how quickly they turn what they believe into a cause . . . and that cause, if you don't watch what you say, into a fight! When they pursue a goal, they do it like the Roman army. Maybe there's no bloodshed, but when they go after an objective, it's with a formidable single-mindedness.

The Greeks also had a god of war, but they called him Ares not Mars. Oddly enough, the Greeks didn't respect Ares half as much as the Romans respected Mars. In fact, the scholarly and aesthetic Greeks thought the belligerent Ares was a real jerk, a nincompoop. (Had the Greeks spoken Yiddish, they would have called Ares a *klutz*—which roughly translated means a clumsy twit who's always tripping over his own feet, spilling soup down his shirt, and burning the toast.) The Greek Ares was ridiculed as a reckless bully who rushed into everything without looking where he was going. Rash and impetuous, he lacked skill and finesse, and as a result, he lost a lot of the battles he fought. Some Aries people behave a bit like the Greek god of war. They want things now, and to an Aries that means yesterday. They impulsively charge into something, without really thinking about the best way of approaching it. Their bolshy manner and their lack of tact, cunning and patience often means they don't achieve half the things they set out to do. Slow down, Aries, take time to plan your best line of attack, and you'll be more successful, not only in your career, but in your whole life as well.

The Aries temperament

A few years ago an Aries woman, the mother of two boys, became very concerned about the education standard at her local school. She made it her business to talk to every parent in the neighbourhood, and within a month had launched a campaign to revolutionize schooling in the area. Her enthusiasm and clear thinking, to say nothing of her attractive personality, brought her to the attention of the media and turned her cause into a national issue, Now that her boys are growing up, she's planning a career in politics. That's Aries initiative for you.

Whatever an Aries woman or man believes, they often have the ability to convert others to their thinking, by the sheer force of their will and determination . . . to say nothing of the famous Aries temper! The problem is that Aries can put just as much passion into a political cause as they would into making sure that everyone in the family squeezes the toothpaste tube FROM THE BOTTOM!! If you happen to be invited to dine out with an Aries, pray that the soup is hot, that the wine isn't corked or the service slow. Otherwise, you may see some well-meaning waiter disappear through the floor, as your Aries host or hostess carries out a short, sharp death sentence on the establishment.

Like the ram on the farm, Aries people have a talent for hitting the mark and getting right to the heart of the matter. They find immediate answers, spot obvious connections, notice weak spots and recognize the strongest line of approach. Their special gift is intuition, a faculty which lies somewhere between guessing and knowing, and which is the essential attribute of the fire signs.

Every human being has a creative ingredient—divine, if you like—a vital , empowering, demanding force. You'll appreciate what drives the powerful Aries engine if you recall those times you've been energized and excited by a sudden thought or a totally new idea. It's the fire that moves great artists, like the Aries painter Vincent Van Gogh, who spoke of a burning sense of certainty which took hold of his whole body and compelled him to act, regardless of the consequences. Many Aries people, at different times in their lives, are taken over by passionate beliefs and convictions. For all you Ariens, there's no denying the force of your beliefs and nobody would want to take them away. (As if anybody could—examples of Aries people with strong convictions include St Teresa of Avila, the mystic Padre Pio and Ulster's Reverand Ian Paisley!) But such an all-consuming energy demands, for the sake of safety (not to mention sanity), that you learn a sense of balance and proportion. Besides, all your fervour could be a bit much for friends or family. Secretly, they'll develop the habit of taking you with a liberal pinch of salt!

Aries children as young as the age of four are all set to take on the world, and twenty years later they still don't know where to draw the line. It was Freud who first wrote about the Oedipal stage, a period we all go through when we're endlessly, forcefully testing our limits—and proving to the world at large (and our parents in particular) how strong, fast, brave, independent and clever we really are. If you've ever tried to pin down a healthy four-year-old, then you've handled raw Aries energy; it's about as easy to restrain as Mars himself. But, as any parent learns, behind that tough, 'I don't need you any more' facade hides a surprisingly sensitive child whose greatest fear is being left completely alone. Deep inside most Aries people is the dread that when they've shown their anger and had their say, there might not be any pieces left to pick up.

Some Aries people insist on cutting off from such painful, difficult feelings. They just don't want to look at what might be happening inside. Sooner or later, though, they'll find themselves crashing against life very painfully. Then again, there are other Aries individuals who are terribly aware of all that is going on inside. A good example is John, who came for an astrology consultation feeling a bit confused: 'All my life I could never really take astrology seriously because all the articles I read about Aries say how bold, dynamic and assertive we are—and I've never been like that.'

It turned out that John's difficulty stemmed from childhood. He had well-intentioned but very strict parents who believed that children should be seen and not heard. As a result, John learned early that it was wrong to say what he thought and inappropriate to show his strong feelings. When he reached maturity his parents were no longer around. But by that time he had so thoroughly taken in and swallowed their attitudes, that he didn't have a clue about who he really was in his own right. Constantly criticizing and checking himself, he felt inadequate and defeated by life. But the astrology reading confirmed John's suspicion that perhaps he did have something valuable to offer. Nowadays he works successfully as a careers adviser, drawing on his painful past and natural sensitivity to encourage other people. In his own way he has become, as he says, 'dynamic and assertive, after all!'

Most Aries people feel the need of a strong,

supportive relationship to help them through their ups and downs. But it really isn't everyone who can cope with a Ram. Their adventures through life can be exciting and enjoyable, but actually living with them can be quite an ordeal. Nonetheless, Aries people would be the first to point out that as partners, their good points far outweigh their bad ones. A woman married to an Aries for many years corroborates:

When he's having a dull time at work, things can get very hard at home. He's bad-tempered, he doesn't seem to know what to do with himself. Nothing pleases him and, what's worse, he says that I'm not appreciating him enough. Things can get really bad between us. But just when I think I can't take any more, he somehow knows things have gone too far. He'll slip out quietly and buy me something romantic so I'll know he loves me . . . and we're back where we started twenty years ago.

The dashing knight in shining armour figures somewhere in the life of every Aries. They might be looking for one to rescue them from the things in life that even they find too much. Or else—man or woman—they're ready to get into armour and chain mail themselves to fight off a dragon of a mother, or save a lover from a fate worse than death. The Aries taste for romance never dies.

All Aries people—though some of them aren't aware of it—hate it when life settles down too much, when things get too humdrum and familiar. At home or at work, they like an adventure, a bit of romance . . . or failing that, a battle. That four-year old in them can never quite stop believing in fairy tales. Aries refuses to accept that life has to be only about unpaid bills and wrinkles. There's nothing wrong with that belief!

Aries people have a lot to offer the world . . . and for the most part they know it! If they can learn to accept that other people's view of life has some validity as well as their own, they can be truly strengthened by any opposition and difficulty they meet in life. Even failure has its lessons, and the road to success doesn't always run in a straight line.

The Aries types

Ariens born between 21 March and 31 March You're very dynamic and go-ahead but you need all the lessons you can get in patience and diplomacy. Without an outlet for your abundant energy, you'd be lost and miserable. Stop being so proud, it wouldn't hurt you to let others see your more vulnerable side now and then.

Ariens born between 1 April and 9 April You're expressive and probably creative, but you try too hard to win appreciation from other people. Unfortunately, it doesn't always come when you need it. You'd be a lot happier if you could learn to give approval to your own successes. And don't forget, nobody can get it right all the time.

Ariens born between 10 April and 20 April You belong to the boldest breed of Rams—plenty of big ideas, ambitious schemes and boundless enthusiasm. Watch out, though; your tendency to ignore limitations and restrictions could mean you end up banging your head against a few brick walls. Fortunately, you're incredibly resilient. And you're right—there's always tomorrow to look forward to!

Aries and work

The astrologer Dane Rudhyar once described Aries as the force which propels a seed to germinate. The first sign of the zodiac, Aries has a lot to do with birth and getting things started, and Aries people are right in their element in any work where they can initiate new ideas or help to get something new off the ground. When we come into the world, we arrive head first . . . not a very graceful way of going into things, but in that particular circumstance, apparently the most effective. For the rest of their lives, Ariens continue to do things head first (it's no accident that the head is the part of the body ruled by this sign). Observe an Arien really getting into work or about to go on the warpath, and you'll see the head out in front while the rest of the body tries to catch up behind. The head is often the most alive and energetic part of an Aries body. While they're working away at something they enjoy, Arien eyes are bright and magnetic, their expression eager and anticipating.

Boredom is the great enemy—life never travels fast enough for most Aries people. Sitting still and doing nothing is the hardest thing of all for you Rams to do. Maybe it's because you fear that when opportunity comes knocking, you might be out to lunch and miss it. Stop worrying that one day the rest of life will sneak off when you're not looking. Remember to keep yourself fit and well. Watch your diet and avoid the temptation just to eat fast foods all the time, If you are plagued by headaches and migraines, take it as a signal to let up and relax.

Rather than being discouraged by opposition and adversity, most Aries people seem to thrive on it. Remove the obstacles, and you cheat them of the thrill of winning. Achievement for them is best measured in terms of the odds they have had to beat to get there. Rather like Indiana Jones in Spielberg's *Raiders of the Lost Ark*, Aries people have a knack of getting into tight corners from which there's no apparent escape route. But at the last minute, just when all seems hopeless, something magical happens, and a way through is found. However, it's worth making the cautionary reminder that one famous Aries, Harry Houdini, never did escape from his last impossible situation. Still, he followed an Aries motto: If you gotta go, go with a bang!

The mythical figure of Jason is often quoted to help lesser mortals understand the essence of Aries. In the beginning of the story, Jason's uncle is the king, and Jason is a minor. But the young Jason is soon to come of age, and must take over the crown, his natural birthright. In other words, the power is 'out there'—his uncle has it—but the time has come for Jason to claim it for himself. This encapsulates the main task of Aries people: to find the power to direct their own lives, rather than allowing something or somebody else to tell them who to be or what to do, Aries is all about becoming the predominant creative force in one's own life.

Before his uncle will let him take over as king, Jason has to go on a quest. His mission is to retrieve the golden fleece from a faraway land, where it just happens to be guarded by a dragon that never sleeps (now what about that for a challenge, Aries?). Like Jason, in order to find their power and strength, Aries people must embark on some kind of quest—to do something to test their power and prove their worth to the world. Jason knew from the start that he would meet a host of unspeakable dangers on his journey. So what did he do? He ordered for the journey the biggest boat that had ever been built. With all that flash and panache, it's not surprising that heroes like Hercules and Theseus quickly heard about him and came to join his crew. There's something about the sheer audacity of an Aries that makes other people want to follow. It may sometimes be a case of the blind leading the blind, but a little bit of belief can go a long, long way.

What the working Aries isn't good at is appreciating his or her own achievements. They get so into the habit of looking ahead at what's still out there to be conquered, that they don't stop to take in and enjoy what's already been won. For this reason, an Aries will benefit from sitting down at the end of a day and trying the following exercise:

1. Write down a list of your achievements today.
2. Now add to that list all the basic tasks you do in a day but which you take for granted—such as making the bed, doing the dishes, watering the plants, etc. These things are achievements as well.
3. Read over your list and congratulate yourself on what you've done today.

Aries careers

Not every Aries is destined for immediate career sucess. Their natural addiction to challenge means that some Aries people fall down again and again, and have to dust a lot of dirt off before they finally make it. The famous Aries entertainer Charlie Chaplin made a brilliant career doing precisely that before he went on to more serious acting.

To act means simply to do. Aries people are the great doers of the Zodiac, so it's not surprising that they should also make very good actors. There is a world of difference between acting and pretending, and Ariens in general, don't pretend. This sign produces punchy personalities like David Frost and naturally dramatic people who take themselves and their work earnestly. Strong character actors like John Gielgud, Marlon Brando, Alec Guinness, Spencer Tracy and Rod Steiger have made their mark through the integrity of their work and their sense of authenticity, Other Aries actors—William Holden, Gregory Peck, Dirk Bogarde, Richard Chamberlain, Omar Sharif, Eddie Murphy and even diminutive Dudley Moore—have all exemplified different images of masculinity. Aries actresses Bette Davis and Joan Crawford, towering myths of Hollywood's heyday, cornered the competitive market for the aggressive heroine. Gloria Swanson, Mary Pickford, Debbie Reynolds, Doris Day and Julie Christie are other vibrant female rams who've succeeded admirably in one of the toughest professions of them all.

The challenge of performance, the struggle to achieve in a field where unemployment statistics are high, along with the innumerable natural hazards of a stage or screen career, are the right kind of incentives to lure a willing Ram into the world of entertainment. But talent alone, as many performers have proved over the years, is no guarantee of success, and is less the commodity in demand than stamina and *chutzpah*. Witness the energy and dynamism of such Aries legends as Elton John, Bessie Smith, Aretha Franklin and Diana Ross (who poignantly portrayed another Aries, Billie Holiday, in the film biography *Lady Sings the Blues*).

Aries dramatists Sean O'Casey and Samuel Beckett have carved themselves a niche in twentieth century drama. But if you're more into Aries fiction or poetry, charge along to a bookstore and get something by Henry James, William Wordsworth, Thornton Wilder, Algernon Swinburne, Charles Baudelaire, Emile Zola (author of *J'accuse!*), or Isak Dinesen (her autobiography was the basis for the film *Out of Africa*) to inspire you in your career in writing. Aries artists who need encouragement to express their innate creativity need look no farther than the works of fellow Rams Leonardo da Vinci, Van Dyck, and Dutch Ram Vincent Van Gogh.

Obviously the military would be one choice of career for Mars-ruled Aries, and there are many people born under this sign who could employ their natural leadership skills to rise to a high rank. Of course, not every Ram wants to be a Rambo. William Booth was a Christian soldier who used his fighting Aries nature to found the Salvation Army and wage war on poverty and neglect.

What could be more appealing to a typical Aries than a career full of danger and excitement? The controversial Aries psychologist Wilhelm Reich had his books banned, was thrown out of several countries and died in an American penitentiary for his views on sexuality. Wilbur Wright the early American aviator and astronaut James Lovell are examples of the high-flying Ram. More ordinary civilian services can provide their fair share of glamorous and genuinely daring professions. Fire-fighting, for instance, is a common Aries career choice. The rescue services—land, sea and air—and police work also ask real bravery and offer a suitable mission for a knight of the twentieth century.

Leaving behind the realm of obvious high adventure, let's turn a moment to the financial world. Don't stifle a yawn, Aries, nobody's suggesting you become a teller at the local bank, unless you consider that occupation *your* personal challenge in life. It's a big mistake to imagine financial dealings are dry, civilized affairs. Take, for example, the stock exchange, where many Mars-minded Rams might make a killing every morning before lunch. All those split-second risks and decisions—now there's something that would really get your adrenalin pumping! The savage world of investment carries a coronary rate equal to none.

With the possible exception of jealousy, more people are killed over money then anything else. This isn't intended to suggest that crime might be a suitable Aries career—the risks and possible rewards of armed robbery may be tantalizing, but you of all signs would really hate life behind bars. Although an Aries in high finance may enjoy sailing pretty close to the wind, the perils of floating a company or launching a new big idea are dangerous enough, without the added pitfalls of illegality.

An Aries who's a good sport can find in the sporting life the perfect medium for their talents. Anything exhilarating, dangerous or competitive would use up all that excess energy they have. Round-the-world yachtswoman Clare Francis needed all her Aries drive and courage to make it as far as she did. And golfer Sevvy

Ballesteros didn't get where he is today by just selling American Express cards on British television.

That Aries love competition is no secret, but their sense of what's competitive is an individual one. In farming, you're up against the elements, and studies have shown a high proportion of Rams in the field. And what about a good courtroom battle?—Aries also scored high in the legal profession. Many Rams are drawn to the challenge of teaching—another line of work where you're bound to have the occasional fight on your hands. And there's always the battle of the sexes—Hugh Hefner, the founder of *Playboy* magazine, is one Aries who's aroused a lot of women's anger on that front. Of course, Aries model Samantha Fox has managed to arouse quite a few men in her time as well.

Some Aries professionals set up in business for themselves, which makes sense for a sign that doesn't mind going it alone. Others might prefer the challenge of a large organization, where they can revel in the cut and thrust of the fight to the top. Alone or in a team, there's always room though for another Aries entrepreneur like Florenz Ziegfeld, the mind behind the famous Ziegfeld Follies. When it comes to challenging other people's doubts and defeating cautious scepticism in order to attract investments for a new venture, leave it to an Aries. All fire signs love to speculate, but it's important they learn to distinguish between an enterprise with potential and mere wishful thinking. Not every Aries has a golden touch. A quick, sharp mind could be the very instrument on which you cut yourself badly. But if you must insist on inflicting pain, you might even be able to profit by it—one survey showed an extraordinary proportion of dentists born under the sign of Aries.

High-powered selling work often pays a very low basic salary—something which usually deters the more security-conscious signs, whose stomachs just aren't strong enough for the get-rich-quick professions. But the need for security is not high on the list of Aries priorities. If you're a fast-thinking Ram with the gift of the gab, you could make a pile selling almost anything to anyone. An Aries woman who made her living selling cosmetics used to brag that she could get her foot over the threshold before they'd even opened the door! All the selling professions—advertising, public relations, publicity work and personal representation—are potential targets for the Aries eye to follow. An actress who had an Aries agent commented during a chart reading:

I really never knew I was such a talented person till I heard my agent discussing me over the phone. At the time I'd hardly done anything, but he sold me as if I was just a week away from the top. You know, from that moment on I started believing in myself more . . . and somehow from that moment the work started flooding in.

Aries people with a flair for words have forced their way into journalism—some hot on the trail of a high street supermarket thief; others in such sites of conflict as the Middle East. In radio and television journalism too, Rams seem happier than most working under fire. It's not surprising that studies have shown more Aries people to be in politics than any other astrological sign; some, like Liberal leader David Steel, trying desperately to force their own middle path between the extremes of right and left, others, like Labour leader Neil Kinnock or left-winger Tony Benn, simply determined to alter the course of the government in power. If you're a Ram with an axe to grind, the political arena may be just the place for you to do it.

Aries compatibilities

Aries/Aries *(Fire/Fire)* Fantastic—if you see eye to eye; a big headache for both of you if you don't. You'll get along great when your talents are allied in the completion of a task, a battle with fierce competitors, or against a boss who won't give an inch. But in most situations it might be a good idea to work apart; in your own separate rooms or, if things between you get really bad, in separate towns!

Aries/Taurus *(Fire/Earth)* The hare and the tortoise. You want to move; Taurus isn't ready. Now things are starting to move, and already Taurus wants a tea break. Aries, never underestimate this steady but frustrating sign and learn from its perseverance. Yes, Taurus needs to be pushed now and again, but it wouldn't hurt you to slow down and let things happen in their own good time.

Aries/Gemini *(Fire/Air)* Mercury (the ruler of Gemini) can move every bit as fast as Mars . . . the only problem with busy Geminis is that you just can't count on them being around when you really want them. But you'll love their sharp eyes and quick wits—not to mention their willingness to try anything once. They have a knack of picking up the things you miss. You could go places together.

Aries/Cancer *(Fire/Water)* Now here's a riddle for you: What could a Ram and a Crab possibly do for each other? Without imagination and patience, not a lot. The Ram rushes in head first; the Crab approaches everything sideways. You might try telling Cancer people how totally misunderstood you feel—that line could really get them eating out of your hand. Whatever you do, don't lose your temper; otherwise, one day when you really don't expect it, you'll feel the Cancer claw . . . where it hurts.

Aries/Leo *(Fire/Fire)* The lion in the Bible may have lain down with the lamb, but when it gets together with a Ram, expect something a little more dynamic. These signs can spur each other on like no other pair. But remember, Aries, always let the Lion believe it's running the show, or there will be hell to pay. Leos are capable of unparalleled love and generosity, but they do demand a lion-sized loyalty in return.

Aries/Virgo *(Fire/Earth)* Slow down here. Virgo finds you a bit too restless and unpredictable. Anyhow, it's about time you took some sound lessons in practicality and patience—and earthy Virgo couldn't be a better teacher. Everybody knows you're great at lining up the targets, but skilful Virgo's self-discipline and fine eye for detail will help you hit your mark every time.

Aries/Libra *(Fire/Air)* Did it ever occur to you that your methods can be a little crude at times? No? Well, you're about to be enrolled in Libra's famous finishing school—a kind of commando training in social refinement. Leave it to Libra—the sign of tact and diplomacy—to finally teach you the art of sensitive relating. Take heed, Aries, you've finally met your match!

Aries/Scorpio *(Fire/Water)* Don't play with that bee in Scorpio's bonnet—you're sure to get stung, and this sting is lethal! Your Scorpio colleague may seem quiet, but there is much more going on there than meets the eye. Make an effort to understand one another and be friends. Otherwise, you might live to regret it.

Aries/Sagittarius *(Fire/Fire)* Running out of inspiration? Do your batteries need recharging? Seek out a Sagittarius and you'll soon remember what real living is all about. Impromptu parties over lunch, tennis in the boardroom—work will seem more like play with you two around. But be warned; when the going gets tough, Sagittarius is apt to get going . . . somewhere in the Tropics, probably.

Aries/Capricorn *(Fire/Earth)* The Goat is a natural

climber, and this combination could be a real uphill struggle for you. You're unimpressed by practical limitations, but Capricorn never thinks about much else. And your flash-in-the-pan successes don't mean much to this hard-working sign—solid achievements carry more weight. One thing you can count on; when you've gained the unconditional approval of a Capricorn, you really know you've arrived.

Aries/Aquarius *(Fire/Air)* You two can be so much into your own things, you might just as well be on different planets! But when you're getting hot under the collar about the same issues, try teaming up—there's nothing the two of you couldn't pull off together. Providing you share common principles and objectives, you'll stand by each other till the end . . . even if you do lose radio contact now and then.

Aries/Pisces *(Fire/Water)* Try letting the Fish swim in and out of your life without getting any more involved than you need to. On the surface Pisces is a pushover: Fish people will say Yes to almost anything you want. But watch out when the tide turns, and that same Fish will say No to everything it said Yes to the day before. Confused?—you will be! Inconsistencies aside, if you ever need a shoulder to cry on, your Pisces colleague is the one to turn to.

The Aries boss

It's not so unusual for an Aries to excel as a boss. After all, Rams have natural leadership potential, and provided it doesn't turn sour, vindictive or despotic (Nikita Khrushchev was an Aries), nothing could be more valuable in any work situation. And then there's all that ram-like vim and verve, that fearless attack capable of reviving the most flagging dead-horse establishment. Rams who are sure of their own capabilities hate to see anybody else's light hidden behind a bushel. They can be a regular fairy godmother to all those bedraggled Cinderella types who have plodded on uninspired for years. Aries bosses know quite instinctively that a demoralized team of people will want to do as little as possible. What's more, they know what kind of carrots appeal to which horses.

Of course, you can't please all of the people all of the time. Aries bosses should expect to meet resistance from other people. Some employees need to be pushed, and a Ram boss is just the person to do it . . . often with outstanding results. But not everybody appreciates being told how to go about their work, and the Aries boss may be judged by some as an intrusive critic.

Rams at the helm don't like working with a quarrelsome or mutinous crew. When they're boss, they rather like things to stay that way. And, though they enjoy a challenge, it's much better if it comes from an outside competitor and not from the ranks of the people they employ. If you fall foul of an Aries boss, expect to be ignored or fired. Remember, they really don't take kindly to criticism, especially if it's personal. How could anyone suggest they aren't the best?

Aries bosses always look so in charge of things, it's hard to imagine them down in the dumps. But if they suffer a lot of defeats and setbacks, they'll begin to question their worth and ability. If that's the case, a few words of support and encouragement will do them a world of good. An Aries boss will teach you a lot about how to go out there and get what you want in life. And the best way to repay them is to be their friend.

The Aries employee

Hire an Aries and things will get jumping. If your staff looks more tired and jaded than usual—if it seems everybody has midweek blues on Monday morning—a new Aries on the scene could have the effect of an effervescent tonic. Be warned; employ an Aries today and expect to see some changes by tomorrow . . . if not by tonight.

For a start, you know that invoice forms have always been stored in the corridor. That is to say, they *were*. Aries decided to put them in the cabinet by the window in the main office, so more people can get to them. And remember that rubber plant you've had for eight years—the one everyone has to walk around each time they cross the room? You'll now find it in the corridor where the invoice forms used to be. Oh, by the way, while you were at lunch, Aries took down the empty shelves in your office because there were none in reception. And see that chart on the wall—it's a new idea to show this month's figures as they come in and compare them with last month's . . . etc, etc.

By now, you've got the message—Aries employees work fast, but they can go a bit too far. You're going to need all the authority you can muster to point out that *you* are the boss and that they have only been here one day. However, after an Aries worker explains the reasons for the changes, you may begin to wonder if there isn't something in them after all. Rams can be persuasive people.

Now, if you're wise, you'll sit down and take the weight off your overheads. Think about it for a minute; maybe there are a few things that once upon a time you thought of altering and for one reason or another, you just never got around to doing. Thought of anything yet? Now, try saying to your Aries worker: 'You know, Aries, I've often wondered if anything could possibly be done about x, y, or z. Never mind, I suppose that would really be asking for a miracle . . .' Wait a minute, did you say miracle? Aries at your service!

Aries employees aren't coy about ambition. Nor, for that matter, are they secretive with their thoughts about bosses who are ineffective or reluctant to change. A sensible boss will overcome initial anxieties and allow

Aries employees plenty of room to run around and exercise their new ideas. It's true you'll need to hold them back now and again. But the last thing you want on your hands is a bored Ram.

You'll just have to live with the fact that an Aries is determined to climb the ladder of ambition . . . four rungs at a time, if possible. Today's filing clerk may well be next year's chairman of the board. You've got to hand it to them, they're great workers. If you don't hand it to them, they'll probably take it away.

The Aries colleague

If you have a typical Aries colleague, you'll know it. They're not hard to spot, and should you fail to notice them, don't worry—they'll come up and let you know just who they are. You'll realize fairly quickly that they're the kind of people who wield a lot of influence at work. The boss probably values them for their enthusiasm and sharp judgement. But if you're honest, you might have to admit you resent them a little.

Rams are committed competitors, and unfortunately they can attract a lot of envy and rivalry. An Aries co-worker might even enjoy being the centre of attention in this way—although he or she would never say as much. Certain other colleagues may secretly try to undermine their Aries rival. All these unpleasant undercurrents can be avoided if the Aries employee could learn to function better within a group, rather than always having to be Number One. But if you're stuck with a blustering, overassertive Ram, then your best defence is to stand your ground and confront him or her squarely and honestly. Aries people respect directness (providing it isn't too vindictive) and, believe it or not, they sometimes borrow a lesson from their opposite sign, Libra, and compromise when they have to.

When they're working hard at something, they really get into it. Sometimes they don't even stop for lunch.

(Can you imagine a Taurus or Cancer not stopping to eat?) It's hard for Rams to see why other people don't feel the same way, and they could become pretty moral about it, righteously pointing out all they've done compared to everyone else.

An Aries often takes the attitude that if a job's worth doing, it's worth doing all by yourself. If they aren't in charge, they find it hard to work as part of a team, and they're very much happier when they have a particular area that's their own responsibility. But it's also the Aries worker who'll be the first to speak up for the group, the one person who's prepared to face the manager and stand up and fight for everyone's rights.

Humour acts as a safety valve for Ariens who tend to take themselves a bit too seriously. They're usually fun to have around, and their natural playful side will have others rolling about the floor. But unfriendly colleagues take heed—treat your Aries co-worker badly and you're liable to become the next target for the Ram's dart of humour. Fortunately, an Aries is usually an asset, rather than a liability. When all is said and done, they're more likely to bring magic than malice to your place of work.

Taurus

Element: Earth
Symbol: The Bull
Ruler: Venus

The Sign of the Bull

If you want to know Taurus, it's time you got acquainted with the bull. He's an animal too long maligned in our culture. Say 'bull' to anyone and they'll very likely say 'bull to you too'. Try asking them what picture they first associate with the word *bull*, and the chances are they'll describe an angry hunk with spiked horns and steaming nostrils. In wise and ancient civilizations, the bull had great dignity as a sacred symbol of power and potency; but in modern times, it seems people can only think of him as a destructive, raging beast.

Take a trip to the country on a warm summer afternoon and you could get a very different picture. Stop and watch the bull in the quiet corner of a field, meditatively chewing the cud, blissfully scratching his rump against a convenient tree. The most violent act you're likely to see him perform is an occasional tail-flick to keep passing flies at a distance. His fixed expression carries all the serenity you might observe in a person who feels good about life and content with his lot. The scene is an idyllic tableau of peace and tranquillity. However, before you're tempted to throw aside the cares of the modern world and climb over the fence to join him, BE WARNED: the field you are about to enter is *his* field; and those cows over there (though they may not seem to concern him too much) are *his* cows.

Understand that, and you're on your way to understanding Taurus.

Taurus people, like the bull, prefer the simple life. What they call 'simple' is anything that doesn't upset or bother them too much. They crave material security—and that doesn't just mean money in the bank. They only feel secure when things stay precisely as they are; and *things* include other people, as well as everything else Taurus people think they possess. For a typical Taurus, it's literally earth-shattering to think that life is a constant state of flux and that people and circumstances are changing all the time. Well, it's as if they were to wake up one morning to find the whole landscape had altered overnight.

All cattle, including bulls, are reluctant creatures, slow to react. The old expression 'waiting for the cows to come home' describes a very long wait for something which is bound to happen . . . one of these days! This couldn't be a greater contrast to Aries the Ram, who is in his element charging around from one thing to another. Taurus the Bull is so much into standing still he could easily take root. Yet if you really want to provoke him into a fury, you can. All you need to do is move too quickly or try to push him too far.

Venus, goddess of love

Taurus is the most sensual of the earth signs. Taurus people relate only to what they can see, smell, taste, hear or touch. What isn't tangible might just as well not exist. They're happiest eating, sleeping or having sex, and some of them don't ask much more of life than that. They're habitual creatures; when they get used to something being a certain way, they don't like it to change.

In Aries we met Mars the god of war. Now meet Venus, goddess of love. Perhaps you've never seen her, but she's never far away, humming a tune, causing a gentle breeze to blow, filling the air with her sweet perfume. She's always around when we fall in love, or anytime we're in the company of someone special who makes us feel good inside. When we step into Nature—the right setting for a romance—the sweet sounds, soothing colours, the gentle harmonies combine to conjure up Venus for us yet again. And whenever we sit down to an intimate meal, tasting good food, drinking a fine wine and listening to the right music—once again we are gently haunted by the goddess of love.

But love, as most of us discover, isn't always as beautiful as it at first seems. The same can be said for Venus. In astrology, the love goddess rules two signs, Taurus and Libra (it's typical of Venus that one sign isn't enough for her). As the ruler of Libra, Venus is quite refined—she likes candlelight dinners, *nouvelle cuisine*, intelligent conversation and fine art. As the ruler of Taurus, Venus is a bit more down to earth—she prefers big banquets with tons to eat, a roll in the hay, and then a good snooze. The Taurus Venus loves the natural world, knows good value when she sees it, and cares deeply about the people close to her and the things she owns. She's dependable and true and, as with so many Taurus people, life is an awful lot richer just for having her around.

The Taurus temperament

Aries the Ram is energetic and itching to get moving. Taurus the Bull has just as much stamina, but he won't be hurried. Taureans have all the time in the world, and demonstrate their real strength by standing firm. (Have you ever heard of Thomas 'Stonewall' Jackson, a confederate general in the American Civil War? He was a Taurus who earned his nickname, appropriately enough, after his famous stand in the first Battle of Bull Run!) A Taurus can maintain resistance indefinitely against any attempt to move or change him or her.

In our pressured, high-speed world, it can be tough for all you Taurus people to keep up your natural slow and steady pace. But you'll always be much happier when you're allowed to take your own time and develop gradually rather than change suddenly. The second sign of the zodiac is very much in tune with the cyclic, dependable patterns of Nature, and Bulls instinctively recognize that things need time to grow, ripen and mature,

However, you've got to admit it, Taurus, there's something irresistible about finding a nice comfortable corner, staying there and doing absolutely nothing. You really love a rut, don't you? Preferably when it's fur-feather-or money-lined. But even when you're covered in barbed wire, you'd sooner stick to it rather than do anything to alter things. There are a lot of Bulls around just plodding along in bad jobs, sour relationships and poor health. Secretly fearing that any change is bound to be for the worse, they conclude they're safer with the devil they know. Taureans are masters at something called *selective perception*, the talent for ignoring what they don't really want to see. Taurus the Bull can be a bit of an ostrich!

While the explosive Aries child screams: 'I will! I will!', the Taurus youngster growls through clenched teeth: 'I won't! I won't!' Not surprisingly, little Bulls—and bigger Bulls—provoke frustration in other people . . . but all to no avail. You can call them stubborn, stupid or plain masochistic. You can offer advice, lay down the law or threaten murder. Scream, break windows or tear all your hair out—Taurus people will do nothing until they're good and ready.

If you live or work with a Taurus, you won't need to be told they're creatures of habit. The trouble is, with a Taurus, a habit can become a religion. If you find it hard to understand why Taureans can't be just a little bit more flexible, you probably haven't heard yet that Adolf Hitler was born in late April. All Taurus children have a little dictator in them and they have ways of getting what they want. You can probably imagine the scene . . .

The family is all set for a day's outing. But there's something about the way little Taurus is acting that says he doesn't want to go. (Maybe it's the way he's digging his feet into the ground.) Meantime everything, including the dog, Grandma and the barbecue, has been packed into the car and everybody's waiting.

'Taurus, are you coming, sweetheart?'
'I don't want to go.'
'Come on, you'll enjoy it when you get there.'
'No!'
'Wouldn't you like a chocolate sundae, Taurus?'
'No!'
'Well, what do you want then?'
'I don't want to go!'

And that's it. Taurus wins game, set and match. Remove the little Bull by force and you're sealing the fate of a pleasure trip already clearly doomed. Nothing, not even murder, will alter that rigid determined expression. So when dealing with a difficult Taurus (child or adult) remember Lesson Number One: If Taurus won't go to the mountain, better start thinking about how you might bring the mountain to Taurus.

Taureans like life to fall into a predictable pattern. Take food, for instance (most Taurus people are happy to). Bill is a one type of Taurus. His girlfriend claims he has an inner clock—with an alarm that booms like Big Ben when he hasn't eaten.

If he's agitated, he has to have chocolate. Sometimes there isn't any chocolate around, so I say 'Well, how about some cheesecake, or would you like some water-melon?' But no, nothing else will do—it *has* to be chocolate. He gets really upset when there's something he wants to eat and he can't have it. It's like a nightmare for him . . . and me!

To fully understand and respect the temperament of any sign, you have to see its essence—which in the case of Taurus means going back to Nature. As you push your trolley round the supermarket, or when you make a mortgage payment, it's not always easy to appreciate that you're engaged in a struggle for survival which is still as fierce today as it was in the lives of our cave-dwelling ancestors. Of course, in some senses, we've come a long way; the wooden club, the flint-headed spear and the poison dart eventually had to give way to the plastic credit card.

However, the fact that our fish, meat, roots, nuts and fruits come pre-packaged in cellophane doesn't remove the fact that we'd die without them. Not only do we need to eat today, we need to know that something will be around for tomorrow too. And we have to think about other things, like keeping dry and warm, for instance. No sign is more concerned with ordinary creature comforts and the fulfilment of basic needs than your sign, Taurus. So what might seem like caution, greed or sheer stubbornness in your character are respectable relics of a strong survival instinct. (Of course, everybody knows you can be plain greedy and downright stubborn too, but that's another story.)

If you want to see this instinct at work, watch a newborn baby. His mind doesn't yet deal with information in the way that an adult mind can: he doesn't intellectually understand the importance of nutrition, tactile stimulation and the conservation of energy. But, like any animal, his body instinctively knows that he needs to be warm, fed and held. And when the source of all that warmth, food and comfort has to leave the room, he fears that she might not come back again, that he'll be abandoned and die. The newborn baby only counts on what is right there in front of him. And that's just about the same way a Taurus sees life as well.

Taureans rarely put effort into anything that gives no rewards or satisfaction. They do, however, know a good opportunity when they see one. The sign of the Bull may seem slow and in many ways inflexible, but watch how quietly and efficiently they can adapt to a new social environment. From nowhere they produce a steady flow of winning charm and an appealing expression, which may well get them an invitation to dinner, if not the offer of a room for the night. One Taurus socialite claimed she could detect people with money through lead walls, and smell a fat wallet through asbestos clothing. In many Bulls the instinct for survival has developed into a social art form.

Fulfilling our needs in the present day means having enough money, something which Taurus people usually manage better than most. Some Bulls seem to have been born with a golden touch; from others, life asks a little effort now and again. Any Taurus who sincerely believes that money is unimportant really needs to do a bit of homework. Conversely, the Bull who lives by the maxim that *only* money counts can become bitter and jaded—'a person who knows the price of everything and the value of nothing', as Oscar Wilde put it.

The Taurus types

Taureans born between 21 April and 30 April It hurts you that life can be so demanding and disappointing. But have you considered that your definition of pleasure may be a bit too narrow? Free some of your natural sensitivity in a creative outlet ... do more to bring out the best in other people ... aim to do one really different thing each day. You'll give a whole new energy to your life.

Taureans born between 1 May and 10 May It's important for you to see things done to the very best of your ability. That's fair enough, but don't get too hung up and self-critical or you'll drive yourself (and everyone around you) crazy. Try seeing your good points, rather than just the bad ones. Aim to relax, and learn to trust youself just a little bit more.

Taureans born between 11 May and 21 May
Success brings you rewards others admire, but don't let your sign down—make sure you give yourself plenty of space to enjoy the life you've worked so hard to build. Don't just bury yourself in your work. Let yourself go, and really indulge that Taurus appetite for pleasure now and then.

Taurus and work

Like trees whose roots go deep into the earth, Taurus people have a strong grip on life and a solid, practical outlook on the world. They need to feel the ground beneath their feet. Which means that in whatever job they do, they like to know where they stand. They really can't be happy in any work where everything is in a constant state of change or upheaval.

As you can imagine, a Bull might feel rather precarious climbing the ladder to success. And yet they are spurred upwards by some worrying facts about working life. Whoever employs you has power over you: they can make decisions that concern you without your having any authority to stop them. If you work alongside other people, your colleagues are entitled to have their own ideas, which could be very different from yours. Not only that, you have to share a place of work with others. They may upset your plans, disrupt your routines and even borrow your possessions. What a thought for a Taurus! Some people may be very willing to muck in with the crowd and take whatever comes their way, but Taureans quickly calculate that in order to have proper control over their own lives, they need to rise above the rest and get to the top. Promotion promises a safe route to happiness—the more power a Taurus has, the more secure he or she feels.

Meantime, the maturing Taurus is steadily acquiring (as Bulls do) some of the little comforts that money can buy. More things need more space, and there may even be a family around at some point. Life begins to get a little too hectic for the Taurus who likes a bit of peace and quiet. The Taurus needs to know there is at least one place where life can be controlled and fairly predictable—home sweet home. The Bull values privacy; the ideal Taurus home would be a centrally heated castle complete with moat and drawbridge to keep unwelcome visitors away. But castles cost money, and often the only answer is a better job. So once again the poor Bull is prodded on to climb another rung.

Taurus really doesn't have a head for heights, and a rung at a time is fast enough. Once a Taurus has been in one place for a while, it's hard to imagine ever moving again. But at every stage of the way, Venus stands with her hand out saying 'What about my share?' So the food and the wine and the holidays get a little more expensive every year, and each day the Taurus has a little more trouble getting up in the morning.

Getting up may be difficult, but holding things up is no problem at all for Bulls—much to the exasperation of those who work with them. Many Taurus people are so addicted to applying the brake, they forget there is an accelerator too. And some take a very long time before they'll even turn on the engine. Try this exercise if you're a Taurus who needs to get moving.

1. Make a list of all those things you'd really like to do: things you'd like to see, people you want to visit, things you'd like to try, etc.
2. Now make another list of all the routine, everyday things you do: the way you normally spend your money, what you normally eat, who you usually visit, etc.
3. Notice all the things you want that you don't give yourself,

and all the things you do now, that you'd rather stop.
Even in very small ways, ask yourself what you can begin
to do about that, and write down what comes to mind.
4. Periodically re-read the list of things you'd like to do, and
check off the ones you've managed to accomplish. Update
your list from time to time.

Taurus careers

There's a touch of Venus in every Taurus. Taurus men
and women are frequently physically attractive
(Rudolph Valentino, Audrey Hepburn, Ryan O'Neil,
Candice Bergen, Ann-Margaret, Gary Cooper and
Tyrone Power, to name but a few). Even in the heavier,
bovine types there's usually a hint of Aphrodite's
features in the eyes or the bone structure. In recent
surveys, Taurus showed up prominent among artists,
which shouldn't be a big surprise when you consider
the input of Venus in the sign. If you know you're
creative, start thinking about a career in painting, sculpture, any kind of design work, or even ceramics. Yes,
it's true, you could end up being a Bull in a china shop!

Venus herself married Vulcan, a craftsman god. She
was fascinated by his ability to forge, shape and make,
while she could only look and appreciate. There is a
deep, often hidden, creative side in Taurus which can
only be released through the discipline of a craft. The
typical Bull, who hates to try anything too new, may
be daunted by the thought, but Taurus artists frequently
achieve an enduring fame. Maybe you have a Taurus
talent with words like many famous writers—Shake-
speare, for a kick-off. What about Charlotte Bronte,
Emily's Taurus sister, who created the sensitive but
steadfast governess Jane Eyre. It took an adamant
Taurus like J. M. Barrie, author of *Peter Pan*, to write
about a never-never land. And have you ever read
Rebecca, the bestselling tale of an unnamed heroine
who goes through hell as the second Mrs de Winter,

written by another evocative Taurus, Daphne du Maurier? And it had to be a sensual Taurus like Vladimar Nabokov, the creator of *Lolita*, who could so aptly describe a middle-aged man's lust for a pubescent girl. (Of course, Taurus is an economical sign, and some of them prefer to use as few words as possible, like Samuel Morse, for instance, dot, dot, dot.)

Considering they're Bulls, Taurus people are surprisingly good on their feet. If you happen to be a very agile Taurus and you feel a certain magic twinkle in your toes, don't wait for somebody to do it for you—enrol yourself in a dance class today. The late Taurus Fred Astaire may have been heavily inspired by the luxury-loving Venus, but he certainly didn't get to the top of his profession by lying around in bed all morning. We can safely assume the same for other Taurus hoofers like Shirley MacLaine, Margot Fonteyn and the famous choreographer Martha Graham. You find dancing rather sissy? Would you prefer a few rounds in the ring with boxing Bulls Henry Cooper, Sugar Ray Robinson or Joe Louis? Or how about warming up in the bullpen with the famous Taurus baseballer Willie Mays?

You won't be unique if you're a Taurus who wants to pursue a musical career. You need only to hear a few bars of Wagner, Tchaikovsky, Brahms, Prokoviev or Erik Satie to recognize the sensuality of a Taurus composer. For lighter tastes try Taureans, Irving Berlin, Burt Bacharach or Sir Arthur Sullivan. And if you play an instrument, you may have been inspired by skilful Taurus interpretations from international performers like Duke Ellington or Yehudi Menuhin. But most important for the world of music, Taurus rules the throat and therefore the vocal chords, accounting for the warm quality of great Taurus singing voices. Famous Bulls who have traded golden notes for green ones include Dame Nellie Melba, Ella Fitzgerald, Alice Faye ('America's singing sweetheart'), Bing Crosby,

Perry Como, Barbra Streisand, Glen Campbell, Stevie Wonder, Cher, Tammy Wynette and Janet Jackson . . . and surely many singing stars of the future who for now will have to content themselves with singing in the shower! Of course, if you can't sing to the gallery then you could always play to them. It's been a lucrative life for Taurean performers on stage and screen, like James Mason, Jack Nicholson, Shirley Temple, Al Pacino, Jimmy Stewart, Glenda Jackson, Philip Michael Thomas (it seems that in Miami, vice pays very well), and Eastenders Anita Dobson and Leslie Grantham, better known as Angie and Den.

Even Taureans who could never rank as musical geniuses could learn to tap out a pretty good tune on the keys to their safe-deposit boxes. There are many examples of Taurus people who have joined the ranks of the super-rich. Take, for instance, the late William Randolph Hearst, whose life story was immortalized by Orsen Welles (a famous performing Taurus) in the epic film *Citizen Kane*. In business, Bulls have a sixth sense about money. They generally know when a deal looks as if it will work—or not, as the case may be. It's no big surprise then that statistics show many Taurus people working with money—in every kind of big, big business they're earning it, managing it, lending it and, best of all, holding on to it. Not for Taurus the dubious speculative venture, the investment 'that couldn't possibly fail' . . . but probably will. Some of you Bulls may have been blessed with a kindly old-fashioned naivety, but you don't have air instead of brains. Like an animal that senses the earthquake before it hits, you instinctively know when something is not a sound proposition.

Banking is a favourite Taurus profession. Well, if you have to leave somebody sitting on your money, a strapping Bull is a pretty sound bet. And if you're looking for insurance, you'll want to be sure you're well covered, so you'll look around for a Taurus to give you protection. Or should you have a little money to spare (a legacy or a small nest egg), and you want some expert advice on what might be a good investment—you know the sign to contact. There are hundreds of well-covered Taurus stockbrokers and investors just waiting to help you, and if you were born under the sign of the Bull, this could very well become your field too. But no matter how you finally choose to earn your money, you'll still need a shrewd Taurus accountant to make sure the tax man doesn't get more than he really deserves. (Of course, the tax man may turn out to be a woman, and she'll probably be a Taurus too!)

Working with money is wonderful, but it can be earned in other ways. A Taurus needs to use all his or her common sense and good judgement to choose a line guaranteed to bring in a dependable return. And what can you guarantee better than the demand for food? Diets may be very much in style, but nobody likes to be hungry for long. A good baker, for instance, never goes out of business. Bread isn't just a food, it's a way of life—the mixing, the kneading, the proving, the baking. And after the baking, the sight, smell and taste of good warm bread. It's Taurus to a T. (Talking of which, television's Mr T turns out to be a Taurus too—as if you couldn't guess by just looking at him!) The mention of food unveils a whole smorgasbord of career possibilities for any Taurus who enjoys making it as much as eating it. There's money to be made in the preparation of smoked and cooked meats, pâtés, cheese and a thousand savoury items, all in demand and each a possible career in itself. And don't neglect your Taurus sweet tooth—who can better recognize perfection in confection and learn how to create it?

Another natural profession for Bulls is building. You're into permanence, and the idea of leaving something behind you—a house, an office block or even a small town—warms your heart. Taurus people plan every move, so how about making some money out of it as an estate agent or architect? And if you're a city-born Taurus who has never felt right in smoke and pinstripes, have you ever thought about the life you might be leading in pastures green? Probably the most famous living Taurus woman, Queen Elizabeth II, is a country girl at heart, happiest spending her private life among horses and dogs. Taurus is right at home down on the farm, growing corn or raising livestock, far from the savage human jungle. In fact, Bulls seem to take to agriculture, forestry, landscape or market gardening, and the whole range of outdoor professions like ducks to water, hens to corn, or sheep to pasture. Probably what they enjoy most is the certainty that you get out of the earth what you put into it . . . sooner or later.

If you care about animals and you've inherited a Taurus way with them, you may want to consider a profession where you can tend to their welfare and survival. Apart from farming or breeding anything from prize bulls to silkworms, there are an increasing number of wildlife sanctuaries in which the natural environment is rigorously preserved to ward off extinction. Domestic pets in distress also present a need, and you might want to run an animal-care establishment where they can receive the kind of love and attention you have to give. Or how about taking doggies walkies, like the strong-minded Taurus trainer Barbara Woodhouse?

The oils, essences and extracts of plants processed by a Taurus can become the lotions, creams, beauty preparations and perfumes favoured by Venus herself. The beauty industry has never been so diverse. A Taurus who ends up in this field is well suited to help others improve their looks, health or sense of wellbeing. Apart from hairdressers and beauticians, there are many different types of massage and physical therapies now practised where the Taurus talent for touch is an obvious asset. And in the fashion world, what better sign is there to transform the raw material of natural fibres—wool, cotton, linen or silk—into something both beautiful and practical?

The Bull may not be in his element right at the top of the tree, but it hasn't stopped plenty of Taurus people from getting there. They're rarely short of an opinion or two—in fact, it's amazing just how far some Taureans travelled on just one or two opinions. Their ideas are often appealing because they are so simple, or appalling because they're so extreme. On second thought, it may not be a very good idea to encourage a Taurus to enter politics. Taurus Adolf Hitler, for instance, would never have won prizes for broadminded fairness, and the Iranian Bull Ayatollah Khomeini isn't about to, either. Then consider Oliver Cromwell, a Taurus who managed to keep England a bundle of laughs for eleven years. And what about the female Bull Eva Peron, who makes Cruella de Ville look like a saint? Then there was Robespierre, who kept the blood flowing in France; and Lenin, who turned Russia Red. And, of course, the notorious Taurus Niccolò Machiavelli—with a name like that he couldn't really have made it as a bank manager, could he?

There's no doubt about it, for a sign that seems by and large committed to staying where it is, Taurus has made an enormous impact on the course of history. There are plenty of present-day examples, like the Papal Bull, John Paul II. Golda Meir was the Taurus premier who held Israel together through crisis after crisis, ably aided by Moshe Dayan—a real Bull fighter. Harry Truman was the President born in Taurus who said 'the buck stops here' and brought the war between America and Japan to an awesome conclusion. And you don't have to look too hard to see how the face of world politics has been permanently altered—for better or for worse—by the economic theories of another Taurus, Karl Marx. Ever thought of making a career in political economics? Or how about in philosophy, like that very utilitarian Taurus, John Stuart Mill?

If, like many people born in your sign, you are drawn to caring for others, never forget the example of Florence Nightingale, a woman of heroic perseverance. First she nursed troops in impossible conditions during the Crimean War; and then, in typically Taurus fashion, she retired to bed until the age of ninety and worked from there, totally transforming the care of the sick in English hospitals. And would the world have been the same without the birth of Sigmund Freud on 6 May 1856? He taught us that all is not quite what it may seem on the surface, and that something primitive and uncontrollable lurks behind even the most civilized facade. No Bull could argue with that!

Taurus compatibilities

Taurus/Aries*(Earth/Fire)* You're bound to admire all that Aries energy, drive and bravado, even if it leaves you dizzy from time to time. Remember, the Ram's forte is starting things; yours is finishing them. Provided you don't stand in their way, and they don't try to push you too fast, this could be a profitable and productive match.

Taurus/Taurus *(Earth/Earth)* As with all same-sign relationships, you two can bring out the very best or the very worst in each other. If you're not careful 'You scratch my back, I'll scratch yours' could pretty easily turn into 'You stay in your rut, I'll stay in mine'. Go to your Taurus colleague for understanding and support—but for real stimulation, look elsewhere.

Taurus/Gemini *(Earth/Air)* The terrible Twins are sometimes quite a handful. How can you possibly deal with a person who's in two places at once and is nowhere to be found when you really need them? Try following these simple instructions: Take Geminis once per day with a little salt. (Caution: it may be dangerous to exceed the stated dose.)

Taurus/Cancer *(Earth/Water)* Crabs really appreciate someone who isn't in a hurry to get anywhere. But watch out—even a dry earth sign like you could be totally swamped by watery Cancer. The Crab's always on the lookout for someone to mother—and with your need for security, you could be just the person. Accept them as they are, and you'll make a very compatible duo.

Taurus/Leo *(Earth/Fire)* Leos really enjoy working alongside a Taurus, even if the Lions' behaviour suggests they're the ones doing you a big favour. Lavish Leos with praise, spoil them with little gifts now and then, and you've got a friend for life. Of course, you won't see things their way all the time, but you had better keep that to yourself.

Taurus/Virgo *(Earth/Earth)* You should be in some kind of earthly harmony with your Virgo cousins, but the truth is they may find you slightly slow and undisciplined, maybe even a little naive. There's always something in a Virgo to respect, even though you could have some trouble coping with a sign that turns even the simplest task into a *magnum opus*.

Taurus/Libra *(Earth/Air)* Some Libras might seem a little too sugary even for your sweet tooth. They're famous for their diplomacy, but infamous for taking over. 'You don't mind if I just do this?'—that's a Libra statement, not a question. Nonetheless, if a job needs to be done to perfection, you two are the ones to do it.

Taurus/Scorpio *(Earth/Water)* Bulls like peace and harmony, which are about the last things you'll get with a Scorpio. Never mind, you still can't help being fascinated by their penetrating gaze and mysterious ways. You're both so different you're bound to learn a lot from one another. Just be careful not to cross them—a battle with a Scorpio is a battle for life.

Taurus/Sagittarius *(Earth/Fire)* Who is this person who swoops in and out, completely oblivious to your needs, and makes sarcastic comments to you and then disappears for days? The relationship between Sagittarius and Taurus makes Tweetie Pie and Sylvester look like the best of friends. Take the time to settle your differences, and you might be able to find some common ground. But work together comfortably? You must be joking.

Taurus/Capricorn *(Earth/Earth)* If you thought you were slow and reserved, wait till you get to know a Capricorn. They're so cautious about life, they even make you look daring. Okay, so neither of you is a ball of fire, but when it comes to making money, you two have got what it takes. Just remember, Capricorns give only as much as they get. So don't be stingy, and you'll never regret teaming up with a Goat.

Taurus/Aquarius *(Earth/Air)* You may be the embodiment of Patience, Taurus, but no matter how you play it with this sign, every meeting is a bit like a phone call with a bad connection. You begin talking about something quite practical and ordinary—and then suddenly you're debating the state of the world recession and a new charter for human rights. The Bull and the Water Bearer live in two different worlds, and it's probably just as well if it stays that way.

Taurus/Pisces *(Earth/Water)* The Fish is rather famous for its dramas, so you can count on being regularly entertained (or exasperated) when there's a Pisces in your working life. Sure, they may drain you at times; but if you're ever in some kind of trouble and need a bit of advice, Pisces co-workers are the ones to turn to—chances are they've been through it themselves.

The Taurus boss

Taurus bosses fall into two main categories. First there are the Ebenezer Scrooge variety, who'll resist change as if it were the advance of an invading army. You had better take a crash course in sign language, because these kind of Taurus people are deaf to any opinion but their own. (Did somebody mention a salary rise? Humbug!) But the second category of Taurus bosses— the naturally wise and sensitive ones—are more flexible and supportive. They're always around when things get difficult, holding it all together like some kind of superglue. They won't grudge offering their workers encouragement and more incentives—they know from experience that the occasional pay rise has a similar effect to ploughing fertilizer into the soil.

No matter where you stand on the earth, there's always a horizon—and a Bull isn't very keen to see beyond it. Everything in life has its limits, but especially Taurus bosses—who'll only allow an employee so much leeway before they draw the line. That's not altogether a bad thing. There are times when clear boundaries are not only necessary, but helpful—a young person just starting out in a job could learn a lesson or two from a strong, firm Taurus boss who knows better than any other sign how to say 'This far and no farther'.

Tranquil Taurus people like peace, and they'll usually do anything to avoid upsetting other people. Somehow they imagine that every difference of opinion will herald the start of another Hundred Years' War, so rather than confront you with what's bothering them, they keep it all in and quietly simmer away inside. They're really incredibly patient, but if you push them too far, watch out! When a Taurus blows, you don't want to be around. If you think the Incredible Hulk is over the top, just wait until an angry Bull gets hold of you.

The Taurus employee

A Taurus makes an excellent second-in-command, not because they're in any sense second-rate, but because the position is often a much more secure one. Even if they enjoy a little bit of the limelight, too much of it doesn't seem to agree with them. The power just behind the throne is less conspicuous, and a stronger vantage point for using their talents to support and consolidate things. Who better to hold the fort when the boss is out of town, than a solid, reliable Taurus?

You can lead a horse to water but you can't make it drink—with the Bull, you'd be lucky to get it to the water in the first place. The last quality an employer should expect from a Taurus employee is adaptability. It isn't totally true to say that Bulls are incapable of making fast adjustments in rapidly changing work situations, but their systems really find it hard to cope with too much change. In fact, if they're subjected to disruption over a long period of time, their health and self-assurance will visibly suffer. Taurus people function best when they feel confident and secure. So support them when they need it, give them a lot of time to work things out, never move their desk to a new place or ask them to change their day off—and they'll always come through.

A truly masochistic Taurus—and there are quite a few—can remain unfulfilled and financially unrewarded in the same employment for a very long time. They'll put up with terrible working conditions, difficult bosses and bleak prospects—things that would have driven away any other sign years before. So what's the payoff? (With Taurus, there's always a payoff!) Staying in the same job—no matter how awful it is—means that at least they don't have to face the trauma of uprooting themselves. Nobody loves a rut more than a Taurus.

If you're a Taurus, you need to feel valued, and money is the currency you understand best. But more than that, you need to feel good about the work you are doing. So if you've been sitting around in misery, hoping nobody will see what's really going on, don't cheat yourself any longer. Go out and get yourself a job you really want.

The Taurus colleague

When you first meet your Taurus colleague, you may be charmed and impressed by somebody friendly and easy-going who obviously wants to get to know you. She or he will give you a complete picture of how things are, and probably even ask you out to lunch (*who* said the Taurus would pay?) Don't be fooled into thinking you're being offered a warm welcome. That easy-going charm is the Taurus first line of defence— they can appear all peaches and cream on the surface, but underneath it's a different story.

When you want to understand the less obvious side of any astrological sign, look to its opposite sign. For Taurus, the sign to read up on is Scorpio. Every Taurus has a hidden Scorpion side, which means no matter how firmly their feet are planted on the ground, they like to dig beneath the surface of things now and then. So if you thought the questions at your job interview were tough, they weren't half as probing as what the Bull is trying to find out over a very pleasant lunch!

After that first encounter, your working relationship will quickly gel . . . one way or another. All Taurus wants to do in that initial reconnaissance exercise is to see how you are going to work out. Even if they can't be sure, rather than live in doubt they'll make up their minds about you very quickly. Taurus usually has pretty definite opinions about life (dogmatic is another way of putting it). What doesn't concern them, on the other hand, really doesn't interest them, and probably never will.

If you passed with flying colours, you've got yourself

a great workmate, a thoroughly reliable person whom you'll grow to treasure. But Bulls make demanding friends. They find it difficult to share, and it threatens them to see you close to somebody else. You might say they're insecure and jealous, but as the Bull understands it, something either belongs to you, or it belongs to me, but it can't belong to us both. And something is either right or it's wrong. Confusing, isn't it? So look out—because if Bulls are confused, that's when they get angry.

If you can accept the famous Taurus temper when it happens (which isn't very often), you're with an absolutely loyal and trustworthy person, who'll be just the right tonic after you've had a hard day at work. The very sight of a friendly Taurus colleague may become as cheering to your soul as the prospect of a familiar landmark after a long and gruelling journey.

Gemini

Element: Air
Symbol: The Twins
Ruler: Mercury

The Sign of the Twins

If you were born when the sun was in Gemini, the sign of the Twins, you'll understand yourself a lot better if you think for a minute about what it means to be a twin. Twins have always been set apart as different or special—after all, most babies make their entrance into the world alone, but twins come as a set. Certain ancient cultures even believed that when two children were born at the same time, one of them was really a god who had come to life in human form. (Goodness knows how they figured out which one; it must have caused an awful lot of sibling rivalry!) The toughest problem for twins—especially if they're identical—is that other people expect them to think and feel alike about everything; they find it hard to accept that each twin is a separate individual in his or her own right. People born under the sign of the Twins have a similar problem—a Gemini looks like one person but inside they're really two different people who don't always get along together.

The most famous twins in mythology were Castor and Pollux. They went everywhere and did everything together, although they were different in one *vital* respect—Pollux was divine and immortal (he would never have to cope with any nagging decisions on life-insurance policies), but Castor was a mortal human, who eventually would have to die. And one day, after a very savage fight, he did. Pollux cried so loud and long over his brother's death that Zeus agreed to grant

70

Castor immortality as well. There was, however, a catch--from that day on the inseparable twins had to live apart. When Castor was down on earth, Pollux had to stay up with the gods on Olympus. And when Pollux wanted to come to earth and mix with mortals, Castor would then have to go up to Olympus to take his place. If you're confused, just think what Geminis feel like; one part of them is in one place, and another part is off somewhere else entirely. You meet them one day and they're as high as can be, happy and full of hope; the very next day you run into them and they're down in the dumps, dragging their feet along. In fact, the only time Castor and Pollux ever got together was when they happened to pass one another, heading in opposite directions. It's the same with Geminis--you really don't know if they're coming or going. Chances are, they aren't sure either.

Mercury, the messenger god

Mercury is the ruler of Gemini, and his character tells us about the fast-thinking people born under this sign. Even as a babe in arms, no one could keep hold of Mercury. As soon as he was born, he was immediately fidgety (a common Gemini problem) and just couldn't wait to explore the world outside his nursery. His mother, Maya, laid him down for a minute, and in a flash he was out over the side of his cradle and off to find some amusement. If Mercury seems rather precocious for a day-old baby, you have to remember he was a baby god. His divine little mind was buzzing with ideas and teeming full of mischief. Just for starters, he decided to play a trick on his big brother, Apollo. Artful and more daring than the average child, Mercury couldn't be satisfied with only hiding the car keys, putting salt in Apollo's coffee, or tying his shoelaces together. Mercury's first brainwave was a plan to steal all his brother's cattle, without getting caught at it (not many infants think of doing that!). Brushing over his own tiny footprints as he went, Mercury marched the herd away *backwards* (to totally confuse anyone who might be hot on their trail) and hid them in a field miles from anywhere.

Apollo, however, unlike Mercury, wasn't born yesterday, and it didn't take him too long to work out what had happened. He was livid. But by the time he got around to Maya's place, his baby brother was back lying in the crib, gooing and cooing sweetly to his mother. When Apollo leant forward to make his accusations, the tender infant broke wind violently in his big brother's face. Realizing he would get nowhere fast with this impossible child, Apollo blew his top. Mercury sat up coolly in his cradle, reproaching Apollo with big innocent eyes, and said: 'Brother, how can you imagine that a tiny, helpless little baby like me could have done such a terrible thing to you?' Watch out! Like their ruler, Mercury, some Geminis can turn on the charm and get away with almost anything.

Mercury was part liar, part thief, and an irresistible charmer to boot. But there was much more to him than that. In fact, like any young child who learns quickly to please (because he realizes just how much he is at the mercy of powerful adults), Mercury could adapt and become whatever a situation demanded—just like a versatile Gemini. With this gift, he fitted in anywhere, and earned the job of messenger to the gods. Acting as a guide for confused mortal souls in all their dealings on earth, he was even able to travel with them after death into the dark underworld, where no other god except Pluto was allowed. Sometimes in heaven, sometimes on earth, sometimes in the deepest underworld— Mercury certainly got around. His ability to see everybody's point of view made him an ideal diplomat, and he was often called in to repair the damage caused by the gods in their ungodlike feuding and persistent infidelities. But despite his serious importance in an adult world, the god Mercury remained a child forever. The same could be said about most Geminis.

The Gemini temperament

Like Mercury, people born in Gemini are as curious about life as a young child. No matter what age they are, the world is a fascinating place, begging to be discovered—and there are never enough hours in any day to take it all in. People born in the element of air don't want to get stuck in one place like boring old Taurus or get swamped in their feelings like a soppy Cancer. If you're a Gemini, you need to feel free to breathe, move, get about, circulate, travel, run, jump, dance, swim, see new places, meet new people, do new things. You welcome change, you thrive on variety—new sights, sounds, tastes, smells, and plenty of new ideas. Your ruler is Mercury, the spokesman of the gods, and everything in life says something to you in its shape, its song, its colour or its movement. But probably nothing means more to you than words, For the small Gemini child eager to discover life, words are the key—nothing is more fun than learning what something is called and then figuring out how it works. MUMMY, DADDY, MILK, TEDDY, GARDEN, STREET, CAR, MONEY, AIRPORT, PLANE . . . with every new word a Gemini learns, the whole world opens up into a bigger and more exciting place.

When something has been named, that's not the end of the story. The conquest of life continues. Geminis also love to move and change things around. So if the CAT gets put in its BASKET, and the TOWEL goes in the WASHER, then what would happen if you put the TOWEL in the BASKET, and the CAT into the WASHER? Oh dear, a little Gemini's logic can seem a bit cruel to an adult (the Marquis de Sade was born in this sign)! But never mind, that's just their way of playing. And, don't forget, when they're playing, they're learning.

Most Geminis have a very playful side to their natures. You'll notice it often in their sense of humour. Life amuses them. Words, like objects, can be shuffled around, hidden, mixed and muddled up:

'My dog hasn't got a nose'.
'Your dog hasn't got a nose? Well, how does he smell?'
'He smells terrible!'

Gemini is very much the joker in the pack. The Twins delight in humour, they appreciate wit, and they're often very amusing people. A joke involves putting together objects, ideas or words that don't, by convention, belong in the same place. There's an anarchy in Gemini humour, and nothing is quite sacred—not even other people's feelings. In olden times, the courts of kings and noblemen always had a resident jester who occupied a very important position. Although the order of access to the king for everybody else was limited, the jester was allowed close to him at all times. The clever clown had a role that would have delighted Mercury himself. He could poke fun everywhere, deflating the self-important in a most infuriating way ... and there wasn't a thing anyone could do to stop him!

But Gemini is the sign of the Twins, and every Gemini is two people (which is probably a conservative estimate). No Gemini can be a bright, happy butterfly every day. There is also a deeper and more serious side to this sign. Remember Castor and Pollux—when one went up, the other had to come down? Geminis who try to live it up all the time often come down to earth with a crash when they least expect it. Look at Gemini actress Joan Collins, famous in recent years for her portrayal of Alexis Carrington in the TV soap *Dynasty*—both on and off the screen, her life is never short of ups and downs. Geminis are complex people who swing back and forth from happiness to sadness, from hope to despair in their search for fulfilment. Who can listen to Judy Garland, the Gemini who sang about life on the other side of the rainbow, without recalling her own sad story? And there's Marilyn Monroe, the Gemini who brought pleasure to millions, but couldn't find any joy in her own life. Another famous Gemini, John F. Kennedy, died tragically in the process of imparting his fresh young dream of new hope to the world. Don't be fooled by a Gemini's frothy exterior—there's much more to this sign than meets the eye.

Even the most buoyant Gemini can run aground in a relationship. If you are the kind of person who enjoys the challenge of a jigsaw puzzle, then a Gemini makes an ideal mate. But don't expect your Gemini partner to only have eyes for you. They're so interested in everything else going on around them, you're bound to feel left out a lot of the time. Most Geminis just like the fun of flirting, although some are notorious for carrying on more than one love relationship at a time. Whoever said a bird in the hand is worth two in the bush, certainly wasn't a typical Twin. If this strikes you as rather immoral, think back to Mercury and you will appreciate that he wasn't moral in anything he did. But if you like paradoxes, you can also run into some very inflexible Gemini moral crusaders (Mrs Mary Whitehouse of the British Viewers' and Listeners' Association is an example). A Gemini not into adapting will sooner break than bend for anyone. And they'll argue their point very convincingly.

What you'll probably notice first about a Gemini are those eyes. Quick, bright, attentive. They miss nothing. You may have run into some very flighty Geminis with a disconcerting habit of looking all over the place while they're talking. Relax. They're not bored (otherwise they would have left you half an hour ago). And they aren't being rude—they just hate to think they could be missing out on something! Besides which, the sign of the Twins is the only sign in the Zodiac capable of doing two things at once . . . and giving both their undivided attention. On the other side of the coin, if you happen to meet the dark, questioning stare of a Gemini in a serious mood, you may wonder for a moment if you aren't being interrogated by a reincarnation of the Grand Inquisitor!

Mercury rules the hands, and most Gemini people like to keep them occupied. If you're at a party and you see somebody gesticulating like an Italian traffic cop, you're probably looking at a Gemini. A Gemini may also be the one clouding the room with tobacco smoke— that's another way they've learned to keep their hands busy. But if you fall into the category of a heavy-smoking Gemini, you should think seriously about taking up crochet; your sign rules the lungs, and there's no proven link yet between crochet hooks and cancer. All you Geminis could do with looking after yourselves a little better. With your hurried life style, you may be too busy to eat properly, and you don't always give yourselves enough time to rest and unwind. You can only get away with this for so long before your nerves are shot to hell. Learn to treat your body with the respect it deserves. When your health goes, everything else could too.

The Gemini types

Geminis born between 22 May and 30 May Bright, lively, outgoing, inquisitive and communicative, you're the most mercurial of all the Gemini types and the most difficult to pin down. Never at a loss for words, you always manage to find something to say about everything . . . even if other people haven't a clue half the time what you're on about.

Geminis born between 31 May and 10 June You're probably the most creative of all the Gemini types, so take time to develop your skills and talents. You're also warm and sociable, and have a real desire to be liked by people. But be careful, you're pretty idealistic, which means you might be disappointed when others don't live up to your high expectations.

Geminis born between 11 June and 21 June   What's obvious to everyone else doesn't interest you a bit. With your insatiable curiosity, you love the weird and wonderful, and look at life from a highly individual angle. Your tendency to try anything once just to see what it is like will get you into some pretty tight corners at times—but leave it to you to figure a way out.

Gemini and work

Mercury was the original jack of all trades, so finding work isn't usually a problem for a Gemini. But after a while, when the list of previous occupations starts to read like an encyclopedia of employment, Geminians may begin to get the feeling they're losing out just flitting around like frenetic butterflies and dabbling in a little bit of everything. When you're young, trying your hand at lots of different things is exciting and a natural part of the process of discovering who you are. However, if this goes on too long, you could end up rootless and lost—you've done a little bit of this and a little bit of that, but you haven't stayed with anything long enough to become really adept at it. Even though no Gemini loves a rut, you're happier in the long run if you've something you can call a career. That doesn't stop you having all the interests in the world, but when you're born in a sign that pulls you so many different ways, its important to find a clear direction.

It's a disappointment to discover that not many jobs are constructed for people who like variety. In a large organization, a multi-talented Gemini could feel cramped just being one little component among many in a big impersonal machine. Others of this sign—like

Jean, a Gemini piano teacher, satisfy their needs for change by having two or more pots on the stove at the same time. During the day, dressed in a conventional two-piece tailored suit, she works at home teaching a succession of serious young music students. But when evening comes, Jean puts her hair up and her face on, and shimmering in sequins, dashes off into town to belt out jazz in an up-and-coming nightclub.

It's true that you can't stand a job that's too sedentary, routine or repetitious. But as you get older and gain more experience of life, you may find you don't have to move around all over the place to quench your thirst for change. Even in the same job, with a little bit of ingenuity (something most Geminis aren't short of), no two days need be the same. And providing you don't too quickly pigeonhole, judge or label others, you'll discover plenty to fascinate you about the people you work with. If you're a Gemini who feels you're going nowhere with nothing to look forward to but pay day, try this exercise—it may help you sort out your priorities:

1. Write down one major thing you would like to accomplish in the next year—something which would make you feel good about yourself.

2. Each month sit down and make a report on how you are doing. Have you been working steadily towards your goal, or have you been so diverted in other directions that you have neglected it? If the latter is the case, retrace how and when this has happened. It may be that you need to keep more of a rein on that part of you which is easily side-tracked. Or it may be that your goal is no longer important to you. See if you can figure out which.

3. If your goal is still important to you, then take the time to refocus on it. If you are no longer interested in that goal, it's okay to choose another one. But if you keep changing each month, then you need to look more closely at why you are so terrified of making a commitment.

Gemini careers

By now, it will come as no surprise to learn that versatile Geminis are so clever at so many different things, they have a lot of trouble deciding on one path to pursue. Let's look more closely at the kinds of careers where their potential talents can be best expressed.

Geminis have a way with words, and are truly fascinated by their meanings and their effects. Words can disturb us, amuse us or confuse us. They can jump out at us from a letter or a printed page. They have the power to provoke, enrage, intimidate or reassure. Geminis often like to keep a dictionary or a thesaurus nearby, and it isn't surprising that many of them use words—written, spoken, and sometimes both—as the central ingredient in their working lives. Many public figures past and present, famous as communicators, were born in Gemini—Prime Minister William Pitt the Younger, Presidents John F. Kennedy and George Bush, Prince Philip (whose quick Gemini tongue gets him into trouble from time to time) and Henry Kissinger (who in his role of international diplomat and messenger would have done Mercury proud). A person who notices everything, including every bit of news and gossip . . . someone who has the kind of charm that can get them through doors that are closed to other people . . . the sort who mixes well and fits effortlessly into any social group . . . is just the kind of person who could make a career in the media. There are Gemini newscasters, radio and television commentators, disc jockeys, chat show hosts (like Geminian Joan 'Can We Talk' Rivers), stylish public relations experts (like image-maker Charles Saatchi), publishers and media magnates (like newspaper mogul Robert Maxwell) and —according to statistics—many, many Gemini journalists and reporters all working with words. What's just as important for a Gemini, is that these occupations deal with what's happening *now*. Geminis hate to miss a thing.

Geminis are born fact-gatherers, but they're not averse to disseminating a little fiction now and then. The catalogue of famous creative writers born under this sign is an international *Who's Who* in literature. *A* is for Arthur: Arthur Conan Doyle, author of the Sherlock Holmes books (did *you* detect the Gemini in him?). If you prefer literary heavyweights, Jean-Paul Sartre was also a Gemini (among his many works is an autobiographical piece, simply called *Words*). If you're looking for words to lead you to a mystical inner world, try the works of William Butler Yeats. Or if you go for the Arthurian legend, read *The Sword in the Stone* by T. H. White ('The best thing for being sad is to learn something'—Merlin). For the more featherweight taste, and a popular bedtime read that inspired nearly a dozen films, what about the James Bond books by Gemini Ian Fleming? If quick thrills and macho mania make you cringe, but you like a good story tightly written, get hold of Dashiell Hammett's detective books. There's another good read in the short stories and personal anecdotes of Lillian Hellman, the Gemini playwright and cinema screenplay giant who lived with Hammett for many years. The list continues with Russian Gemini Aleksandr Pushkin, German Thomas Mann, American Saul Bellow and terribly English G. K. Chesterton; the playwrights Jean Anouilh, Ben Jonson and Terence Rattigan; poets Walt Whitman, Gerard Manley Hopkins and Federico Garcia Lorca; Gemini women writers Elizabeth Bowen, Fanny Burney and Françoise Sagan. Geminians will no doubt continue to add to the list of great and popular fiction, so long as there are people who enjoy reading. Or listening. Let's not forget Gemini songwriters Cole Porter and Sammy Cahn whose immortal lyrics still linger on in almost everyone's head. And what about Bob Dylan, another

Gemini, considered by some to be the mouthpiece for the sixties generation.

Not every Gemini is scrupulously honest. (Who would be, if it meant spoiling a good story?) Travelling from fame to infamy, there are Gemini writers who have made a highly lucrative living, exploiting a typical Gemini weakness—gossip! The most notorious, but by no means the only example, is Hedda Hopper (reputedly born 2 June 1890)—a woman who made Hollywood hell for the indiscreet. Before we leave writers, and passing from the notorious to the sublime, let's add to our list the name of Queen Victoria. She was not known in her day as a writer—when you have a title like the Empress of India, it tends to obscure your creative talents. Her secluded childhood frustrated her natural Gemini curiosity and thirst for knowledge; but her lively personal diaries reveal her sensitive private character and provide an intriguing narrative of the era over which she reigned. Out of a very ugly period of history came the beautiful, haunting diary of Anne Frank, another Gemini who has touched the hearts of millions. (By the way, if you're having trouble tracking down any of these writers, there's probably a Gemini working at your local bookshop who will be very happy to help you. And a typically capable Gemini librarian will surely be able to locate a copy of anything that's temporarily out of print.)

Music is another Gemini talent. During one of his early excursions on the unsuspecting world, the young Mercury met with a tortoise. The diminutive divinity enticed the poor creature into a nearby cave, where he brought its animal life to a swift and unexpected conclusion. From the shell, Mercury made the very first lyre, which he used to bribe Apollo to forget all about the cattle incident. Musical instruments aren't cheap, but a few of you would-be Gemini musicians will have to resort to such extreme measures in order to get in some practice. Musical notes, the shapes they make, their interactions, their harmonies and discords can be every bit as appealing to some Twin types as words are to others. And to prove the point, there's a legacy of Gemini classical music in the works of Grieg, Schumann, Gounod, Stravinsky and Richard Strauss. If you aren't that much into culture but you'd like to perform music all the same, here's a Gemini list to give you some encouragement: Paul McCartney, Barry Manilow, Grace Jones, Prince, Dean Martin, Burl Ives, Benny Goodman, Rosemary Clooney, Judy Garland, Tom Jones and Suzi Quatro. And if you can't play or sing (although that never stopped some people) why not dance like expressive Geminian Isadora Duncan.

After words and music, we have to mention pictures. A Cancer person will most probably remember an event for the feelings it evoked, but most Geminis see things in pictures—frequently 3-D. So it's not surprising to find Geminis behind the camera, in films, television or photography. Julia Margaret Cameron enchanted the Victorians with her pioneering photographs in the pre-Raphaelite style; and the ever-curious Gemini Jacques Cousteau helped show us a world we don't normally see with his remarkable underwater films and photos. Outstanding among Gemini film directors is James Ivory of *A Room With A View* fame. And with the Twins' natural eye for colour, detail and form, it's not surprising that some Gemini painters have left a vivid impression—like the engraver Dürer, the eye-catching Gauguin or the convention-breaking Gustave Courbet, to name a few. Or how about making concrete use of your creative talents by following in the footsteps of the famous Gemini architect Frank Lloyd Wright?

Unfortunately, there are people who have trouble seeing anything. A natural concern with clear vision attracts many Geminis to careers as opticians, optometrists and even eye surgeons. And with their quick and sensitive hands, it's not unusual to find Geminis effectively teaching braille to the blind and visually handicapped, or helping the deaf to develop speech and communicate with sign language.

On any subject, in any setting, an important strength in a teacher is the ability to convey clear pictures. Geminis have an immediate and very creative understanding of younger people—and even the ability to draw out the inquisitive child, eager to learn, in the older student. That's where the famous Gemini humour comes in very handy. It's an established fact (or so a Gemini once said) that people learn quickly and effortlessly when they're amused. Or when they're in love . . . but that's another story.

In mythology, Mercury was famous as the messenger of the gods. He kept people in touch, passing information from one person to another. And if you're a Gemini, you probably enjoy doing this as well. So why not capitalize on it by joining the ranks of postal workers or offering your services in the field of telecommunications? And what office wouldn't benefit from having a friendly Gemini receptionist or switchboard operator, who could smooth talk even the most irate callers.

Dealing appropriately with people means being able to understand where they are coming from. Geminis often have the ability to sense what it's like to be standing in somebody else's shoes. So if a Gemini friend says 'If I were you, I would . . .', it might be worth considering his or her advice. And with the right training, Geminis who have learned to listen as well as talk make first-class counsellors and therapists. After all, one of Mercury's jobs was to guide souls into the underworld, and that is really what psychotherapy is basically about—looking at what is going on beneath the surface level of life.

Mercury, a born trickster, was also a master of disguise. Perhaps that's what takes so many Geminis into the fashion industry (Beau Brummell, the Regency dandy was a Gemini). They bring together unlikely combinations, design new cuts, predict next year's colour, revive neglected styles from Grandma's day and add their own special touches. Their love of dressing up could lead them into the theatre and cinema, where people do it all the time. Take Laurence (now Lord) Olivier as a very typical example of the Gemini chameleon. His detractors always moaned that he was 'more ham than Hamlet' but, through his career as an actor and director, he became undeniably a Gemini legend for all time. As an energetic young actor he loved to sport wigs and false noses, alter his body shape, his walk and his speaking voice—employing an outstanding Gemini gift for mimicry with every role that he took on. (The extraordinary impersonator Stanley Baxter is another Gemini performer.) And don't forget Al Jolson, another versatile Twin, who starred in *The Jazz Singer*, the very first Talkie, and told the world in true Gemini style 'You ain't heard nothing yet!' Other Geminis who have made or are making their mark include Bob Hope, Clint Eastwood, Michael J. Fox, Brooke Shields, Priscilla Presley, John Wayne, Errol Flynn, Jane Russell, Johnny Weissmuller (You Tarzan, Me Jane), Judy Holliday, Rosalind Russell, Beryl Reid and *Hill Street Blues* cop Bruce Weitz.

There are lots of Geminis around with great big stars in their eyes. Many make it to the top, like Donald Trump, the fabulously wealthy American casino owner who's left his mark on the Manhattan Skyline; some, like Wallis Simpson, who *almost* became Queen of England, don't get quite as far as they would like. Of course, success depends on what you're looking for. Many Geminis are looking for a line of work that will give them a more ordinary satisfaction, a good income and sound career prospects. If nothing we've mentioned so far suits you, how about using your powers of persuasion as a salesperson?—Geminis are notorious for their ability to talk anyone into anything. You can be with a person, any person, less than a minute and already you know where they buy their clothes, how they voted in the last election, their grandmother's maiden name, and the exact pitch that would appeal to them. Talking of speaking somebody's language, how's your Hebrew? Or your French? Serbo-Croat? Swahili? Geminis make excellent linguists, translators and interpreters. In these kinds of job, you might even end up travelling, although you could be just as happy sorting out travel for somebody else. You're somebody who can get a thrill from a day trip to the next town, so why not make your living planning other people's journeys?

There are many ways of getting around for a living. You could be a bus conductor, a train, lorry or taxi driver—all good Gemini jobs. You could race around like Twin Jackie Stewart, or horse around like Gemini Grand National winner Bob Champion, or chase a ball around like nimble Gemini Wimbledon champ Bjorn Borg. Of course, if tennis doesn't appeal to you, why don't you use that playful imagination of yours to invent your own game? Unfortunately, we don't know the sign of the person who created Trivial Pursuit, but it sounds just the kind of thing a Gemini would think up. Do something comparable, and you'll be laughing hysterically all the way to the bank.

Gemini compatabilities

Gemini/Aries (*Air/Fire*) You need constant stimulation, and an Aries is the one to give it to you. When you team up, anything is possible—especially hot new ideas that could make you both a lot of money. Born friends, you'll enjoy working together almost as much as you'll enjoy playing together. But face it, there aren't many who could keep up with the two of you, and probably quite a few who would be happier not to!

Gemini/Taurus *(Air/Earth)* A Taurus is bound to be annoyed at times by your lively energy—as a bull feels harassed by a gadfly. In any work situation, a Gemini may leave the Bull wondering what it was that just flew past him. All right, Taurus is a bit slow and stifling at times, but if you hang around long enough to watch, you could learn a lot about the value of patience and perseverance from this sign.

Gemini/Gemini *(Air/Air)* When you look into the mirror, some days you like what you see, and other days you don't. And that's pretty much how you'll feel working alongside another Gemini. But when you two put your four heads together, you'll never be short of ideas and schemes. Whether you ever stop talking about them and get around to doing them is another story, and stories are one thing the two of you will never be short of.

Gemini/Cancer *(Air/Water)* Your casual observations and some of your innocent, off-the-cuff remarks will cut sensitive Cancer to the quick and put you in their bad books for months. Perhaps you'll never fully understand why they take life so seriously, but for your own sake, just accept that they do. Okay, you might get exasperated by the moody Crab's ups and downs, but when was the last time you won a prize for consistency?

Gemini/Leo *(Air/Fire)* Leo is a child at heart, so you two kids should have a great time working together. You know how to please, you're thoughtful, witty and attentive—all the things Leos pride themselves on. Of course, they won't admit it, but they do get a little jealous when you go off and play with someone else. Never mind, just keep remembering to laugh at all their jokes, and they'll forgive you anything . . . eventually.

Gemini/Virgo *(Air/Earth)* Not a bad business combination. You'll like their dry sense of humour and their common-sense approach, even though they're a little too down-to-earth at times for your taste. They'll find you witty, inventive and clever, even though you're a little too over-the-top at times for their liking. But together you'll do the job and do it well. Just don't make a steady diet of one another, that's all.

Gemini/Libra *(Air/Air)* The very best of friends—your air sign affinities make for mutual understanding. You both like compliments, and you both know how to give them. Of course, Librans have a lot of trouble making up their minds, and you can be pretty indecisive at times. Let's just hope you two never have to come to any joint decisions, or we'll be here all day.

Gemini/Scorpio *(Air/Water)* Gemini is one of the few signs capable of outwitting a Scorpio. Your relationship is a bit like a chess game—each person trying to figure out what the other one will do next. You'll love Scorpio's insight and depth; they'll respect your clever observations. But the Scorpion's intensely emotional nature will occasionally be too much for your rational mind to bear. What's even worse, Scorpio demands the one thing you find the hardest to give—your total commitment.

Gemini/Sagittarius *(Air/Fire)* Sagittarius is restless, enthusiastic, and loves a good time. A lot like you. They'll take you places you're afraid to go on your own, and you'll point out things they usually miss along the way. Once you stop nattering all the time and get down to it, you two could work well together. Sagittarius has vision and big ideas; and you're just the one to provide the practical details to help realize them.

Gemini/Capricorn *(Air/Earth)* Down-to-earth Capricorn really isn't the easiest sign for you. They like sure-fire ideas which are known to work, while you're full of bright new schemes and fancy, chance gimmicks. Besides, they moan a lot, and that's guaranteed to drive you up the wall. But you'll learn to respect the way they stand by their principles, even if you don't agree with half of them.

Gemini/Aquarius *(Air/Air)* Great minds think alike, and you two probably will. When other people at work really aren't speaking your language and you need a bit of company with imagination and something different, freshen up your life with a dose of the Water Bearer. You may find them downright stubborn at times, but their timing is perfect—they'll always show up just when you need them most. And even better than that, they know when to keep their distance.

Gemini/Pisces *(Air/Water)* Pisces swim in and out of work situations almost as cleverly as you weave your way through them. But how could you not love the Fish? They're gullible enough to be taken in by nearly everything you say—no matter how many times you change your mind or point of view. It's true, you may find their inscrutable emotions a little infuriating at times, but that makes them all the more fascinating to try to figure out.

The Gemini boss

If you're a typical Gemini man or woman, you'll pride yourself on how well you fit in at work, and how easy it is for people to relate to you. But take heed, things can alter dramatically when you become the person in charge. Geminis who see promotion as the means to greater personal freedom are in for a rude awakening. Even if you're working for yourself, you'll start to feel very uneasy as the full weight of responsibility comes to rest on your shoulders. When it dawns on you that you're in control of the working lives of a large number of people, there aren't many of you who can hold onto that favourite Gemini catch phrase *'That's not my problem'*. Colleagues you once considered agreeable and capable will turn overnight into demanding, obstructive or incompetent oafs with serious comprehension difficulties. As boss, if you choose to make it your business to field every tricky situation that comes your way, you'll wind up with ulcers. You're a sharp troubleshooter, but even a well-weathered Gemini in charge will be driven crazy trying to hold it all together and please everybody.

With a Gemini, it's often all or nothing. Most of the times, a Gemini boss will rise to any challenge and look tirelessly for fresh strategies to cope with each new situation. But if everything gets too much, and *your* Gemini boss gives up in despair, then you'd better beware. That's when the other side takes over . . . and that's the side that doesn't give a damn. Gemini, like all thinking types, can suddenly decide to switch off the central heating and be very cool and aloof to everybody. Geminis believe there must be a solution to every difference of opinion, and sometimes the most effective way they have of proving that philisophy is to shut out anyone who doesn't agree with them. So one morning when you arrive at work you might notice that the WELCOME mat has been taken in. From that day on, the boss's office can be codenamed FORTRESS GEMINI, with a snarling Scorpio secretary keeping guard at the door. When the sign that's interested in everything and everyone changes its tune, nothing matters but its own concerns. Geminis who take that position aren't unique, but it can make them very, very lonely. And that's not easy for a sign that likes to relate.

So to all you Geminis with your sights set on the top, a few words of caution. Remember that you need to enjoy what you do. If you're happy being a boss, you can be one of the best. But when the pleasure in your working life goes, you need to do something about it, or you may as well give up working.

The Gemini employee

A Gemini in employment enjoys being described as an asset. And Geminis with the will to get on certainly know how to impress you with dazzling displays of their varied talents. Geminis have charm, and they know how to present themselves. They usually dress well, they can be very entertaining and they're incredibly well-informed. When you visit a company and you're greeted by a Gemini employee, you can be sure that he or she has made it their personal business to know everything there is to know about you. And what better way to learn all that's going on than to keep on good terms with everybody? Managers always find Geminis useful; directors find them indispensable; and the chairman of the board will find them absolutely everywhere!

With a Gemini, there are always two sides to a story. People born under this sign not only have sharp eyes, they can have a sharp tongue too. If Geminis believe they're being treated unfairly, they have a full battery of effective medium and long-range ammunition to inflict on a less than perfect establishment. George's story is a case in point. He was working in a large advertising concern and doing very well. But then his boss started giving a younger colleague all the interesting contracts that came in, and our Gemini friend George was left dealing with the cement companies and spare-part wholesalers. Very soon George had had enough. Over lunch with a co-worker one afternoon, he drew up an entertaining list of his boss's faults; 'unimaginative', 'tasteless', 'bigoted', 'inefficient', and so on—each adjective bringing to mind an amusing anecdote about the manager's imperfect character. Unfortunately, just as he reached the chapter headed 'mentally deficient', his boss, who happened to be sitting behind him at the next table (and who, with all his faults, had never been deaf), turned round and gave George his marching orders.

If you appreciate your Gemini employees, they'll sparkle for you. Gemini is often the resident comedian, supplying a steady flow of wisecracks and funny stories to keep a working team alive and happy. They're friendly, caring and attentive to their colleagues. They'll be the first to volunteer to organize the surprise party when somebody has an important birthday. Of course, that'll mean making a few calls to order food and bring in some of their old friends (your monthly phone bill will double within two hours). They'll even take time during their lunch hour to drive quickly round the corner to collect the hors d'oeuvres, the savoury dips, the crispbreads and the wine. Of course, in the process, they're bound to bump into somebody they haven't seen for years . . . and with the heavy lunch-hour traffic, you'll be lucky if they're back at their desk by three-thirty. Okay, so no work has been done in the meantime, but can you really be cross with anyone who's being so thoughtful?

The Gemini colleague

Ever wonder how news travels so fast when there's a Gemini around your place of work? Well, here's the answer. Any Gemini baby that's delivered into this world comes with an in-built radio receiver. How else do they always manage to be around when something's happening? Male or female, they make a great Clark Kent, there to sort out every crisis and get all the news in to the bargain. Is it a plane? Is it a bird? No, it's a Gemini, here to help fix the photocopier about to explode; deal with an awkward customer; calm down a manager who's blowing a gasket; compose a difficult letter; mend a broken heart. They'll be there with tea, sympathy, two asprins, a dry handkerchief, a screwdriver, a gin and tonic, a sledgehammer, a hundred words of good advice, and whatever else you need. Problem solved? They're off—there's always something else that a Gemini really *must* be doing!

But your Gemini colleague's flighty habits could undermine even the happiest work relationship. If the will-o'-the-wisp in question is in short supply once too often when there's a pressing job to be done, you might get angry with them and speak words the Gemini will find hard to take. At a given moment, there's usually one bane in a Gemini's life. Rub a Twin the wrong way and one day it will be your turn. In contrast to their normally talkative selves, they'll become deep and impenetrable. If you try to make conversation, they'll respond with a wafer-thin comment that slices you through. Even if you ignore them, the atmosphere becomes charged like an impending thunderstorm.

Fortunately, most Geminis like to travel light and they'll eventually discover a reason to cast off old resentments—and you'll be relieved and grateful to be working with the sign that has the gift of being able to look at every situation from more than one perspective. But then again, you could be working alongside a more relentless and unforgiving Twin—in which case you'll simply find yourself attacked from every possible side. You might as well give in because they never give up—there's nothing quite so persistent as a grudge-bearing Gemini with a point to prove.

Cancer

Element: Water

Symbol: The Crab

Ruler: Moon

The Sign of the Crab

If you have trouble understanding what Cancer people are all about (and who doesn't at times?) try getting to grips with a crab. With Cancer being a water sign, water is where you'd expect to find crabs, but they like to come out and see what's happening on dry land too. A crab can stay still for so long on the same rock that you're tempted to think it's dead (precisely the thought that might run through your mind with a very slow Cancer person). But if you want to grab hold of it, you won't get the chance—it'll be back safe in the water before you can touch it. That's elusive Cancer for you!

Cancerians move like the crab: sideways. They're not quick to begin things and they often take the long way round—London to Edinburgh via Peking. But they can move fast when they want to—try taking away something that belongs to them and you'll see. These people are sensitive souls, so don't be fooled just because some of them appear confident and on top of everything. They act tough and strong to protect themselves, just as the crab grows a tough shell to cover that very vulnerable body.

For a Cancer, letting go of the past and starting a new phase in life can be painful but necessary, which is what growing is for a crab. Every now and then all crustaceans—the crab family, in fancy language—grow so much they start bursting out of their shells (that's no comment on your weight problems, Cancer!). They find

93

themselves a dark corner under a rock where nobody can see them—like sensitive Cancer people going through a difficult time. Life is hell for crabs until they get out of the old shell and the new one gets comfortable. Cancers who recall the pain of changing jobs, moving house or starting another day, will know just how they feel!

It's amazing nobody has thought up a dance called the crab. All you Cancer people could pick up the moves in no time: two steps forward, one step back, and repeat . . . over and over. That's how most Cancerians move through life. They start out to do something, and then they wonder if they're doing the right thing. In friendships and deep personal relationships, for no obvious reason, they're very close one minute and far away the next, leaving other people confused and asking 'Did I do something? What did I say?'

Cancers need to get away, be alone or lose themselves in a crowd for a while, and then they're usually fine. Getting to know the little ways of the human Crab may take you a lifetime, but if you don't give up on them they'll never give up on you. At the same time, you'll have to accept that their vulnerability makes them awfully defensive. You're liable to get pinched very hard if you ever start messing around with Cancer the Crab!

The moon, ruler of Cancer

If you live or work with a moody Cancer and the ups and downs are driving you loopy, it's worth taking time to observe the monthly cycles of the moon. The new moon peering out of the dark sky might remind you of a Cancer tentatively entering a new situation. When Cancers get used to new people and places, they relax and become more confident, like the moon gradually growing brighter and fuller. But having done all the waxing it can, the moon begins waning again, until it disappears completely. Now you see it, now you don't.

Cancer people are always disappearing too, behind work or a book or something. You need to bear in mind that the moon doesn't ever leave. It travels in a perpetual orbit around the earth; even when it's behind a cloud, it's always there, although it doesn't look that way. When you're getting to know a Cancer, you'll discover that he or she is never as far away as you think.

Pale and mysterious, eternal yet ever changing, the moon has always been an object of fascination. Many of the world's early civilizations were matriarchal (i.e. they were run by women) and the moon was worshipped as a goddess. It's easy to understand how people long ago saw the moon as the face of a great big mother looking down at her children in the dark. We make a connection in astrology between the moon and a person's early home, something very important for all Cancerians. Some of them feel as if they're tearing their hearts out when they leave home. And the most important thing of all about home for Cancers is MOTHER. Wonderful or awful, mothers have a huge influence on Cancer children, as many adult Cancers will tell you . . . for hours and hours.

The word *lunatic* comes from the Latin word for moon. It doesn't mean that Cancerians are mad, but they are extra sensitive to the magnetic influence of the moon on the earth. The moon affects movements of water, as you can see with the tides; and when you consider that the human body is seventy per cent water, you'll appreciate that we're all susceptible to its influence. Cancerians in particular are often aware of the full moon once every month. It doesn't make them sprout hairs or howl in their sleep, but as people who live or work in big institutions can tell you, it's often a time when things get a bit out of hand. The sign of Cancer teaches us about something we prefer to forget—our own natural rhythms and cycles. People are a part of nature, like the seasons and the tides, the pattern of night and day, and the life cycles of plants and animals. Technology may have made many things possible, but it doesn't remove the fact that changes and cycles are a part of life. So if you're a person who regularly complains about all the moods a Cancer goes through, ask yourself if you aren't perhaps a little more changeable than you would like to admit.

The Cancer temperament

After a jaunt through Gemini, you're probably tired of rushing around. So relax now and let Cancer look after you. Crabs love taking care of things and people, but their emotions in any situation are as fickle as the weather. They are celebrated for their moods—some of them have more changes of feeling than Imelda Marcos had shoes—and they aren't very good at hiding their little fluctuations. A Cancer in a carefree mood makes everybody smile; but meet a drab and droopy Crab for lunch and you're saying 'farewell' to joy for the rest of the day. Many people lose patience with a temperament that seems so indulgent and childish. Cancers do behave a bit like children, but that isn't necessarily a bad thing—in fact, part of the trouble with our very 'adult' world is that many grown-ups have lost touch with the part of us that never grew up. Cancer people are only too aware of it. Cancerians who remember a bright and happy childhood radiate a glowing playfulness through to old age. If some of the memories of the early home are sad and hurtful, a Cancer can carry feelings of unhappiness right into adult life. A small cut made in a young tree becomes a large scar when the tree grows big.

Some of the things that Cancer has to teach us about life concern memories we'd sooner forget. Most of us can recall quite clearly something unpleasant or painful which happened a long time ago when we were children. For instance, imagine you were ignored or rejected when what you really needed was love and attention, and imagine that, for some reason, the rejection kept on happening or went on for a long time. The pain a small child would feel in that situation is far too big to just go away. So you'd grow up with a 'hurt child' inside you, and it wouldn't matter whether you were twenty-five, fifty, or seventy-eight, you'd still be nursing that pain from early life. But we're living an adult life now, and it isn't practical or convenient to go around acting like a hurt child, even though that's what we might be feeling some of the time. However, when you're at home and in private, there's really nobody to stop you giving yourself the kind of love and attention now that you didn't get when you were very young. All of us—not only Cancers—need to realize that as adults we can start to do something for that inner child. No matter how old you are, it's never too late to have a happy childhood.

Cancers love to take care of other people, but they like to be taken care of as well. In their eyes and smiles you'll often see a waif-like sweet sadness that appeals to the mother in each of us. But it's a bad Cancer habit to believe that other people are there to look after them all the time. Not everybody wants to play mother, and demanding that they do can put a strain on even the very best relationships. Some Cancers need to be reminded that they left the nursery a long time ago. If they keep trying to get another person to do everything for them, they'll never grow up.

Even if you're not a Cancer, it's hard to forget your own mother. Many Crab people find making the break hard to live with. Either they're calling up Ma to get her opinion on everything that happens, or they save a fortune in phone bills by never leaving home in the first place. Don't imagine, however, that it's all love and harmony in Cancer; there are Cancer people who hated their mothers (to hear them talk, you'd imagine they grew up with the Wicked Witch of the West). Thank God, few have solved their grievances as drastically as infamous Cancer Lizzie Borden, who had a sinister idea of the best way to bury the hatchet with her parents.

Holding on and letting go is a real Cancer dilemma. People born under the sign of the Crab can hold on forever to just about anything—tired relationships, boring (but secure) jobs, old feelings, beliefs long outgrown and bad habits. There's a habit common among Cancers of stashing away things, just in case they might need them some day. Most Cancer homes are stuffed with what looks like junk to anybody else—old clothes, empty boxes and jars, cards, packets, magazines, programmes, string, buttons . . . anything, really. There's nothing more desperate in the world than a Crab who needs something and can't find it.

The private world of a Cancer is private. Crabs don't take kindly to intrusions or disruption, yet, like the best of mothers, they can be loving, indulgent and forgiving most of the time. If you make good friends with a Crab, you'll always be treated like one of the family. The sign of Cancer rules the stomach, which accounts for the digestive upsets Cancers have to endure when they're miserable. It also explains the millions of Cancer people who are such excellent cooks you'll never want to leave the dining table, and marvellous home-makers who like to create an atmosphere of contentment for those they love. To complete the entertainment, Cancers always have a tale to tell. Some of them never shut up, especially when it comes to talking about the past.

Home is a magic word for a Cancer. It means haven, a refuge, a shell into which a crushed, weary Crab can retreat and recuperate. A home is a place to grow whole again, to get back a sense of identity and belonging that the harsh world can easily take away. A homeless Cancer is a sorry sight to see. But getting too homey with a Crab can have its drawbacks. Cancers are known for their generosity and kindness, but don't forget they usually expect something in return. It's hard to work out the ground rules where Cancers are concerned because they have a habit of changing; but if you offend them you'll know all about it—although they're unlikely to communicate the fact directly. Instead Cancerians behave rather like the American skunk, which emits a pungent odour affecting anybody or anything within a three-mile radius. When somebody upsets a Cancer at a party, everybody's evening will be ruined.

Don't believe that sensitive means weak—it doesn't, and Cancers aren't, whatever they pretend. They can appear very sweet and gentle, but they're devastating when it comes to the crunch. Of course, they're vulnerable inside, but on the outside they can be as hard as nails when they need to be, just like the crab. If you're in a life-and-death situation with a Cancer and there's only a life belt for one, the Crab won't be the one left behind!

If you haven't yet seen the tougher face of the Crab, don't take the first opportunity to test it out with a Cancer friend or lover. Force the Crab into a tight corner, and out will come the famous Cancer pincers—and then you'll be sorry! They don't always fight fair, either. Some Cancers will hit you when your back is turned, or get you below the belt. Never imagine that they've forgotten all about something. The Crab never forgets. A steely determination is often the last thing other people expect from Cancers but many of them don't show their true colours and full strength until the second half of life (after the age of thirty-five or so). Once Cancer people set their sights on a target—somebody or something they really want—nobody in the world will stop them. Does it really surprise you that both Julius Caesar and Nancy Reagan were born under the sign of Cancer?

The Cancer types

Cancerians born between 22 June and 1 July The most Cancerian of Cancer people. Of course, you're very sensitive—but you must learn to control your feelings. Your subjective reactions to other people can create a lot of trouble for you. Take some time every day to re-assess where you're going, and be a little more objective. Otherwise, your dreams and goals can become very unrealistic.

Cancerians born between 2 July and 12 July   You have tremendous determination and you're capable of achieving very high ambitions, but watch out—your stubborness could be your downfall. The most jealous and intense of all the Cancer types, you'll also need to exercise some control over your negative feelings as well. And don't be surprised if you turn religious when you get older—no one is more fascinated by the deeper meaning of life than you are.

Cancerians born between 13 July and 22 July You're so sensitive to anything floating in the atmosphere, you pick up the feelings of whoever you're around. You're also compassionate to a fault, so be careful about falling prey to every hard-luck story you hear. If you learned to be more disciplined, you could really make something of your natural creative gifts.

Cancer and work

We're talking here about one of the most ambitious signs in the whole zodiac, but who'd believe it? Most Cancers seem to be much happier curled up in front of the fire watching television, preferably nibbling, than out waging war on a competitive world. There are many different definitions of security: a comfortable armchair is one, money in the bank is another. Maybe they can get by with very little when they're young and just starting out in life. But the older they get, the more Crabs start to feel the pinch!

Old habits die hard with Cancerians. Because in early

life many Cancer people feel strongly dependent on other people, later on they can find it very hard to believe they have it in them to make it alone. Some end up as the woman behind the man, or the power behind the throne—the one in the background who helps others make it to the top. If you like it that way, fine. But even if you have had your share of personal failure in the past or you haven't got very far, it doesn't necessarily mean you have to take a back seat to other people for the rest of your life. Keep reading. In the next section on Cancer careers, you'll get a true picture of your possibilities, and you'll see just how much some Cancers have actually been capable of, no matter how insecure or shy they might have felt inside!

Work and career are not just about achieving ambitions or a higher standard of living. In most cases, work involves social interaction. Crabs, with their tendency to cling to the past and get stuck in old patterns, can benefit from mixing with and meeting other people. If you're a Cancer person who hasn't yet managed to find success in your work or chosen career, it may be that you need to do something new. If you've tried several things already but nothing has worked, be adventurous and try the following short exercise:

1. Make a list of all the things you feel have gone wrong for you in your career. Don't forget to include the times when other people have stood in your way, when you've hoped for a promotion and didn't get it, or when a pet project of yours fell through.

2. Now look at the list and being as honest as you can, ask yourself what part you might have played in helping to set up some of these difficulties and disappointments. Were there any advantages to be gained by not being successful? For instance, did not getting what you want serve to win you other people's sympathy? Or did the failed promotion mean that you didn't have to risk the possibility of not being good enough at a better job? (These are what

psychologists call 'secondary gains'—the hidden benefits of an apparently unfortunate situation.)

3. Now look to your future. What do you need in your work to feel more happy and fulfilled? Remember the problems you have had in the past, but now imagine new and more creative ways to handle them. Take some time to picture yourself better able to deal with the various obstacles and challenges which might be in the way of realizing your goals and ambitions. Ask yourself what is the next step you need to take to get closer to achieving you goals. Now picture yourself taking that step, and as soon as you can, get out there and do it.

Cancer careers

Yes, of course there are some Cancers who don't like children (could it be that they really can't take the competition?) but you'll have to travel a long way before you run into a Cancer who isn't into taking care of people, animals or something. A nurse's uniform doesn't suit everybody, but if we took all the Cancers out of the health service, we'd all be in a bad way. Cancer people have a natural potential to be good nurses, doctors, midwives, social workers, teachers and therapists—anything which involves looking after others. With your healing presence, you make people feel better just by being there. And even if you are a moody Crab a lot of the time, you still have enough tenacity to deal with the most stressful, long-term or acute cases. Linda, an experienced Cancer nurse, never had any big problems—she actually felt nourished working with sick or distressed people:

I know it sounds strange, but sometimes I arrive at work in an awful mood, especially if there's been trouble at home before I came out. But as soon as I'm on duty and helping people who really need my assistance, I'm lifted right out of my misery. My husband says I only really love him when he's got a virus or a toothache!

Underneath it all, Cancer is a tough sign. Although it's one of three in the element of water, most Crabs would thank you kindly for something stronger. Some people born under this sign could feel quite at home in a pub or a bar—in front, behind or under the counter. So the friendly bar person who serves your favourite tipple the way you like it and mixes a harmless-looking cocktail with a pinch of something wicked, will probably turn out to be a Cancer. Crabs might also consider working in a brewery, or starting a business of their own selling the finest liquor and wines. What about all those intimate and romantic little teashops, coffee houses and licensed inns where lovers make their trysts under the protective eye of an understanding Cancerian? More adventurous Crabs literally take to water—fishing, working on board ocean liners, ships, ferries, or anything to do with the sea.

Drink goes well with food, and food suits Cancer very nicely (some Crabs eat their way out of a depression; others eat themselves into one). Cancer's ruled by the milky moon, which accounts for the number of Cancer people who become the cream of dairy workers, making or selling milk products like yoghurt and cheese. If this is your sign, you may have it in you to be an excellent chef, cook or restaurateur. Cancers who can stand the heat of the kitchen usually have the kind of temperament that goes with all the legends about good chefs, but they also have the skill to prepare a meal you'll be over the moon about. And if you're a Cancer who feels like getting away from the hectic pace of living, how about managing a small family-style country hotel where you can offer others your very personal attention and a place to get really comfortable and relaxed?

Cancers have a way with the public and a natural ability to arouse other people's emotions. Emmeline Pankhurst was a Cancer feminist who campaigned tirelessly to help bring the vote to British women. And have you ever seen copies of the most famous poster to come out of World War I? Above the words YOUR COUNTRY NEEDS YOU were the uncompromising moustached features of another powerful Cancer orator of his day, the Secretary of State for War, Lord Kitchener. Lord Mountbatten, of Burma the last Viceroy of India and later First Sea Lord of the Royal Navy, was another popular Cancer crowd puller. Iva D'Aquino was an infamous American Cancer who came to the attention of the American public when she went on trial as one of the 'Tokyo Rose' women broadcasters delivering Japanese propaganda over the airwaves during World War II. Less dramatic and far better known modern Cancer communications include newsreaders Sue Lawley and Alastair Burnet, and the controversial, caring Crab Esther Rantzen, who recently has done so much to help the plight of abused children.

The field of child care and education is growing fast, and Cancers would find it the perfect milieu. It's not just an accident that Lady Diana Spencer worked in a nursery before she became the Princess of Wales. Her sign is Cancer, and look what she has done for the image of motherhood since giving birth to Prince William, also a royal Cancer. Being a mother used to be considered a career in itself, and it's certainly more work than any full-time job. If you're in doubt, get hold of the biography of Cancer matriarch Rose Kennedy, mother of John, Bobby and Ted. You might not want to bring up children, but maybe you have a talent to raise their spirits, like that famous Cancer ringmaster P. T. Barnum.

From nurseries we move on to gardening and landscape architecture, other careers in which Cancers can flourish. Some Crabs have five thumbs—but they're all green, and the plants in their homes are usually so luxuriant and thriving they threaten to take over the entire living space. If you enter a house where you have to cut a clearway through to the bathroom, you're probably in a Cancer residence. Or how about beekeeping? That was the profession of Cancer Edmund Hillary before he scaled greater heights and conquered Mt Everest in 1953.

Cancers might like to extend their care for the family and home into personnel work or even more widely into the community, where they could be active figures in local government or on borough councils. Or they could set their sights on something higher, like an office in national government, where genuine concern, Cancer charm and a helpful mask of manners can take them a long way—Edward Heath, Cyril Smith, George Shultz and ex-Presidents Calvin Coolidge and Gerald Ford are Cancer people who have made it in this department.

Remembering how much you Crabs love to take care of property, even somebody else's, it's no surprise that many of you could become clever curators or accountants, and persuasive estate agents with an eye for a bargain. The bank manager in your home town was possibly a very capable Cancerian. And don't forget the Cancer housekeeper or butler, the type who would give a lifetime's service in a happy employment (the Cancer actress Jean Marsh not only had a starring role as the maid Rose in the popular television show *Upstairs, Downstairs,* but she was one of the people who originally conceived the idea for the series). And your love of things of the past might attract you to the lucrative world of antiques and heirlooms. A slightly unscrupulous Cancer person would have just the right line in old-world charm to con any sweet little old lady out of her family china—at 1930's prices. Most Cancers aren't criminals, of course; but if a chance to make some money occurs, they can be as cold-blooded as the crab itself.

That same love of the past and tradition makes some Cancer people passionate patriots and historians. Academically minded Cancers could also become anthropologists or archeologists—after all, this sign would travel any distance in search of mummy! A great many Cancer people go into various kinds of archive work, where they can indulge their love of collecting things. (Why not? Their own homes are usually stuffed with relics, old newspapers and miscellaneous memorabilia from days gone by.) And there's that most specialized of Cancer occupations—genealogy, the study of the origins of families. Incidentally, many Cancers who love to preserve the moment and look back on the past are attracted to photography. You might consider making your career from sensitive exposures, like the French photographic pioneer Cancer-born Henri Cartier-Bresson. Or by exposing yourself to the camera, like top Cancer model Jerry Hall.

Combine the love of home with some practical training, and Cancers could make it as architects, interior designers and manufacturers of carpets, hardware, domestic appliances and china (Josiah Wedgwood was born in this sign). Other Cancer people with a talent to please and a strong artistic flair might be drawn into the fashion industry. Elizabeth Emmanuel, Hardy Amies and Pierre Cardin all became highly successful Crab couturiers. If you can't design or make or mend, but you feel you could sell, your Cancer charms will help you sell anything to anybody. Even shy Crabs who prefer to stay in the shadow are not afraid to put other people in the limelight. They might carve careers as literary or theatrical agents, personal managers or entrepreneurs, where they could encourage the development of young talent, protect innocents from ruthless exploitation—and make ten per cent into the bargain.

Are you a future Cancer artist? While many born under this sign like to paint or make music purely for their own pleasure and recreation and may be content to remain in obscurity, Cancer's sensitivity would find expression and understanding through a career in the arts, like such famous Cancer painters as Rembrandt,

Degas, Whistler (remember his mother?), Chagall and David Hockney.

In the course of a month the moon moves through every sign of the zodiac, giving people born under the sign of Cancer a natural understanding of all types of temperaments—the perfect qualifications for the acting profession. Such incomparable performers as the moving Meryl Streep, the great character actor Charles Laughton, the versatile James Cagney, and that old smoothie George Saunders are (or were) sensitive Cancers who made it to the top in this tough profession. And talking about moving performances, don't forget that Ginger Rogers was a Cancer dancer whose award-winning role as Kitty Foyle proved she could act as well. Barbara Stanwyck was the Cancer star in the classic film *Double Indemnity*, playing a very wicked woman you wouldn't want to take home to mother. And remember Melanie Hamilton, Scarlett's maternal sidekick in *Gone With The Wind*? She was played by another great Cancer actress, Olivia de Havilland. If you prefer your Cancer women seen and not heard, you'll adore Theda Bara, the silent screen's original Vamp. But don't forget that Cancer men also can be pretty seductive: pin-up boys Eddie Kidd and Tom Cruise, the naughty Chris Quinten of *Coronation Street*, heart-throb Harrison Ford, and macho moon-man Sylvester Stallone all prove the point.

Most of you Cancer people love a good story. How about *The Old Man and the Sea* by the water-loving Crab writer Ernest Hemingway? If you think you can write, all you need is some paper and a pencil, and you could make a fortune—Cancer Neil Simon did with his plays *The Odd Couple, Barefoot in the Park, The Goodbye Girl, Brighton Beach Memoirs,* etc. For something a little heavier, try the Cancer talents of literary genius Marcel Proust, who wrote all about one of Cancer's favourite subjects—the past—in his multi-volumed masterpiece *A Remembrance of Things Past*;

the visionary George Orwell, who expressed a Cancer concern about the future in *1984*; and the romantic George Sand, whose private love affairs were as intriguing as her plots. All you Crabs who feel persecuted by life will quickly relate to the inner world of fellow Cancer Franz Kafka. And how could anyone ignore the Cancer novelist whose books have sold more copies than the Bible and become a religion for romantics all over the world? We're talking, as if you hadn't guessed, about the colourful Barbara Cartland.

All water signs love music, and rhythmic Cancer is no exception. Illustrious Cancer composers include Igor Stravinsky and Richard Strauss; Stephen Foster, author of '*My Old Kentucky Home*' was born in this home-loving sign—along with trumpet man Louis 'Satchmo' Armstrong, drummer Ringo Starr and singing stars George Michael and Cindy Lauper. Two Cancer songwriters, Richard Rodgers and Oscar Hammerstein, knew just what the sentimental public wanted when they collaborated to produce such all-time hit shows as *Oklahoma, South Pacific, The King and I* and *The Sound of Music*. Of course, if you can't sing, play or write it, you might still be able to make a fortune through it—like another Crab, the high-flying record-empire builder Richard Branson.

Ballooning may not be your thing, but that doesn't mean you aren't a sporting Cancer at heart. One of the most celebrated personalities on the tennis courts in recent years is the moody Crab Illie Nastase. Tennis-player Arthur Ashe and golfers Tony Jacklin and Nick Faldo are other Cancer front-runners. What about you?

Are you still waiting for your vocation? Deep-feeling Cancers who get the calling enter the religious life as priests, nuns and monks. Although they aren't always comfortable in the limelight, they are often the medium for an important spiritual message, hence the many powerful Cancer preachers. Mary Baker Eddy was an evangelical Cancer who created her very own church—

the First Church of Christ, Scientist. John Calvin, the French-born religious reformer, was also a Crab. A far less famous but equally determined Cancer was Francesca Cabrini, a nun eventually canonized by the Catholic Church for her devotion to her work as a missionary and, in particular, the welfare of children.

If you are a Cancer, you don't need a pulpit to preach. Two sisters, born under the sign of the caring Crab, Ann Landers and Abigail Van Buren—America's most famous agony aunts—got their message across every day of the week to countless newspaper readers across the country. But if you're really looking for a Cancer to inspire you, look no further than Helen Keller, the deaf and blind woman who overcame her handicaps to become a leading light in the field of education. Her story is one of sheer courage and determination, and a lesson to us all.

Cancer compatibilities

Cancer/Aries *(Water/Fire)* Fire and water make steam, and you're the one who is likely to be doing all the hissing when impulsive Aries is around! What else could happen, given your love of peaceful surroundings and the Aries tendency to barge in and take over. A good working relationship will take a lot of effort and understanding from both of you.

Cancer/Taurus *(Water/Earth)* You wouldn't think that a Crab and a Bull had a lot in common, but they do. But both Cancer and Taurus hate being pushed around and goaded by other people. The Bull needs a lot of time, and you're no speed merchant yourself; so you'll be happy to plod along at a Taurus pace. With your intuition and the Bull's practicality, there could be a nice profit waiting for you when you get there. And after work, you couldn't dine out in better company.

Cancer/Gemini *(Water/Air)* A Gemini fluttering into your place of work can play havoc with your nerves and offend your sense of privacy. Gemini wants to gossip or chatter; all you crave is a bit of peace and quiet. You feel like talking; Gemini is nowhere to be found. It's a pity your moods clash so often, because when you hit it off, you can make a lively, friendly team . . . although neither of you would win any medals for consistency.

Cancer/Cancer *(Water/Water)* You might think that this is a great working combination, and it could be—even if you do talk mercilessly about one another after work! Nobody can read a Cancer like a Cancer: but put two watery Crabs in the same office pool, and there's sure to be the odd skirmish. If you can overcome all the petty irritations and pull together you could unite to topple any opposition.

Cancer/Leo *(Water/Fire)* Leos can take pretty instant likes and dislikes to people, but they might be stumped to know where they stand with a fickle and unpredictable Crab. When it comes down to it, somedays you'll be in the mood for the Lion, and some days you won't. But whatever happens, always give Leos the impression that they are in charge, even if you're really the one pulling all the strings.

Cancer/Virgo *(Water/Earth)* You're a bit too sensitive to enjoy being criticized, but there's a lot you could learn from a sharp, clear-thinking Virgo. Try to remember they only have what's best for you in mind, and do what you can to make this relationship work. With your good taste and Virgo's practical, discriminating nature, you two could go far together—especially in any work looking after the comforts and needs of others.

Cancer/Libra *(Water/Air)* Librans love a harmonious and peaceful work atmosphere. On those days when you're feeling open and optimistic, your two signs couldn't be better mates. But just wait until you happen to be in one of those 'stinker' moods, when nobody can do anything right. Libras have a lot of diplomacy and tact—just as well, they'll need all they can muster to deal with you.

Cancer/Scorpio *(Water/Water)* Which would you prefer—to be pinched by a Crab or stung by a Scorpion? Sooner or later we all have to bow to a champion, and you may have to admit you've met your match in Scorpio. If there's ever a dispute between you, you'll discover Scorpio's talent for taking revenge even beyond the grave. Should it come to that, it might be a good idea if you found yourself a different stretch of water, preferably oceans apart from a vengeful Scorpio.

Cancer/Sagittarius *(Water/Fire)* A breezy Sagittarius will think nothing of making a dozen blunt suggestions about how you could improve yourself, and then make off with your typewriter for a while without so much as a by your leave. Just wait till the glib Archer tries telling you, 'come on, it's not the end of the world!' All in all, this is a very trying working relationship, at least until you've learned to accept that yesterday is gone with the wind and tomorrow is another day—and that's not very likely!

Cancer/Capricorn *(Water/Earth)* There are times when Cancers just can't cope with the idea of work. Not so for a typically stolid Capricorn who will put duty and responsibility before everything, especially feelings. Opposites have a lot to teach one another even if they don't at first attract. Capricorn are steady and disciplined—everything you're not. Given time, you could learn an awful lot from the Goat.

Cancer/Aquarius *(Water/Air)* Idealistic Aquarius lives in the head; feeling Cancer lives in the heart. Aquarians love anything new; you're most at home with the old and familiar. Obviously, there are going to be a few problems here. And yet, if the ideals of Aquarius contain a real concern for others, and if you're a caring Cancer who shares that picture of the world, you and the Water Bearer just might hit it off.

Cancer/Pisces *(Water/Water)* Cancer couldn't find a more sympathetic colleague or ally than compassionate Pisces. Your happy work relationship with Pisces is likely to spill over into a good friendship outside business hours, especially in the local wine (or is that whine?) bar. There is a definite danger (and it's the only definite thing about this partnership!) you'll get along so well that nothing ever gets done. So don't let things degenerate into an orgy of sentimentality, and this could turn out to be a very creative and supportive combination.

The Cancer boss

When things are going well, you couldn't wish for anyone better than a Cancer boss. They'll make it their business to take a personal interest in you. Even in the male of the species, those Cancer mothering qualities ensure a fair degree of thoughtfulness. Should you need to take some time off, your Cancer boss is likely to be sympathetic. But don't make the mistake of thinking that you are his or her special favourite: Cancer will mother everyone and everything in sight.

A Cancer manager-owner will likely be in business for money first and last. So, despite a talent for being sympathetic, if output is affected or threatened, don't expect understanding to go on forever. Cancer bosses who are personally making a lot of effort to reach deadlines and high productivity levels will quickly run out of patience with other people's delays and short-comings. It will warm their hearts to see staff develop their individual talents and skills. But more than anything, they enjoy seeing their employees work. Anybody who gives of their best to a Cancer boss will only get the best in return.

If you're a wise Cancer boss, you'll make good use of your God-given charm and tact to remind others gently about what might have been overlooked. You'll get much more work out of your employees if you keep them at a distance from one of your famous Cancer moods. If you're a high-powered Cancer boss, they could need special protection. You'd be well advised to hire yourself a personal assistant, somebody with a cool, even manner—Virgo, for instance—to do your relating for you. But just be sure that she or he can cope with a Cancer boss's most lethal weapon—Chanel Number Skunk!

Cancer bosses are caring and receptive. Okay, they sometimes find it hard to speak about what is going on inside them, but they're the right people for others to open up to. The fact they're so good at covering up their own thoughts and feelings makes them quick to spot when others are doing the same. And because they often hide their own light under a bushel, they have a knack of noticing the hidden talents and abilities of employees. In the end, if you've got a Cancer boss, you can count on being well looked after—even when you really don't want to be.

The Cancer employee

Cancer people are usually diligent and eager to please, but don't expect them not to have ideas of their own, and whatever you do, don't forget to appreciate them. Cancer employees want to put their personal stamp on everything they touch: they'll automatically re-arrange work programmes, schedules and even the office furniture–all to the advantage of the company. Of course, their efficiency has its drawbacks as well. When they are not around, nobody else has a clue how things work or where things are. Needless to say, this is very much how a Cancer worker likes to be–indispensable. How warming to the little Cancer heart to feel missed and needed. Not to mention that indispensability gives the Cancer employee a firm base to stand on when the subject of a salary rise comes up–which, by the way, is likely to be regularly and often.

Yes, Cancer will help to turn the working environment into a home from home. They know how to make people feel comfortable. (They also know how to make people feel uncomfortable, which is usually a clue that they need a rest and should take some time off and get away for a while.) Their working relationships can be close–and all the more productive for it.

Cancer employees will often take on much more than they need to, and they expect to be paid for it. Bosses take heed: if your Cancer worker appears to be shouldering a heavy load, make sure to give an appropriate reward–for no one is more resentful than a Crab who feels unappreciated. Cancer's hoarding nature can store up dozens of grievances against you. True to nature, rather than openly sharing their negative feelings directly to your face, Cancer employees would rather take the opportunity to discuss these injustices with their fellow workers. Apart from Scorpio, it's close water-sign cousin, no sign rivals Cancer's capacity for revenge. So if there is a cool draught coming from the typing pool, or if you feel cold-shouldered by your closest associates, start paying attention to that Cancer employee who is working so quietly and dutifully in the corner. He or she may well have something do with it.

Cool Cancers can perform acrobatic feats of management and complete impossible deadlines; they have a way of performing best when the going gets tough. Wise bosses should aim to hold on to Cancer workers as long as they can. The way to do this is simple—keep them happy. Otherwise, the more ambitious Cancer worker will use the job to accumulate experience and expertise, and then move on. If the gleam of ambition is clearly visible in those innocent Cancer eyes, it's a good bet that when they finish working for you, they'll have learned what it takes to be your most serious rival.

The Cancer colleague

Most Crabs in any new working situation will discover that their charm and innocence are definitely on their side. They could find themselves pretty quickly adopted by a colleague (probably another water-sign person), responding to that first impression of gentle shyness. So the newly arrived Cancer might feel like Little Red Riding Hood or Pinocchio, duly warned and protected from all the dangers and pitfalls of the new job—the forest of office procedures and red tape; the witch in Room 343; or the wolf upstairs in the accounts department! The new-found protector will probably have underestimated Cancer's ability to give as good as they get . . . sooner or later.

All the support and caring you might expect from a good Cancer boss can also come your way from a Cancer colleague. Unless, that is, you're both after the same promotion. In which case, look out for competition. Cancers can be quite unscrupulous, especially with their tongues, in private and behind closed doors. Just remember that the Crab's habit of accumulating property also extends to the boss. Cancer co-workers, who usually promote a happy family atmosphere at work, won't necessarily be quite as familial if they imagine you get on better with your employer than they do.

Hidden ambition is likely to lie behind the breaking up of a friendship. At their most paranoid, your Cancer fellow employees might suspect you of plotting against them at work. Their natural reaction to this would be to initiate a little character defamation in self-defence. Don't forget that Cancer's memory for injury is as famous as the elephant's. And yet even in this unpleasant situation, if something serious happens to you and you really need help, the first person there with the oxygen mask will be your Cancer colleague.

The positive side of a Cancer at work is strong and supportive. Unless they create them, Crabs hate bad feelings and will do anything to reconcile people and dispel misunderstandings. They will go out of their way to help you. They'll drive you home when you're sick, make you tea when you're tired and fed up, and offer to cover for you if you have to take time off.

If you have a Cancer colleague and you appreciate that she or he is going through some kind of stress, even a small gesture of support can work wonders. Asking 'What's the problem?' might be a bit tactless and intrusive, but a kind voice and a gentle hand on the shoulder will convey the important sense that you're there if they need you. However, if you personally have caused the upset, stay well away and resist being apologetic until they are ready—and then do all you can to show that you are truly sorry. Stop at nothing. Don't ignore the situation and think it will go away, and don't imagine you can wear a Cancer down—you *never* will!

You are fortunate if you have a Cancer working alongside you. They can be excellent team workers and won't shirk responsibility, especially in a crisis. Not to mention the fact that when you leave, they'll probably be the ones who organize the collection!

Leo

Element:	Fire
Symbol:	The Lion
Ruler:	The Sun

The Sign of the Lion

Shake yourself dry after the watery world of Cancer the Crab, and feel the warm glow of the fiery sign of Leo. It's the classiest sign of them all. From now on, everywhere you walk you're on red velvet carpet. Does that surprise you? It won't if you're a Leo. It will seem only natural that your sign belongs to the lion, king of all beasts, the timeless symbol of courage, pride and regal dignity.

Observe the lion. He's in his element lying out in the sun, looking almost as quiet and tame as a fireside cat. But don't forget that he's a powerful puss, more than a metre broad at the shoulders. When he opens his great molars, you'll agree that any animal capable of lunching on a full-grown giraffe deserves an awful lot of respect. Every seasoned bush traveller has learnt that when you're dealing with a lion you never take anything for granted. And that's more or less the formula to follow whenever you come across a Leo!

The lion has a reputation as a killer. If you're out in the bush at night you'll probably hear his terrible roars as he psyches himself up for the hunt. And as soon as it's daybreak, he's up and about again before anybody has had time to forget who's really in charge. Noble and dignified, always standing with his best profile against the sun, the lion's bright regal eyes search the horizon for any signs of visitors. In demand everywhere he goes—on a brief walkabout or stopping off for refreshment at a local watering hole—the lion just loves to hold court. Even a shy and self-effacing lion (and they're few and far between) will rarely say no to the lion's share of attention.

Inexperienced travellers—safari package tourists and foreign film crews—are sometimes tempted to overstep their mark with the lion, simply dying to get that once-in-a-lifetime snapshot . . . forgetting that the lion is also very partial to a quick snap! Of course, it's possible that the lion may have recently eaten. If he's peacefully enjoying his digestion, the visitor would be quite safe. But you never can tell. After all, the lion doesn't like to follow rules, he prefers to make them. So does a Leo.

The sun, ruler of Leo

The sun is a great big ball of fire 92,957,000 miles away, but we'd be nothing without it. With its powerful magnetic attraction it keeps the earth moving in a perpetual orbit around it. Once upon a time, people worshipped the sun. To judge by the number of Leos who bask in its rays at the least opportunity, the cult never went out of fashion.

Like the sun, Leos don't enjoy being just another face in the crowd—they infinitely prefer to be at the centre of what's going on. Whether they know it or not, what a Leo loves most is a good audience. Their instincts tell them what they have to do to get one and, more important, they're very good at holding on to one once they've got it. They're born performers. Dressed to kill, some Leos will stop you dead in your tracks with all their jewels, their glitter, and the dazzling colours they put on. Others, apparently more sober and serious, grab your attention with their gracious dignity and refinement. There are Leos whose minds are so brilliant they'll blind you. And scintillating social Leos who'll astound you with their clever insights and entertain you with their witty comments. Wealthy Leos will flabbergast you with their lavish hospitality; and even Leos who have little or nothing will impress you with their stylish simplicity, reminiscent of royals in exile, who nibble smoked herring pâté on crispbread with an expression of ecstasy as if they can recall banquets with beluga caviar in the old country.

The ancient Greeks prayed to the sun god Helios, who drove across the skies from morning till night in a stately golden chariot pulled by nine dazzling white horses. One morning his teenage son, Phaeton, decided that he wanted some of the glory his old man was always getting, so he borrowed the chariot for the day. But as soon as the big wheels started to turn, Phaeton knew he'd made a terrible mistake. Nobody needed to tell the blinkered horses there was somebody inexperienced in control. They promptly went crazy, soaring and diving through the sky, dragging the chariot high and low. The earth was getting badly scorched, the seas were drying up, people and animals were running riot. When Zeus, King of the Gods, got wind of what was happening, he had to stop it the only was he knew how. He hurled one of his terrible thunderbolts, and poor Phaeton fell to his death like a shooting star.

In a manner of speaking, what happened to Phaeton can happen to anybody who takes on something they aren't ready for. Leo people have an innate tendency to try to handle more than they can deal with, so they'll hopefully learn something from Phaeton's mistakes. It's great to follow your ideas and try to get what you want. It's important to believe in yourself. But if you go over the score and you set up targets that are beyond your human capacity, you can expect sooner or later to run into disaster. Napoleon and Mussolini proved that point. They were Leos who achieved extraordinary heights and then blew it by going just that bit too far.

The Leo temperament

If you take out a camera in a crowd of people, you get some amazing exposures. A Scorpio is likely to do a quick left turn and look the other way; a Capricorn will probably start organizing everybody for a big group picture; a Cancer is suddenly going to remember an urgent date with the dentist and scuttle out of camera range; you'll see Libras in mid-sentence and mid-smile, subtly adjusting their coiffure and straightening their clothes. But where's Leo? Whatever direction you point the lens, you'll find a Leo beaming back at you, ready and waiting for you to click the shutter.

Of course, some Leos are more introverted. But even the most mouse-like of Lions still have something that makes you remember them. Just watch a Leo turning up late (which is often their style) for a social occasion. They'll make their gracious apologies for being a nuisance and insist on slipping in quietly without troubling anyone. But they might just as well have arrived wearing the crown jewels—that's how unobtrusive they manage to be.

If the rest of the world doesn't recognize the marvellous qualities a Leo possesses, it usually isn't for the lack of advertising. Leo men and women need to express and share their talents with the world. They're frequently capable of getting other people to blow a trumpet for them, but whatever they have to resort to in order to proclaim their merits, they can't be happy unless they're in the limelight. Leos aren't exactly competitive—just don't get in their way, that's all. A Leo sun doesn't take kindly to being eclipsed!

People born in Leo aren't necessarily loud and bombastic. But when they've made their views clear (and sometimes even when they haven't), they'll expect you to conform to the edict. Leos have straightforward, obvious standards of behaviour—straightforward and obvious to them, but rarely to anyone else. So the rule is simple; if a Leo expresses an opinion and you happen to think differently, air your views tactfully, or shut up and talk about the weather. With a Leo, it's easy to feel you've said the wrong thing—something like the sensation you'd probably have if you went along for tea at Buckingham Palace in your pyjamas. Leos are easily offended, although, to be fair, they'll usually forgive you if you grovel enough. When a Leo likes you, it's probably because they find your ways and your ideas pleasing and even entertaining. But what might do for you, would certainly never do for a Leo: For Lions, only the best will do.

Less than four hundred years ago, King James VI of Scotland became the first king of Great Britain. The crown rather went to his head. In fact, he said right at the beginning of his reign: 'I am the head and the whole island is my body.' James believed in the Divine Right of Kings. He was convinced that the thoughts and opinions of a king or queen were always right . . . because it was God's will that put them in power. There's something about that attitude that doesn't invite contradiction—which can be a bit like trying to argue with a Leo.

Yet working or living with a Lion can be a magical experience. The heart is the part of the body associated with the sign of Leo, and Leos need to love almost as much as they need to be loved. At their very best, you'll find no warmer, more loving or generous people than those born under this sign. They are adept at falling in love, and just as proficient at falling out of it again. Unfortunately, the latter has much the same consequences as falling out of a tree, except that broken hearts don't mend as neatly as broken bones. Too bad that Leos never learn. Where did they get their ideas about love? Could it have been from fairy tales or glossy magazines? Maybe that's why they never quite get over the shock that the honeymoon doesn't shine forever. Love for a Leo is always *the real thing*. Clandestine affairs and dark intrigues can be fun up to a point, but too much lying or pretence is a strain on the heart, and mystery doesn't become the sign ruled by the sun. Besides, Leos hate to be caught cheating . . . and they hate a cheater even more. In their minds, all Lions inhabit a mighty castle, and when they're seriously wounded in love or friendship they retreat to its highest turret—not a bad place to go when dark revenge is in your heart and you desire nothing less than to smother the traitor in boiling pitch or hurl a couple of boulders in his or her general direction.

To a Leo, love is more precious than gold. So if they seem to be testing you, it's only because they want to be sure they're making a sound investment. Don't let their demands drive you away—that's just the price you have to pay when you go after something as sought after as a Leo's affections. When Leos give, they usually expect something in return, so you shouldn't be too surpised to find a tag attached to everything they offer. Leos are loyal, generous and devoted . . . provided they know you put them before everybody else. They are supportive, helpful and encouraging . . . provided you show a devoted uncritical interest in them. And they're unusually broadminded, sympathetic and understanding people . . . provided you never do anything to offend them.

Someone born under the sign of the Lion may look like an arrogant adult with a terribly inflated self-opinion, but underneath it all a Leo is like a small child who desperately needs to feel loved and appreciated and who's greatest fear is that of rejection. When we are children, winning mother's love is more important than anything else. If we are the most special person in the world to her, she'll make sure we're kept safe, protected and well fed. But if somebody else is more important to her than we are, then we're in big trouble. She might go away to be with that person, and then she won't be there to save us should a big hairy beast come along to eat us up. To a baby, survival is equated with being special. Not being special could mean disaster. In their heart of hearts, even the most grown-up Leos still believe their survival depends on being Number One. That's why they want to be the most important, the centre of attention, the best thing around. Second best is a little dangerous, and it just isn't good enough.

If you were lucky enough to be the mother of a Leo, you'll probably remember times like this. It's three in the morning, and you're still pacing the carpet with baby Leo, who just won't go to sleep. The feed has been given, both ends seem comfortable. So why aren't we tired, then? Baby Leo wants you to play–again. You have already played peekaboo for half an hour, but your lovely Leo is still awake. You sang the 'Eensy Weensy Spider' more than twenty times, but no change. If you play hunt the bunny rabbit for much longer, your arm is going to drop off. But wait! The little eyes are closing, the breathing's getting deep and peaceful. Now you can safely put the little Lion down and get back to your own soft pillow. BUT NOT FOR LONG! It's almost four o'clock now–where does baby Leo get all that energy? Wide awake again and wanting more attention! How else can a Leo be sure you really care?

Now, mother's love may well suit Leo to a T, but it can't go on forever. There are other important things around to consider–father, for instance. Good or bad, the father in the early home leaves a very deep impression on the Leo child. There are some wonderful fathers, and to young Leo they can seem like a hard act to follow. And there are not-so-wonderful fathers– angry, neglectful or critical ones, or ones who just aren't there. Leo children who never felt wanted or loved enough by their fathers can have a hard time believing in their own value and worth later in life.

More than anything, a Leo hates to feel ignored, forgotten or left out–and some of them will go to any lengths to protect themselves from such humiliation.

There's a story told about a famous London actress, a Leo, who had the lead role (what else?) in a West End play. She discreetly mentioned (on at least ten occasions) she was about to celebrate her fortieth birthday (for the third time since she turned fifty, a seasonal rival commented). The company manager decided that a surprise party was in order. Everybody was sworn to secrecy until the great day arrived. But theatre life is never short of off-stage dramas, and, as the curtain came down, the stage manager suddenly remembered that he hadn't ordered the cake, the flowers or the champagne. He was desperately scouring the yellow pages when the lady's dresser appeared to reassure him: 'Don't worry, she was afraid you might forget, so she asked me to order everything last week.' You don't always have to remember how important a Leo is. If you forget, they'll happily remind you.

The Leo types

Leos born between 23 July and 1 August   A natural lover of limelight and glory, you are the proudest of all the Leo types. So long as you're valued and admired, you'll give your all—but you won't waste a minute on people who don't appreciate your style and talents. And when you turn off your warmth, it can get very chilly!

Leos born between 2 August and 11 August   What a performer! You're the most expansive, expressive, effusive and idealistic of all the Leo types. You're also the most foolhardy, so look before you leap. No matter how obnoxious you get, people still seem to love you. How do you pull it off?

Leos born between 12 August and 23 August   When it comes to getting things done, you're the Leo to do it. Once you get going, nobody can stop you—not even when you run smack up against them. You were born to lead—why else would God have made you so domineering?

Leo and work

The working world isn't just sitting around waiting for all you Leos to step up on to the throne. The road to success is usually a long, steep and rocky one, and chances are you'll have to walk it like the rest of us. But, along the way, you'll encounter people who'll welcome you with open arms and joy in their hearts, as if you were the rising sun. On the other hand, there are bound to be others who'll take one look at your face and wish you had never appeared on the horizon.

Ultimately, it's up to you to make it all happen. You'll have to learn to live with the little disappointments that will come your way from time to time. You look so natural at the top of the pile, its unfair that you should have such a hard climb getting there. But without a struggle, how can you prove what you're really worth? No matter how much appreciation you get from other people, it's what you feel about yourself that really counts. And you're happiest when you achieve something that you've had to work hard for. The saddest Lions are the ones who refuse to face reality—like the reality that the sun is a great big ball of flaming gas. Leos who loll around fantasizing about all the wonderful things they're capable of doing can end up talking a lot of hot air. So please don't just live in the realm of possibilities—put your money where you mouth is and do something concrete to realize all your potential.

That famous Leo pride can work two ways. It can make you afraid to try anything in case you might fail; but it also means you totally refuse to be beaten. It takes *real* class to apply yourself to anything that comes your way. But you'll also need to learn to bend and adapt now and then, which doesn't come naturally to your sign. When you fasten on to an idea, you can be so obstinate, you'll never let go. It takes *real* Leo nobility to get rid of that habit. Whatever happens, don't forget that although you're a star, you're not the only sun in the galaxy.

Here's an exercise which could help launch you on the right path to sucess:

1. If you aren't already well-established in a career, take a minute to reflect on what you really want to do. (Keep thinking, you'll come up with something.) If you are already in a line of work you're happy with, consider how you could achieve even more in your field.
2. Now ask yourself if your goal is realistic or not. If it isn't, adjust it to something that is ultimately within your reach. Then go on to the next step.
3. List all the things, small and large, that you could do to take you nearer your goal. Pick out one item on the list which you could get started on today.
4. Now go and do it!

Leo careers

When we're talking about Leo careers, we might as well start at the top. That's where so many of you Leos intend to end up, isn't it? (Some Leos literally get to the peak in their professions, like mountain Lion Chris Bonington.) It's impressive how many department heads, managers, company directors and presidents are born in the sign. Now don't be coy and pretend you'd refuse a commanding role if you were offered one. If you've got it, Leo, go ahead and flaunt it!

But don't expect to rise automatically to the top, like cream rising to the surface of milk. Only a few exceptional Leos are born with the golden spoon already in their mouths. A prime example was Lady Elizabeth Bowes-Lyon, a sweet-faced little Leo, who became, through marriage, the Duchess of York. When

Edward VIII adbicated in 1937, she graduated to the title of Queen Elizabeth—and brought a popular, new and very Leonine style to the monarchy. Today she's so clearly at home receiving the adulation she inspires, it's hard to imagine her being suited to anything less. Getting into the Royal Family, however, may be an impractical career suggestion although history has proved many times over that nothing is impossible where the right Leo is concerned. The Princess Royal is a Leo who instinctively knew what family to be born into.

In her professional life, the Princess Royal has shown a typical Leo concern for children in her role as patron of the Save the Children Fund and through her work in other organizations such as the Riding for the Disabled Association. As a champion rider herself, she likes to see others get a fair crack at the whip.

Leo people can appear very selfish, and sometimes they are. But remember that the sun doesn't only exert a force to draw everything to it, it also radiates an enormous energy outwards. Many Leos are drawn to the teaching profession, perhaps because it's a job where they can be the centre of attention and help other people at the same time.

The child in every Leo wants to play. Some choose to play with their money on the stock exchange; some might like playing with other people's money as investment speculators. Put a very playful Leo in charge of a playground, a funfair or a park, and everybody will have a good time. Better still, give a Leo a playhouse, and you'll have a first-class theatre manager—somebody with panache, a touch of the old-school impresario, complete with cape and fedora, an ivory cigarette holder, and on every finger a ring—gold of course! Best of all, find them a playing field, and they'll go for gold—like that remarkable Leo Olympian, Daley Thompson.

Every sign is associated with a particular precious metal, and gold is obviously the one for Leo. Many

Leos who can't yet afford the real thing aren't ashamed to don gilt and glitter, and challenge the world to spot the difference. Not all Leos are so flamboyant. Some prefer reserve, especially the gold kind, and might choose a career in banking just to be beside the bullion. And with all their golden charms, crafty Leos in search of work could do very well designing jewels or selling ornaments fit for a king (or queen)—a job which has the added bonus of enabling them to rub wrists with the rich, the filthy rich and, better still, the very famous!

As you'd expect, Leo has produced its share of big stars in the entertainment industry. One of the more recent Leo phenomena is Madonna. Her appeal seems to have very little in common with that of the Virgin Mary, but she does have an inexplicable power to draw people. During the Sixties, Mick Jagger, another Lion of Rock, exhibited an earthier style of sexual magnetism that brought him worshippers in their mad millions. Leo people often know exactly how to make the very most of themselves. They can judge just how to dress— themselves or other people. Yves St Laurent and Coco Chanel were both Leo born. Some of them know the right way to undress as well! After all, it was Mae West, the Leo screen star *par excellence*, who quipped: 'Why don't you come up and see me when I've nothin' on?' The effect these Leos have on the general public must have something to do with the influence of the sun—it always makes people break out in a hot sweat or want to take their clothes off. Ava Gardner, Robert Redford, Susan George, Robert Mitchum and Robert de Niro are other movie Leos who have left their audiences breathless, hot and panting for more.

Film is very much a Leo medium. The roll call of big cats in celluloid include names like Dolores Del Rio, Clara Bow, Peter O'Toole, (*The Lion in Winter*), Dustin Hoffman, Shelly Winters, Lucille Ball, Arnold Schwarzenegger and Bert Lahr—who actually got to play a lion, albeit a cowardly one, in the MGM classic *The Wizard of Oz.* (By the way, one of the most famous lions in history still reigns today as the trademark of Hollywood's MGM Studios, and the Lion behind all the scenes of that company was producer Sam Goldwyn, the big 'G' right in the middle of the name.) For style in movie directing, you can't do much better than that craggy old Lion, the late John Huston, or Cecil B. de Mille—the man who turned pics into epics. Only a bold Leo could conceive of films that even today make the Bible seen understated. And we can't forget master of macabre, Leo Alfred Hitchcock, or the innovative Stanley Kubrick, a Lion of a director who rose to fame with *A Clockwork Orange* (orange-growing, by the way is a recommended profession for Leos living in sunny climes). If you're tempted to go into films or theatre, but don't rate yourself as an actor or director, there are careers open to you in set or costume design, hairdressing and wig creation, or even operating the big spotlight at the latest hit show. And if you don't get your own name in lights you could always apply for the job of president of your favourite star's fan club!

Leos love a living legend. Female Lion Madame du Barry, the court favourite of Louis XV, was one. T. E. Lawrence (of Arabia) was another legendary Lion. In more recent times, Jacqueline Bouvier is a Leo who has dazzled the world with glamour and style, first as Jacqueline Kennedy (the First Lady of Camelot, who, like many Leo wives, did so much to enhance her husband's image and popularity); and later as Jacqueline Kennedy Onassis (married to a modern-day Midas). She met and made enough drama in her life to hold centre-stage for over a decade—like a true sun queen, she's the stuff myths are made of.

Leos like anything larger than life. The brilliant Swiss psychologist Carl Gustav Jung was a Leo who shone his light on the unconscious mind through his work with dreams and his insight into the mysterious workings of the human psyche. In the process, he discovered a vast kingdom inside all of us, an inner realm populated by the kinds of characters we're liable to encounter in myths and fairy stories—wicked queens, handsome young princes, damsels in distress, poisonous dwarfs and hungry ogres, to name but a few. Legend-loving lions eat up all that stuff. They even could make some money regurtitating it back again in the form of scripts for American soap operas which owe their huge popularity to over-the-top plots and leading players that seem to have been lifted straight out of old fairy tales.

So how about being a writer? Leos who take up the pen professionally owe their success to their bold romantic flourish and an inspired ability to tell a story. Okay, they'll embellish the truth here and there, but it's all for a good cause—to entertain. Among the tellers of tales born in Leo are Sir Walter Scott, whose books are full of the kind of chivalrous action we'd expect from someone born under this sign. And the imaginative French writer Alexander Dumas, who created the swashbuckling exploits of *The Three Musketeers*. *I, Claudius*, the story of an emperor, was written in true epic style by Leo author Robert Graves, who also created his own version of the Greek myths. An Irish Leo playwright called George Bernard Shaw found great popularity in England, especially with his famous play *Pygmalion*, based on the myth of the sculptor who fell in love with a woman he fashioned out of stone. (There's nothing left to add to his plays, but like a true Leo he took the opportunity to compose enormous prefaces where he put forward his views on every subject under the sun.) Emily Brontë, Guy be Maupassant, Radclyffe Hall and the poet Shelley are among the passionate Leo writers still drawing an enormous readership. Last of all, two wounded literary Lionesses: Dorothy Parker, whose sardonic humour, wicked wit and creative sensitivity make her a cult figure, even today; and Zelda Fitzgerald, a queen of the Jazz Age, whose considerable

writing talents were obscured by the tragedy of her life
and the fame of her husband, F. Scott

If you're born in the sign of the Lion, you'll want to
leave a paw print wherever you go. Henry Ford, a Leo
engineer, made his mark with the Model-T Ford. He
also made his name a legend in the process. That would
warm any Leo's heart, but it's unfair to remember him
only for his cars and the fortune he amassed. Famous
and fabulously wealthy, he nonetheless displayed a
Leo's concern for others. When he heard about the
crowds of hard-grafting farmworkers who were out of
work and starving in the winter months, he moved his
factories into farming communities to give them jobs to
do—proving that a little consideration for others pays
dividends in the long run.

Leos love to express themselves, and they'll do it any
way they can. Apart from writers, actors, actresses and
inventors (like John Logie Baird—the Leo who developed
the first television transmitter), there are the artists. For
starters, we can offer you a range of Leo artists that
runs from the opulent formality of the portraitist Joshua
Reynolds, through the Revolutionary works of the Fren-
chman David, past the English giant of sculpture Henry
Moore, up to and beyond the outrageous, inimitable
Andy Warhol—whose factory not only produced art, but
manufactured superstars as well. There's always room
for more, so potential Leo artists take heed!

You Leos would roar with pride in a job which allows
you to show all your power (Leos could shine in local
or national politics). You'd really be purring in a career
which gave you a chance to express your wonderful
creativity (in which case, politics might not be quite
such a good idea!). But even if you aren't the next
president, prime minister, reigning monarch, leading
film star or hottest new spark in the fashion world,
you'll bring grace, dignity, showmanship and a natural
talent for organization to anything you do. A Leo could
turn slicing salami into a creative art.

Leo compatibilities

Leo/Aries *(Fire/Fire)*   Provided an Aries is willing to play by your rules, you two will get along like an office on fire. They'll like your energy and style, and you'll love the way they make a fuss about things—especially when that thing is you. There's one big drawback, though—the Ram likes being the centre of attention almost as much as you do. If you're going to get along with this sign, you're going to have to learn how to take turns.

Leo/Taurus *(Fire/Earth)*   Taurus people will be cautious with you at first—they're none too impressed with flash and panache. You need time to get to know one another. Then you'll discover you both have a lot in common, like a love of status, luxury and the good things in life. So if you want to bring a budding friendship to full bloom, treat the Bull to a tasty meal, a good glass of wine and the most disgusting dessert on the menu.

Leo/Gemini *(Fire/Air)*   Leo is the king, and Geminis make the best royal jesters. You'll like their sense of humour, the clever way they think and all the great ideas they have—even if half of them never materialize. And when a Gemini values you, you'll be sure to get plenty of good press. But their restlessness is bound to get on your nerves from time to time—especially when you're in the mood for a lively audience, and your Gemini colleague has done one of his or her famous disappearing acts.

Leo/Cancer *(Fire/Water)*   Face it Leo, there are some people you're just too much for. If you insist on being all fire and flare, even the most extroverted Crab will scuttle for cover. You can fool some of the people all of the time, but not a Cancer. They don't miss a trick, and they'll see right through you, vulnerable side and all. Sure, Leos like to expose themselves, but not that much!

Leo/Leo *(Fire/Fire)* This is a most creative and exciting combination. You'll spark each other off, light each other's fire, and compliment one another till you're blue in the face. But make sure you respect each other's territory—put two cats together, and their claws are bound to come out now and again.

Leo/Virgo *(Fire/Earth)* You may have marvellous ideas, but it takes somebody with a bit of Virgo common sense to help you put them into practice. They may also put the brakes on your enthusiasm and frustrate you at times, but whatever they promise, they're going to deliver. And if you're in the mood to be humble and you're hankering after some good honest criticism, look no further. Your Virgo colleague will gladly dish some out to you.

Leo/Libra *(Fire/Air)* You like to look on the bright side, and Libra could help you weather any difficult storm. At last, the perfect audience. They'll flatter and praise you when you're down, and applaud like mad when you're on form. And all they expect is the same in return.

Leo/Scorpio *(Fire/Water)* Apply fire to water, and things can quickly come to the boil. Even the king of beasts will be terrified of Scorpio's highly emotional and volatile nature. The only thing you two have in common is a love of power. Keep your distance, Leo, unless you intend to defer. A meek manner will always win over a Scorpion . . . but can your pride stand it?

Leo/Sagittarius *(Fire/Fire)* It could be your lucky day when life throws you into the company of a Sagittarius. They love all animals, but especially Lions. Work or play, they'll help to keep your spirits high, even if once in a while they cut you to the quick with their own unique form of compliment like 'Goodness, those clothes suit you much better than the ones you usually wear.' They're blunt, but they'll take you places you've never been before—and you won't even have to leave the building!

Leo/Capricorn *(Fire/Earth)*   At first glance, the Goat and the Lion don't appear to have much in common. You love to play and laugh; they love to work and moan. You like a bit of attention; they're anything but flashy. But, believe it or not, you do share some similarities. You both get miserably depressed if you're criticized, and you both desperately want to get ahead in the world. Try teaming up now and again—the results could surprise you.

Leo/Aquarius *(Fire/Air)*   There are days when you'll see eye to eye with your opposite sign, and other days when you won't see Aquarius at all. When you're hot and excited, they're detached and objective. When you're feeling laid back, they're all over you with some new idea. But no matter what, they'll treat you with respect—which is how they treat everyone. How *dare* they treat you the same way as other people!

Leo/Pisces *(Fire/Water)*   Pisces people make good slaves, so you two should get along quite well. But watch out! Fish are rather slippery—just when you think you've got them where you want them, they'll slip out of your hands. If things are going to work at all, you're going to have to learn to accept their moody ways, even if you can't begin to figure them out.

The Leo boss

If you know what's good for you, don't take liberties with your Leo boss. An intrusive question, a flippant comment or an ill-considered criticism could bring your promising career to a speedy conclusion. It's true that the sun is just another star but as far as this solar system is concerned, it's the only star we've got—and you'd better like it that way! After all, the sun is important to us; people used to, and still do, worship it—which is exactly the kind of reverence reigning Lions expect. The spotlight is only big enough for one, and if you stay around a Leo for a while, you'll realize that your place is in the audience. A Leo boss likes to be *boss*. They are often friendly and kind, but you can never forget they're in charge. Everything they touch carries their own personal stamp. A newcomer in the job will quickly learn to recognize the Leo boss's initials: G.O.D. So give her or him respect. But that doesn't mean putting on an act, being ingratiating or insincere. Because if there's one thing a Leo can't stand it's a fawning hypocrite.

Your Leo boss, man or woman, can be a real father to you. If they like you, Leos want to see you get on in the world. They'll take an interest in your private life, and you're sure to get support and wise words of advice when you look as if you need them. The snag is that when Leo gives, Leo also expects. So when your charming and caring Leo boss asks you to do something, it's really more a statement than a question—like 'You don't mind doing this for me . . .' as you're passed enough extra work to fill a whole weekend. When a Leo's in charge, there's not much room to say no.

You need to learn tact for dealing effectively with Lions at the helm. If you think one of their ideas isn't good, don't say so. Don't make personal comments. Don't be clever and familiar—you won't make any impression at all, and your career may never recover.

Praise your boss's 'brilliant' idea, spout anything you can think of which is favourable about it, say something like 'that's fabulous, it'll work so well we could probably also get away with . . .' and then very coyly insert your own better suggestion. No Leo boss likes to have his or her edicts ripped away. Consult the Lion even when you know perfectly well what you're doing. Leo bosses need an employee who'll affirm their value and worth—no matter in what capacity you are employed, your real job is to keep them secure and happy by making them feel important. And the more you do it, the more they'll love you for it.

The Leo employee

Competition for jobs is tough these days, but, if you're a boss, don't even think of telling a Leo employee how fortunate he or she is to be working for you. So far as a blue-blooded Leo is concerned, *you* are the one getting all the favours. Of course, Leo employees aren't petty enough to resent your position . . . they merely expect the veneration to which they feel they're naturally entitled. A Leo enters a place of employment intent on carving a niche—and generally does. It's hard to treat a Lion just like one of the gang. Leos often have immense natural charisma—a glowing, magic quality that draws others to them. You can watch a Leo's personal corner of the building gradually turn into a wayside shrine, where colleagues and visitors automatically gravitate to make their offerings and receive a blessing.

When Leos aren't seeking attention for themselves, they're expert at giving appreciation to a suitable boss. In fact, most Leos have a real talent for helping those they care about to feel good about themselves. If you employ Lions and treat them extra well, they'll gladly respect you back in return. You may never get a Lion to eat out of your hand, but they show their appreciation and admiration in any way they can. Take our advice—follow these few easy tips and you'll always get the most from your Leo employee:

1. Always say 'please' and 'thank you' to them in a sincere and reverential tone.
2. Make them think you can't make a decision without them.
3. Listen to their opinions as if they were holy scripture.
4. Offer them a special assignment in total confidentiality, and allow them special privileges which turn their co-workers emerald green with envy.

If you're a boss to a Leo worker, there may be times you'll think you're being made redundant. At first, it's probably humiliating to have to ask your Leo employee everything that's happening with the business, but after a while you'll get used to it. Lions don't always need to have top billing on the programme—they're perfectly satisfied to know that the whole show would fall to pieces without them. A famous London financier claims he owes his success to Ruby, his tea lady. He never makes a decision or a move without asking her opinion first. There aren't any prizes for guessing her sun sign.

The Leo colleague

Leos always put on a good show. Their public expects it of them, and they hate to turn in a bad performance. Even when they're quite new in a job, you'll see them slowly but surely taking over. They can't help it, and usually nobody stops them . . . because we all know a star when we see one. Before very long, people are falling over themselves—and one another—to get along with the Lion at work. Whenever there's a disagreement among the staff about how something should be done, here's somebody prepared to settle it once and for all. Leos have style—their own style. If people are looking for somebody to lead the way, Leo isn't afraid to go to the head of the line.

Naturally, a fellow worker might become a bit

resentful and envious of a successful Leo associate. Maybe you feel that way about a Leo you work with. Who's surprised? (Not your Leo colleague, that's for certain.) Of course, it is quite understandable that you should want to do things *your* way now and again. And probably some of your ideas are very good. But somehow your Leo co-worker makes you feel that you never get it quite right. You need to face a simple fact; some of us have got it, and some of us have not got it. And Leos are the ones most determined to show the world they've got it, even if it's at your expense. Got it? Right.

Now at some point you may very well have a serious difference of opinion with a Leo at work. If you should fall out, you'll quickly appreciate that you've put yourself in a situation that's difficult to reverse. So what do you do? If you have said or done something really terrible, you should immediately consider drafting a long and unqualified apology—in fact, you should write it in your own blood just to be on the safe side. However, considering we're talking about an angry Lion here, even this may seem a pretty feeble gesture.

But we hope it will never come to that. Just remember to treat your Leo colleague with respect, and you couldn't ask for a better workmate—loyal, kind and incredibly warm to be around. In any event, it's never a bad idea to have the king of beasts on your side.

Virgo

Element: Earth
Symbol: The Virgin
Ruler: Mercury

The Sign of the Virgin

Joanne, an attractive Virgo publisher, had this to say about her sign:

I couldn't believe it when somebody told me that I was born in the sign of the Virgin. I really didn't feel much like a virgin at the time. I'd just married my second husband, and already had two children from a previous marriage—and I assure you they weren't immaculate conceptions!

A lot of Virgo women and men go through the same confusion Joanne felt. Knowing how much you Virgo people can worry about things, we believe that our first task is to put your minds completely at rest. Reaching your full potential in the sign of the Virgin doesn't mean taking a vow of chastity. We have to apologize if astrology has never made it clear before, and we sincerely hope that this has not been the cause of any drastic decisions in your lives.

Any ten-year-old with his first dictionary would be delighted to read out the full meaning of the English word *virgin*. But the word *virgo* comes straight from Latin, meaning quite simply an *unmarried* woman. (Apparently, chastity didn't become such a cherished commodity until after the Virgin Mary made it fashionable.) A woman, then and now, doesn't only exist as the 'other half' of a relationship or a marriage. All Virgo people (men as well as women) feel the need to be self-sufficient and independent of others, no matter how closely they get involved. One of the famous Virgos of this century is the Swedish actress Greta Garbo. She had several well-reported affairs but never tied the knot with any man. 'Marriage?' she once answered an enquirer, 'I don't know. I like to be alone—not always with the same person.'

Virginity just isn't what it used to be. Did you know that Queen Elizabeth I, known in her day as the Virgin Queen, was a true-blue Virgo, born on 17 September 1533. Well, it's a fact she never married—with a list of enemies that included 'Bloody' Mary, the Pope and the Spanish Armada, she had quite enough trouble on her hands. But as for her remaining a *virgin* . . . writers of the period make it very clear that she never wanted for male company, and there's a strong hint she didn't get her other nickname 'Good Queen Bess' for nothing.

The goddess Artemis, the sister of Apollo, is an example of a virgin who got along very well without men, thank you. When she was young, she threw out all her Cindy dolls and demanded that her father Zeus give her a bow, a quiver of arrows and a pair of hunting boots. She was such a fearless huntress, she would have made Rambo look like a Girl Guide! Artemis loved nothing more than the fresh outdoors and plenty of her own company. If she was ever keen on men, it could only have been as target practice!

In earlier Greek myths, Gaea was the first earth goddess, a symbol of the complete woman. She represented Nature, and every living thing came out of her body. Before she arrived on the scene, there was only chaos, but like a veritable Virgo she soon straightened that out. In the beginning, Gaea had no mate or consort, so she created the god Uranus by impregnating herself. Now, by even the strictest Virgo's standards, you'd have to call that self-sufficiency!

Mercury, the messenger god

We first encountered Mercury in the chapter on Gemini. You'll remember that he could be a tricky customer, great at communicating but a quick-change artist, ready to turn coat at the drop of a hat. Now, as the ruler of Virgo, he shows that he has a more reliable side to his nature. When he puts down his roots in an earth sign, he's prepared to stick around. If he promises to take on a job, not only will he do it, he'll do it better than anybody else. That's the good news. The bad news is that Mercury can also be a fussy little nit-picker, although if you're a Virgo, you might prefer the word *perfectionist*.

Mercury was the original dispatch rider. His main job was to travel back and forth between heaven and earth, delivering messages from god to god and between gods and ordinary mortals. He was also famous for giving people good advice. If you needed some help choosing the right toga to wear for the orgy at Flavia's on Saturday night, when you couldn't make up your mind what colour to paint your atrium, or you hadn't a clue what to plant in your arboretum, Mercury was always on hand to advise you. He had very clear ideas about what was appropriate and what wasn't. What's more, he had a persistence that could drive people to despair—if you live or work with a Virgo person, you'll know what we're talking about!

Some astrologers believe that the god Vulcan also has associations with Virgo. Vulcan was the first-born son of Jupiter and Juno (the King and Queen of the Heavens), so his birth should have been quite an occasion. The story goes that Jupiter had all the cigars already laid out and the champagne on ice; but when he saw the newly born Vulcan, paternal pride gave way to disbelief. The little creature in Juno's arms was so ugly that Jupiter immediately decided to get rid of it—and quickly, before anybody found out. Jupiter literally threw Vulcan out of the heavens. He fell to earth with a fearful crash that did nothing for his appearance and permanently crippled him. Naturally, poor Vulcan felt rejected, but he was far too practical to give in to his sense of inadequacy. He buried himself in work, and by sheer hard graft he turned his misfortune into a triumph and became the most sought-after craftsman of his time. His phone just never stopped ringing. There's a hint of Vulcan in most Virgos: they're clever and capable and good at what they're doing, but underneath it all there's a frightened child, always worrying about being good enough.

The Virgo temperament

If you're feeling rather dazzled and overwhelmed after our state visit to Leo, stop for a moment and collect yourself in Virgo's cool green garden. But don't get too comfortable! We may be nearly halfway round the zodiac, but this is no place for slackers. Now we're in Virgo, there's work to be done. So come along, the entrance to the sixth sign is just ahead: a simple wooden gate with the inscription: *Labor vincit omnia* (Nothing beats hard work.)

When the sun entered the first sign of Aries, a seed broke open and the growing tip burst through. Then in the earth sign of Taurus, the root pushed down deep and took a firm grip on the soil to take in nourishment. In Gemini, the shoot pushed up towards the sky, throwing out stems and leaves to reach for air and light. In Cancer the flower bloomed, pollen filled the air and new seeds began to form. When the sun came into Leo, the fruit matured and found its colour. Now in Virgo, the fruit is ripe and it's time to reap what we have sown. And this is precisely what Virgo teaches us—you only get back what you put in.

Where Leo ends, hard work begins. Leos are born expecting recognition from other people; but Virgos instinctively know that it's something you have to earn. This isn't the most happy-go-lucky sign of them all. There's not much about Virgo people that's casual or complacent, despite what they may seem, regardless of what they pretend to the outside world.

Outside is exactly where many Virgos would prefer the world to stay. It's not that they don't like the world, they're just highly sensitive to it. When they step out into life, they want to be sure they're on solid ground. Which is why Virgos spend so much of their time trying to figure out how things and people work. They feel safer when they thoroughly understand the ins and outs of something—whether it's a sewing machine or another human being. They're happiest when there's order around them and everything in its proper place. Virgos may seem terrribly single-minded or obsessive, but that's how they protect themselves from sinking into the terrifying sea of chaos, confusion and contradiction that surrounds us all.

In Virgo's rule book, prevention is better than cure. They like to be ready for everything, and they don't live comfortably with ignorance (their own or anybody else's). Which explains why so many of them read . . . and read . . . and read. Virgo people can't have too much information on even the simplist thing. Ask a Virgo in a restaurant how she wants her steak done, and she'll give you enough information to prepare you for a career in catering! But Virgos aren't superficial browsers, content to garner knowledge simply for its own sake. When you're a Virgo, you're motivated to learn something whenever your Virgo security alarm system is triggered, which is to say at least ten times every day. For instance, your instincts tell you that a hairline crack in the wall could signal the collapse of your entire house. So a do-it-yourself manual will have a prominent place in the library of information neatly arranged on your living room shelves, where you can lay your hands on anything from home repairs to homoeopathy. Yes, another of your big concerns is your body—everything that goes into it and (heaven forbid!) any part of it that might swell up, collapse, turn green or drop off. Virgos can have full-blown nightmares about their bodies. (It took Mary Shelley's Virgo imagination to dream up the horrors of *Frankenstein*.) That tiny spot on your arm is almost invisible without the high-powered magnifying glass and the three-hundred-watt light bulb you're pointing at it, but you're right, Virgo, there's always an outside chance that it could turn out to be malignant.

All the earth signs are strongly affected by their bodies. Whatever you may believe about the immortality of the human soul, no soul on earth goes far without a body that's in good working order. Virgo is aware of the body as a finely tuned vehicle which, like all machines, needs regular servicing and protection. But not every symptom responds to creams and cold cures. The body is an integral part of who we are, expressing in its own unconscious way what we feel and think. A Virgo concerned with health runs a very high risk of succumbing to Grade A hypochondria. If you're born under this sign, you're prepared to go to considerable lengths to prevent your body falling apart. There's probably a corner of your bathroom where you could set up a professional pharmacy with all the tonics, preventions, pills and potions you've collected. And should you be travelling in some exotic land where you can't be too sure what (or who!) went into the soup, an entire dispensary will have to travel with you.

You can only relax about something when you're able to understand what's happening. Virgos analyse and dissect everything and everybody—including themselves. Remember Ibsen's hero Peer Gynt? He got himself into a real Virgo dilemma when he tried comparing life to an onion. He took it to pieces peeling away layer after layer until he discovered that it had no heart. So be careful when you start pulling things apart:

the child who removes a butterfly's wings to see more clearly how the insect flies can only discover that the butterfly will never fly again.

Virgos often feel lonely as children. Even in a large family they somehow get the message that they're going to have to go it alone. At least, that's one side of the story. Deep down inside, they cherish a Cinderella-style dream that one day a prince (or princess) will come along to make everything all right . . . only he'd better be the *right* prince! Virgos are notoriously fussy and choosy about the people they team up with, and in the end they may, like Artemis himself, feel happier to be by themselves. Unlike your Leo neighbours, you Virgos aren't out for a lot of attention, and yet your cool, self-contained demeanour gets you all the admiration you can handle. If people aren't put off by your critical nature, they're usually delighted by your intelligent conversation, humour and wit, and impressed by your obvious desire to improve yourself. Even when you make love, you'll apply yourself with a commendable dedication to getting it right. It can be a real business doing pleasure with a Virgo.

Virgos aren't nuns (if you're prepared to set aside a few exceptions like Mother Teresa of Calcutta!) but, having dispelled the myths about Virgos and chastity, it must be said that when you know a Virgo, you can't help noticing a prudish streak that emerges from them in certain situations. It's not so much that they mind getting close or having a really wild time (they enjoy their physical pleasures every bit as much as fellow earth signs Taurus or Capricorn). But with those of you born under the sign of the Virgin, it's a case of first things first. Other people may be able to have sex while ashtrays are full, but not you.

At heart, Virgo is a serious sign. However calm and sorted out Virgos may appear, they're always stalked by a vague fear that famine, drought or some unimaginable catastrophe is just around the corner. When it comes, they're determined to be ready for it. So be careful when you say to a worried Virgo friend 'Cheer up, it might never happen!' Try to stop them worrying, and it feels to them as if you're removing the whole point of their existence. You have to take into account that Virgos don't just fret over nothing. They keep themselves informed and they have an earth sign finger on the pulse of life. So when your Virgo neighbour starts building an ark, don't just laugh and dismiss him as a crank. Stop wasting precious minutes and go check up on the long-range weather forecast for the next forty days!

Virgo types

Virgos born between 24 August and 1 September

Whatever you take on, you give it your all and see it right through to the end. But must you drive yourself crazy worrying about everything that could go wrong? Relax and have a little more faith in life. Don't push the river, and in the long run you'll get just as much done.

Virgos born between 2 September and 11 September

You can't be happy unless you're doing something. Even on your rest days, it's hard for you to turn off the motor. There's nothing wrong with wanting to make your mark in life, but all work and no play will make you even more neurotic than you already are. Stop being so tough on yourself, and enjoy life a little.

Virgos born between 12 September and 22 September

You're the most creative of all the Virgo types. You're also the most obsessive. Does everything you do have to be a hundred per cent right all the time? And when it comes to relationships, you aren't hard to please, you're almost impossible! Remember, no one comes prepacked as perfect.

Virgo and work

Word has it that every Virgo baby is born clutching a job reference. (If it's true, there's probably a Virgo somewhere with statistics on the subject.) Most Virgo people take to work as easily as others take to drink. In fact, work amounts to an illness for some Virgos; there are more workaholics born under this sign than any other. When they aren't involved in something productive, they feel more out of place than a hen in a dentist's waiting room. Indolence doesn't suit them. Even on holidays they need to keep busy all the time. Travelling with them is like going on an expedition—they need a pack animal (or a masochistic Pisces friend) to carry around all their guidebooks, sun-tan lotions, insect repellents and endless supplies of bottled water.

Virgos don't need other people to motivate them—as with all the earth signs, the sound of the wolf howling at the door is usually incentive enough. But there's no point having a door if you haven't a house to go with it. And, of course, you need curtains, tables, chairs, good quality food, nice clothes, a compact disc system, a jacuzzi, a patio and your own indoor exercise room . . . unfortunately, the best things in life aren't quite as free as they used to be. Virgo isn't one to watch a current account dwindle down to zero. But even when there's plenty of money in the vault, can you really trust the bank employees to look after it? What if a computer goes beserk and forgets to credit the last big cheque you paid in? Worried Virgos open their monthly bank statements as if they expected a cobra to pop out.

A Virgo's idea of heaven is a working situation in which they can play an important and integral role. Each person at work is like a cog, wheel or spring in a finely made watch, perfect and complete in itself, but interacting with everything else as part of the whole mechanism. Nothing pleases Virgo more than to be part of an efficient organization and to see the whole machine ticking over nicely. And yet some Virgos find it hard to get along with others at work. They like the idea of meeting a co-worker halfway, but with their critical minds, the meeting could turn into a collision. Virgo people do all they can to compromise here and there, but they can't resist making a comment when something obviously isn't right. If you're a Virgo who doesn't get a lot from working with other people, maybe you should find a job you could do on your own. But just think how frustrated you'll feel when you get in a foul mood and there's nobody around to take it out on.

Here's an exercise which might help Virgos relate better to employees, colleagues or bosses.

1. Take a moment to reflect on how you feel inside yourself when you're engaged in a task at home or at work. What is your attitude to other people when you're busy working away at something?
2. Now answer these three questions as truthfully as you can. Are you able to ask other people for help and support when you really need it? How do you feel when you're giving out criticism? How do you feel when another person criticizes your work?
3. Take a few minutes to consider what practical steps you could take to improve the quality of your interactions with others.
4. Now make a list of those steps (Virgos love making lists). Your next day at work try to follow these steps. In a few weeks, you should see some real changes, both in yourself and in the way others relate to you as well.

Virgo careers

For Mercury-ruled Virgo a career with words seems obvious. When it comes to choosing the right thing to say and the right words to do it with, discriminating Virgos are the ones for the job. Many could happily end up with successful careers in the publishing field, operating as hawk-eyed proofreaders and sabre-toothed editors. Others might make it into the big league as highly paid journalists and writers, following in the footsteps of such well-known Virgo authors as James Hilton *(Lost Horizon)*, William Golding *(The Lord of the Flies)*, H. G. Wells *(The War of the Worlds)*, Jessica Mitford *(The American Way of Death)* and Frederick Forsyth *(The Day of the Jackal)*. It used to be the case that any adolescent who wanted to be considered a reader had to get hold of a copy of *War and Peace*. This famous Russian novel, describing the lives of people brought together when Napoleon was preparing to invade their country, was intricately created by the great Virgo writer Leo Tolstoy. But if the thought of tackling such a hefty historical tome gives you instant reader's cramp, sample some of the light and witty short stories by the Virgo-born author Roald Dahl. A contemporary American Virgo, always at the very top of the list of best-selling writers, is ghoul gourmet Stephen King, author of *Carrie, The Shining* and other scary tales guaranteed to curdle the milk in your cocoa. For a deadly but altogether more civilized late-night read, follow the inimitable Miss Marple or hair-splitting Hercule Poirot as they pick up the telltale clues that murderers leave behind . . . at least, they always do in the novels of Agatha Christie—born in the sign of the Virgin in 1891, and still taken to bed by millions every night.

Not only are many of you Virgos not prepared to live a life of chastity, some writers born in your sign have been pleased to push virginity a little further towards extinction. Thirty years ago every American teenager had a dog-eared copy of *Peyton Place* wedged under the mattress. Its author was Virgo Grace Metalious. Earlier in this century, D. H. Lawrence, another Virgo writer, was sending temperatures soaring in post-Victorian England with his novel *Lady Chatterley's Lover*, the book that finally said it all. (Life, like many Virgos, is full of irony. One of the greatest architects of the morality that characterized Victoria's reign was the Queen's husband, Prince Albert Saxe-Coburg, also a Virgo. Greatly troubled as a child by the divorce of his parents, Albert fought hard to promote the image of the cast-iron Victorian family—the very values Lawrence challenged in his writing.)

Mercury endows Virgos with talents that make them suitable for other work with words besides writing books. A secretarial job need no longer be the dogsbody profession it once was. In dynamic organizations, this career now calls for a range of abilities including a share in decision-making (something unimaginable ten years ago), as well as more traditional telephone and reception skills and the latest word-processing expertise. For a more artistic Virgo, calligraphy and graphics suit a sign that's so steady, precise and into detail. Bookbinding, which seemed likely to disappear at one time, has come back into vogue again, and could be a highly profitable Virgo profession. Should you prefer working with people, you could be of real service helping children or adults with language or learning difficulties, so why not specialize in remedial teaching or speech therapy? (Virgo-born Maria Montessori devised an educational system to encourage the fullest potential of even the most withdrawn child.) Or you could help out those with problems seeing, by taking up a career in optometry. After all, there isn't much that escapes your eye.

If you insist on making a spectacle of yourself, you might want to get into the technical or artistic side of the entertainment business. Many of the Virgos who have become famous as performers are a long way removed from the image of the virginal prude that the name Virgo suggests. But some came very close. When American cinemagoers discovered Virgo Ingrid Bergman, they believed that she really was as pure as the snow-white character of St Joan she played so convincingly on film. They were in for a shock when she eloped with Robert Rossellini. But Virgos often get a kick out of saying or doing the outrageous, and they do it—as they do most things—very effectively. Hygiene-happy Michael Jackson and the poet Edith Sitwell are very individual cases of convention-breaking Virgos. If there's one thing this sign has got, it's style—the roll call of Virgo celebrities who have caught the public eye includes such favourites as Greta Garbo, Claudette Colbert, Lauren Bacall, Frederic March, Anne Bancroft, Sophia Loren, Raquel Welch, Richard Gere, Sean Connery, Lily Tomlin, Peter Sellers, and that famous television couple Linda Gray (better known as Sue-Ellen) and Larry Hagman, the one and only J. R. Ewing. All these great performers, apart from standing out in their own special way, owe their fame to a peculiarly Virgo gift: timing. And the same could be said about dancing Virgo Gene Kelly, singing Virgos Patsy Cline, Hank Williams and Freddie Mercury, songwriting Virgo Alan Jay Lerner (*My Fair Lady*), and boxing Virgo Rocky Marciano. Yes, Virgo skills score pretty well in the sporting field too. So if you've got your sights set on beating the best, get into golf like Virgo Arnold Palmer; run circles around them like the great American legend Virgo Jesse Owens; or shoot right past them like the French skiing ace Jean-Claude Killy.

By any judge's standard, the sign of Virgo gets high marks for presentation. You'll get a few sloppy ones here and there, but most Virgos somehow always manage to make it appear as if they've just stepped out of cellophane. In the middle of a hectic working day on the hottest afternoon in living memory, when everyone else is constantly checking their underarms for perspiration odour, you can count on a cool Virgo looking as fresh and unflustered as ever. Though the Virgo manner may appear very casual, the effect is as closely calculated as a chemical equation. Socially and professionally, even the quietest Virgo men and women know how to make an impression, so it's natural that people would turn to this sign for advice on appearance and presentation. Sophia Loren and Raquel Welch are two Virgo beauties who have both written succesful books advising other women on how to be as distinguished as they are. And there's always room for more Virgos in any line of work that involves helping others find the style and look that's just right for them. If you're a typically meticulous Virgo, you also could use your natural gifts in the field of public relations, helping a company create the right image, making all the complicated arrangements for an important meeting or exhibit, or grooming a VIP for a gala reception.

Virgos don't only like to look good, they want to feel good as well. The famous Virgo preoccupation with health can give rise to anxious hypochondriacs capable of creating in themselves symptoms of all the terrible maladies they insist on reading about. But with their natural concern for the body and their sensitivity to others, Virgo people can excel in professions which involve them in the health and welfare of others—as nurses, doctors, alternative medicine practitioners, physiotherapists, dieticians, nutritionists and dental hygienists. If you're a Virgo health-freak, why not capitalize on it by dealing in health foods—selling them, cooking them or growing your own on some cosy organic smallholding in the country?

There's a whole natural world around us in which humans occupy an increasingly large part. But as we alter the balance of the eco-system, we threaten our own survival. Virgos concerned with the damage that is being done to the wildlife and vegetation with which we share our tiny planet could find satisfying work as environmentalists and conservationists. In fact, some Virgos infinitely prefer working with animals rather than people. Ken Douglas is a Virgo who does research into animal ailments, and he couldn't be happier with the company he keeps:

I used to be a doctor, but I much prefer my work now. Dogs are much easier to get along with than people, and they don't insist on talking about their illnesses!

Probably Virgo people's greatest talent is their organizing ability. You'll always find a Virgo organizing something or someone—it comes as second nature, whatever line they happen to find themselves in. Richard Attenborough, the Virgo actor turned director, spent years painstakingly organizing the making of his two big films *Gandhi* and *Cry Freedom*. Then there's the famous example of a French Virgo who demonstrated a method of making the most of what you've got. Have you seen pictures of the huge and fabulous Palace of Versailles with its famous gardens and the celebrated Hall of Mirrors? It was all the creation of the 'Sun King' of France, Louis XIV. When you consider the magnificence of his court and the splendour of his reign, you might assume he was born in Leo or some other ostentatious sign. But he was a highly calculating Virgo who—through his excellent administrative abilities—succeeded in distracting his nobles from their pursuit of power (thus adding to his own) by constructing a dazzling showcase which became the wonder of Europe. Louis XIV certainly was crafty, but craftsmanship comes naturally to a sign famous for its technical dexterity, patience and attention to detail. If you're a Virgo who's looking for something steady to do with your hands, try stonemasonry, carpentry, furniture-making, tapestry-weaving, dressmaking, or working as a gold or silversmith. That should keep you busy.

Crafty Virgos also can make good business people, more at home in the boardroom than any other room—except the bathroom. But, like all earth signs, they have a money problem: they can never get enough of it. (Jesse James the outlaw was born in the sign. So too was Goethe, author of *Faust*, the tale of a man who sold his soul to the devil!) The same Virgo people who worry over a skin blemish also like to see their bank account in good complexion. Other people's money is no less interesting, and you'll frequently find Virgos working in investment companies, banks, building societies, accountancy and insurance. A career as an economist, systems analyst or business organization consultant couldn't be more appropriate for a thrifty sign that loves to see things working efficiently. And, Virgo, if you're still at a loss for what to do, why not cash in on your obsession for order, cleanliness, ritual and precision, and become the most sought-after estate manager, butler, dry-cleaner or domestic servant in town?

Virgo compatibilities

Virgo/Aries *(Earth/Fire)* When things at work are running smoothly, and you haven't encountered anything unmanageable for months, it's time for an Aries to charge into your life and shake you out of your complacency. You can send out a chill breeze to extinguish the Ram's bright fire; but you could also help an Aries along by (tactfully, please!) giving them some of your sound practical advice. They probably won't listen, but that's their problem not yours.

Virgo/Taurus *(Earth/Earth)* The Bull's a dependable colleague. Taurus people like life clear, simple and worked out, just as you do. Of course, Bulls are a little slow, and some of them really can't walk and chew gum at the same time (adaptability isn't their strong point), but never mind—there's still something about them you can't help loving.

Virgo/Gemini *(Earth/Air)* Their scatterbrained behaviour will make you dizzy, but you can't help liking the Twins' youthful spirit. They're never short of money-making ideas, and you've got the practical know-how to make them work. Team up, and you'll be heading straight for success. But whatever you do, don't let Geminis take charge of the wheel—they'll probably drive you to distraction if they do. And if it comes to a showdown, the weapons you both reach for will be words—really sharp ones.

Virgo/Cancer *(Earth/Water)* Cancers feel; you analyse. Together you won't miss a trick. But try not to turn the sharp edge of your criticism onto them—they just can't take it, no matter how hard they try. And they don't always say when something's bothering them, so you're left guessing what's wrong. Offer them help when they look as if they need it, and if in return they want to spoil you, relax and enjoy it.

Virgo/Leo *(Earth/Fire)* You aren't envious of the Lion holding court, but you don't appreciate a Leo who's too bold and brassy. Still, you admire anybody so at home with other people. Does it surprise you to learn that Leo people respect your diligent nature and your strong sense of purpose? (If it didn't mean being so dull, they'd probably try to be more like you!)

Virgo/Virgo *(Earth/Earth)* You worry yourself into a frazzle over nothing, and you can hide it from every other sign but your own. You're very happy to put other people under the microscope, but see how you wriggle with a Virgo who lowers the lens on you. Work-wise, though, it's a good combination and you'll probably get along . . . even if you cordially detest one another.

Virgo/Libra *(Earth/Air)* In your efforts to expand your personal fortune, a Libra may turn out your most worthy ally. Even if they can't show you how to make money, they'll certainly teach you how to spend it.

If ever you feel like lashing out and doing something different, your Libra colleague will have plenty of interesting suggestions. Maybe it isn't your forte, but learn a little flattery—with Libra, it will get you everywhere.

Virgo/Scorpio *(Earth/Fire)* Other people may find the Scorpion a tricky customer, but you're one of the few who can understand what these people are all about. They're dark horses, but then you're no Goldilocks yourself. You'll learn a lot just being with one another—in fact, working with a Scorpio could change your whole perspective on life. Best of all, when you 'vant to be left alone', trust your Scorpio friend to understand.

Virgo/Sagittarius *(Earth/Fire)* A little of Sag goes an awful long way. But when your horizons get too narrow and life is too serious, a dose of their happy-go-lucky nature is just the tonic you need. They've got an endearing habit of bringing magic and excitement into other people's lives . . . and leaving somebody else to clean up the mess after they're gone. Three guesses who'll that be.

Virgo/Capricorn *(Earth/Earth)* A Capricorn is right up your street. If you think you worry a lot, just spend a couple of hours beside a groaning Goat. When it comes to moaning, you've met a kindred spirit who likes talking shop as much as you do. And just think, you can criticize them till your heart's content, and they'll probably just agree with every word you say.

Virgo/Aquarius *(Earth/Air)* Aquarius people are exciting, always different, and working with one could feel like a change for the better. But never put yourself in a position where you end up running after them, because within a very short time you'll be worn out. Water Bearers don't want your devotion, they want to feel free—free to leave the room, change their minds, do what they want. Cope with that, and you'll get along fine.

Virgo/Pisces *(Earth/Water)* You can feel so sorry for a Pisces you end up doing everything for them . . . and then you're annoyed that they never get themselves together, so you tell them off. So *they* feel bad, *you* feel sorry, and the cycle starts again. But the good news is that with two sensitive people from opposite signs, each has what the other lacks. Result: A great working team and a strong friendly relationship.

The Virgo boss

Even if you're not into religion, better say a prayer that your newly appointed Virgo boss isn't the same cut as that notorious Virgo, Captain William Bligh, commander of the good ship *Bounty*. You too could turn mutinous, smarting under the lashing criticism of an overexacting Virgo at the helm. Even with a more understanding boss, you'll quickly get the picture that Virgo runs a pretty tight ship.

Virgos in charge have very definite ideas about how a job ought to be done, and they're low on patience when it doesn't turn out that way. Leslie is an American Virgo boss, running a firm of London-based financiers. She admits that it isn't always easy to work for her. But she isn't ashamed of her reputation, either:

I know my standards. I've learned the job from the bottom up, so I know what I'm talking about, and I don't stand for people messing things up. Yes, I listen to suggestions, and I'll use them if they're good, but I'm not here to massage other people's egos. I'm here to get a job done right.

Leslie was anxious to point out that she is normally harder on herself than she is on other people. (We can only assume that she throws herself onto poison darts each evening after work!) Even the playful repartee of a friendly Virgo boss usually contains a reproach—a gentle reminder of what you are doing wrong. But don't forget: underneath it all, Virgo bosses really do want to be liked, and many of them wish they could cut out their tongues after some of the things they say. In the final analysis, to get along with a Virgo boss, it's most important to show them that you accept them for what they are. Despite the fact they dole out criticism like eggs at Easter, they're not all that keen when it comes their way.

The Virgo employee

Virgos have every qualification to make them the ideal employees—they're born servers—practical, thrifty, tidy, precise, and sticklers for detail. If they're happy with what they're doing, you couldn't ask for a better right-hand man or girl Friday. They'll take on any job that needs to be done around the place of work, whether it's cleaning the loo or sending out the boss's Christmas cards. And yet—for all their willingness to serve—deep down inside, Virgos usually feel superior to the work they're doing, and sometimes to the people they're doing it for. But they're cautious by nature and it takes them a long time to move out and move on . . . and a lot can happen in the meantime.

If there's one thing Virgo employees have, it's principles. Plenty of them. If they're critical of how things are being run, they really ought to speak out and have their say. Instead, a lot of them keep mum, and that's when the resentment starts to build up. On the surface, they maintain the facade that everything is just peachy—underneath they're itching for a fight. Self-contained Virgos silently seethe when an employer is around, but as soon as the boss is gone, out pops a very vitriolic Virgo who just can't help unleashing a caustic comment or two. Adept in the art of subtle undermining, an unhappy Virgo employee is potentially as destructive as an army of termites beneath the Empire State Building.

Virgo is a sign often noted for its timing, and a vengeful Virgo won't attack until the moment is right. By then the next job is already in the bag, the evidence against the boss has been weighed and prepared with inimitable Virgo thoroughness, and in the best tradition of Artemis herself, the time has come to move in for the kill. Never forget that Rocky Marciano was a Virgo. When it comes down to it, they know just how and where to hit.

For weeks now, colleagues have felt the atmosphere thicken and gel. A Sagittarius has been taking bets in the men's room as to where, when and how it will happen. It's three o'clock on a Friday afternoon. The Cancer on the switchboard nervously fingers her first-aid pack. Innocently, unsuspectingly, the boss leaves his desk and crosses towards the seated Virgo employee. The audience holds its breath. The boss speaks. The Virgo listens. The final straw settles ... and Virgo strikes! The boss is staggering backwards, but no ... no, he's staying on his feet ... yes, Virgo's giving him a few home truths now ... he's not sure if he can take much more ... and here's another blow to the boss's self-esteem from Virgo ... there's no stopping this Virgo today ... and there goes that Virgo with a quick one in the neck and a sharp knee where it hurts ... and that's it! The boss is out of the fight, and Virgo is out of the building!

Despite the calm, cool and collected front most Virgos present to the world, there's a rebellious side to their nature that comes out at work. They like nothing more than proving their point; and thanks to Mercury, when they know they're right they can usually find the exact words to cut an opponent to mincemeat. Even if they're wrong, they have a way of putting things that doesn't leave you much room to argue. So if you want to save your neck and hang on to your indispensable Virgo employee in the process, make sure you show them the respect they know they deserve.

The Virgo colleague

Virgos are caring friends—thoughtful, obliging, and eager to be of service to others in need. If you want to get the very most from a Virgo colleague, you have to elicit their sympathy. First, make yourself look as pale, tired and haggard as possible. Next, approach them with the task you're needing help with and say something to the effect: 'I've been awake half the night trying to work this out, and I still can't do it.' It's a bait most Virgos can't resist.

If you're ever introduced to a Virgo man or woman who says that work isn't important to them, they're either lying, drunk, madly in love, or badly informed about their date of birth. They make exemplary co-workers—although for every detail you like about them, they'll probably find something to criticize in you. Your Virgo colleague is big on detail; no matter what the subject, you'll find they have very specific tastes and preferences. Virgos possess the most impressive talent for discriminating (sometimes rudely) between what is absolutely right and something that doesn't quite make it. To anyone else, the difference seems trivial. Sometimes it is. But their style of dress, their choice of decor and the way they approach a task are all very carefully considered. Watch a Virgo at work pausing for a moment to draw out those long, critical antennae and begin the subtle process of appraising, adjusting and improving the job they're focused on. They judge themselves mercilessly, and they're capable of being equally unsparing of the people they work with.

There's no doubt about it—it's good to make friends with a Virgo colleague. In a conflict, their greatest weapon is a sardonic withering humour, with an edge as cool as a steel blade. A Virgo may appear quiet, soft-spoken and well-behaved most of the time, but don't be fooled. You've heard about the mouse that roared? When it comes to the crunch, even the most prissy or demure Virgo is capable of cutting the mightiest adversary right down to size.

Libra

Element:	Air
Symbol:	The Scales
Ruler:	Venus

The Sign of the Scales

How do you recognize a person born in Libra? Compare them with other people (a favourite Libra occupation) and you'll notice that they think their way carefully through everything. Faced with a new situation, they hardly ever jump in at the deep end. Instead, they look at it from every point of view before they make a move—*if* they make a move! Some Libras hem and hum and haw so long they never get around to doing anything. They believe that there's a right way of doing everything, and they don't like what other people might say about them if they get it wrong. So they're forever assessing, readjusting and correcting their actions, like an artist trying to paint a really perfect picture. They like to think that everything they touch will turn out beautiful, balanced and fair.

But, of course, no one can always get it right, and somebody's bound to end up feeling unfairly treated. There's a statue of Justice herself dominating the Old Bailey, the setting for many a famous criminal trial. She's an uncompromising lady with a set of scales in her left hand to weigh up everything, and a big sword in her right hand to show she really means business. Like most Libra people, she has her hands full trying to be fair. And sometimes she isn't. Legal systems, like human judgement and Grandma's old kitchen scales, always lean a little bit one way or the other. Sometimes criminals go free, and innocent people carry the can. In any situation, attempting to do what's fair and just can sometimes get you in an awful lot of trouble.

Did you ever hear the case of the poor Tiresias, a poet of ancient Greece? He was walking in a shrine sacred to the goddess Hera, when he discovered two snakes entwined in a sexual embrace. He began to wonder which of the two—the male or the female snake—was getting the most pleasure, so he asked the goddess if she knew. Even Hera didn't know the answer to that one, but she offered Tiresias a chance to find out by changing him into a woman for seven years. She thought that would give him quite enough time to make a fair comparison. Seven years later, having diligently complete his researches, Tiresias staggered back to the grove, looking rather the worse for wear. Weighing up all his experiences, he declared that, as far as he was concerned, woman had a better time sexually than men. Hera was delighted with the result. But her husband Zeus felt Tiresias had let the side down. He was so annoyed when he heard his decision that he struck Tiresias blind on the spot. So you see, Libra, even when you're right, sometimes it pays to keep your mouth shut!

Venus, goddess of love

Venus, also called Aphrodite, rose out of the foaming sea and stirred up quite a lather when she eventually turned up among the gods on Mount Olympus. There had never been anything quite like her—and did she know it! She smiled at all the gods with a mischievous glint in her eye and immediately provoked a jealous squabble among the other goddesses. For years Athene and Hera had been the reigning beauties. Nobody could pretend they weren't appealing, but their charms evaporated when sizzling Venus arrived on the scene. Zeus—this time on the side of justice—organized a beauty contest to determine who really was Miss Olympus.

The prize was to be a golden apple, and as judge he chose Paris, a hunky mortal boy who had a reputation for being good with women. Athene and Hera accepted the challenge, determined not to be upstaged by this upstart surfer Venus.

When Hermes, the messenger god, found Paris ploughing the fields, he told him all about the competition, but the youth didn't much like the idea. Paris suffered badly from a common Libra problem—when he was faced with a decision, he could never make his mind up. So he asked Hermes if this was an invitation he could refuse. 'You always have a free choice,' replied Hermes, 'but, of course, Zeus will strike you dead with a thunderbolt if you say no.' Sorry, all you Librans out there—whether you like it or not, sometimes you can't get out of making a decision.

On the day of the contest, Venus was busy pushing back her cuticles when she overheard Athene in the next tent shamelessly promising Paris that he would never lose a battle in all his life, if he let her win the competition. And only a minute later, as they were lining up for the first heat, the goddess of love heard Hera promising Paris the whole of Asia if he gave *her* the top prize. That did it! Athene and Hera had gone too far with their cheating, and Venus was the one to teach them a lesson. The time came round for the judgement. As Paris stood beside her, the goddess of love undid her scanty little wrap-around and it slithered to the floor, uncovering her greatest assets. When the blushing Paris bent down to pick up her robe, Venus whispered to him through her cool, sweet breath that he could have any woman he wanted if he gave her the golden apple. From that moment on, there was really no contest; the young man made his judgement, Venus got the apple, and Paris got Helen of Troy, the most beautiful woman in the world. The trouble was, Helen was already married to Priam, King of Troy. That innocent little beauty competition started off the Trojan War . . . and Paris got killed in the fighting. So maybe he made the wrong choice, after all. But you can't blame Venus for that—she only did what was fair. As for Paris, maybe he could have chosen better. But what happened to him later only goes to prove that nothing is guaranteed to work out happily, even if you make the right decision at the time.

The Libra temperament

Librans come to life when there's somebody around to relate to. You could say that when there's nobody there to agree with or fight with, they're not very sure who they really are. Libra people need company like a question needs an answer. So visit them, write them a letter, call them on the phone, give them something to respond to, and you'll make them happy. Ignore them, and you've got an enemy on your hands. Friendship can mean a lot to a Libra. A lover can mean everything in the world.

No matter where they are, Librans look for an ally, a special person, somebody who'll be there just for them. They love to get attention. Pay them compliments and you'll get everywhere with people born in the seventh sign of the zodiac. Even the most happily married Librans find it hard to resist flirtation. When someone looks at them in a way that says they're special, or whispers a few words of affection, they're in seventh heaven! Libra is the sign of relationships, and most Libras are on the lookout for the right one. After all, isn't life more meaningful, balanced and complete when you finally meet your other half? That's your theory, Libra; but in practice, other people turn your life upside down.

Librans can make marvellous friends and attentive, ideal partners, but their romantic imaginations often get the better of them. The Libra ideal of love is a bit like the pictures you see in the pages of a glossy holiday brochure; glamorous, affectionate couples sightseeing by the Acropolis or making eternal pledges of love by the moonlit Taj Mahal. In every Libra heart there's a dream waiting to come true. One day a marvellous stranger will turn up out of the blue, and from that moment on, everything that was wrong will be right. The only trouble with perfect partners is finding them. Librans spread their charms as easily as a fishing boat casts its nets—but they're often disappointed with the catch. They may meet a long string of people who will seem to be 'right' . . . but sooner or later every one turns out to be a bit of a letdown. There's always something wrong—already married, too demanding, no money, no manners, bad habits, bad breath . . . for the very fussy Libra, there's never anyone quite good enough. It's a common Libran mistake to assume that relationships with people can be sorted out as easily as you can arrange a head of hair or a vase of flowers. Perhaps that's why people born in the sign of the Scales often feel left up in the air or down in the dumps, just when they think they've worked out all their difficulties. You'll hear some of them complain that they put so much into relating, but other people never seem to meet them halfway.

Librans would like everything around them (their homes, careers, friendships, families and the country they live in) to be as harmonious, tasteful and attractive as possible. Their greatest handicap (one shared by all the air signs) is a habit of idealizing other people. When Librans fall in love, the scene is set for Romeo and Juliet, Bonnie and Clyde, and Rhett and Scarlett all rolled into one. Newly smitten Librans couldn't be happier, as if nothing so momentous has happened since Columbus discovered America, or America discovered the hamburger. If only the honeymoon could last forever! But with the sign of the Scales, everything that goes up has to come down—and Librans often come down hard on anything or anybody who seriously disappoints them.

Libras' high expectations make them one of the most critical and heavily judgemental signs of the zodiac. When a sweet Libra turns sour, run for cover. Each astrological sign is strongly influenced by its opposite—and in the case of Libra, we're talking about pushy, determined, impetuous Mars-ruled Aries. A Libra partner who smiles and whispers 'Your wish is my command', doesn't bother to add '. . . but you can only order what's written on the menu!' Many Libras have no idea just how cleverly they manage to control situations—with the combination of Mars and Venus, they have an assortment of strategies at their disposal; everything from a pout to a punch! Librans are the kind of people who hand the car keys over to you and say 'You drive, we'll go where you want to go.' But if you end up taking them somewhere they don't like, they blame you—and there's hell to pay!

Libra is a sign full of contradictions. Some Libra people are afraid to say directly what they want or feel, because they're frightened you won't like them for it. Instead, they expect you to guess what it is they need, and then they get upset when you don't. But there are other Libras who will tell you precisely what it is they expect of you, and if you can't live up to it, you can just forget about being their friend. Either way, the sign of relating has a lot to learn about relating.

If you're a Libran who's serious about wanting to get the balance right, isn't it time to change your tactics? You could start by accepting yourself more as you really are, complete with your good and bad points. And on the subject of other people, the lesson for you may be to recognize your illusions and make your ideals a little more realistic. Every romantic evening has a morning after. Every silver lining has a dark cloud. Angela, a thirty-year-old divorced actress who was having her chart read, didn't much like the sound of that; 'What a depressing view of life. I know what you're saying, but does it really have to sound so miserable? Surely, life is for enjoying.' Of course, Angela was right. Life is for enjoying. But she herself wasn't enjoying it at all at the time. Her marriage had failed, and she wondered if astrology could help her understand why:

I don't know how my ex-husband, John, could treat me so badly. I made every effort to help him. Do you know, when we met, he didn't even have a job. Of course, he was very different then—he was terribly good-looking and very, very funny. I really believed in him at a time when nobody else did. I knew he was bound to get somewhere as a writer, and he did. He took very good care of himself then, but now he sags like an old armchair. He's changed. He's not the man I married.

As Angela reflected on her marriage, she saw how her critical nature crept out of the closet just as soon as they were married . . . and John, the handsome prince she fell in love with, slowly turned into John, the monster who deserted her. When she acknowledged her part in the break-up, Angela began to learn a very valuable lesson; good relationships can't stay beautiful and gift-wrapped forever. Being with another person is hard work. Over a period of time we're bound to reveal sides of our natures we'd much rather hide. It's easy to hate ourselves for our shortcomings or blame other people for theirs, but nothing and no one can be a hundred per cent perfect all the time. The Danish philosopher Søren Kierkegaard wrote: 'Perfect love means to love the one through whom one became unhappy.' That's a profound thought, but it's one that Librans could learn from.

The Libra types

Librans born between 23 September and 1 October You've got plenty of natural charm—at least, while everything is going well. But some people are uncomfortable with only your smiles and diplomacy, so speak up when things are bothering you. Whether you know it or not, you've also got an artistic streak in you. Don't be lazy—do something with it.

Librans born between 2 October and 11 October You've got an insatiable interest in people—all kinds and from all walks of life. For everybody's sake, give yourself plenty of freedom and variety, and find ways to get around and expand your horizons. A humdrum existence definitely isn't for you.

Librans born between 12 October and 23 October You're hard on yourself, but don't underestimate your potentials. With a little more effort, consistency and confidence, there is so much you could do. Find the right creative outlet for your natural intelligence and sensitivity, and you'll be a lot happier with your lot in life.

Libra and work

Libra's various permutations of character soon emerge in the arena of work and career. At one end of the scale, you'll find Librans who see early on what they want and never look at anything else till they get there. But then there are other Libra people who spend so long vacillating about which job to apply for or whether to try for a promotion or not that they miss the boat over and over again—and end up miffed when some lesser mortal gets something they could have walked away with. Some Librans are completely unable to settle on what career path to follow, and so they get absolutely nowhere. (Let's face it, this sign can have trouble deciding which side of the bed to get out of every morning.) There are Librans who are plain lazy—they feel the world owes them a living. And then there are the Libra snobs, who consider a lot of jobs way beneath their dignity. A Libra woman who had to clear tables to earn herself extra money pretended to her friends that the boss was really her uncle, and she was only helping out while he was short-staffed.

Librans are sometimes talked into doing what they don't really want to do, although usually not forever. Tony, for instance, had no real desire to become a doctor, but his mother and father had their hearts set on a medical career for him. So Tony became a very good doctor, but all he actually enjoyed about it was the glamour and the drama—because what he really wanted to do was to be an actor. At the age of thirty-five, he finally had the courage to pack up his practice and go on stage. It was a difficult change, but a Libran's prepared to do a lot for a bit of attention.

Librans want harmony at work, and they'll do anything to achieve it. They hate crass behaviour, clashing colours, gnashing teeth, and crashing bores most of all. They'll function best in a tasteful working environment—complete with plush carpets, airy decor, flowers on every desk, and big windows with a leafy view. What most Librans like best about work is the human contact it offers. In fact, some enjoy liaising with bosses or co-workers well beyond the call of duty. This is not to suggest that anything improper would necessarily take place. It's just that Librans relish the reminder that where relationships are concerned, they haven't yet played their last card.

Most Libras will benefit from a little introspection. Here is an exercise which will help you Librans to better understand yourself and your relationships:

1. Sit in a quiet place and bring to mind somebody you don't like—maybe someone you work with who really gets on your nerves. See if you can pinpoint exactly what it is about that person that irritates you so much.
2. Here comes the hard part. It is a fact of life that what we

are most intolerant about in others is what we dislike most in ourselves. Now look inside yourself, and see if you can identify a part of you which is like that person you can't stand. For instance, if you can't stand how snotty someone is, see if you can recognize that you yourself can be snotty sometimes.

3. Then bring that person to mind again, and see how you feel about him or her now. Has your understanding changed or softened in any way? If not, don't worry. But try the first three parts of this exercise again at a later time.

4. Now focus on someone you really admire—somebody you like a great deal—and try to pinpoint exactly what it is you respect in that person so much.

5. Here comes the fun part. It is also a fact of life that what we most admire in another person is in us as well. For instance, if you really appreciate someone's grace and good manners, then you have the capacity to be good-mannered and graceful too. If you really appreciate someone's directness then latent within you is the capacity to be as direct as that person. Reflect on ways you can bring out in yourself those qualities you admire in others.

Libra careers

In the days of prehistory, relating to other people was easy. If somebody had something you wanted, you took it from him. If he wouldn't give it up, you hit him over the head with a big heavy object. Gradually things became more civilized. People began communicating in grunts, and within a thousand years, they'd started speaking to each other. It must have been a Libran who pointed out that the time had passed for primitive barbaric behaviour. From then on, people saw that if a person had something you wanted, you could talk and negotiate for it, one human being to another. You could say 'If you don't give it to me, I'll hit you over the head with a big object.' That's how diplomacy was born.

For Librans, relating is a fine art. It's natural, then, that many embark on careers in public relations. If you feel you have your own personal image pretty well under control and that you manage other people comfortably and with tact, why not work promoting someone who doesn't possess your flair for handling even the most delicate situations? And, of course, there's always the diplomatic service–the art of getting other people to do what you want (preferably without drawing blood).

Magnus Magnusson, Melvyn Bragg, Clive James, Angela Rippon, Edwina Currie–with so many prominent public figures alive today born in Libra, it's no wonder it's sometimes referred to as the 'hot-air sign'. So for all you Librans who like to meet, greet and get noticed, there could be the right career waiting in the media. If you can't get into the media, you could always try for politics. As history shows, Libra people all over the world have come to the forefront as leaders and influential politicians, all with ideals of peace, unity and fair play. Of course, their personal interpretation of these Libra ideals, and their methods of achieving them, couldn't be more different. But one thing is for certain; they'll fight like hell to promote their version of truth, beauty or justice–and to set up the political system they think is right.

Alexander the Great was the military Libra type (and there are quite a few of them) who believed that if you really want to bake a cake, you have to be prepared to break a few eggs. When he had broken more than his fair share, he redrew the map of the ancient world and achieved his dreams of a united empire. In very recent years, Bishop Desmond Tutu, Archbishop of Cape Town and winner of the Nobel Peace Prize has made a Libran impact worldwide with his determined vision of peace in apartheid-ridden South Africa. And, by nibbling away at people's consciences, the Libran Boomtown Rat Bob Geldof has gained enormous admiration and inspired millions with a plea to feed the starving in Africa.

We can't discuss Librans who have made history

without mentioning Margaret Hilda Thatcher, a believer in peace negotiated from a position of strength. When in 1979 she became Britain's first woman Prime Minister, she altered the course of politics. (Probably no event has done more to affect the British way of life since the introduction of the tea leaf.) And she showed a whole other side to Libra when she said, 'If your main objective was "please, I just want to be liked and have no criticism", you would end up doing nothing in this world.'

Right at the other end of the political spectrum, we find another Libra fighter, Annie Besant (1847–1933), who sided with the oppressed and poorly paid in Victorian England, organizing the famous strike of the match girls in 1888. Later, out in India, she was imprisoned for her part in the campaign for Indian home rule. And when full independence to India came many years after, it was under the leadership of a powerful passive resister, the wily Hindu Libra Mahatma Gandhi, who preached the Libran ideal of peaceful coexistence. The creation of the Jewish State of Israel was due largely to the herioc leadership of its first Prime Minister, Libra David Ben-Gurion. Mexico still remembers the exploits of the Libran bandit turned political revolutionary, Pancho Villa. And can Argentina ever forget the bloody rule of Libran Juan Perón and his glamorous, extravagant actress wife, Eva Duarte, or Evita, as she is better known today?

Libra is the sign of relating, and you can't think of some Libra people without also thinking of their partners. Once upon a time, marriage was the only career open to a woman; but things have changed. Sarah Ferguson, for instance, an ebullient Libran lady who became Duchess of York after making her vows to Prince Andrew, also has a very Libran career publishing art books. John Lennon, the Libra Beatle who pleaded with the world to give peace a chance, was transformed by his marriage to Yoko Ono. Eleanor Roosevelt, Libra wife of President Franklin D., became an ambassador for him and a colourful world personality in her own right. Libra President Jimmy Carter, always caught (in true Libra style) on the horns of a dilemma, chose on many occasions to be represented overseas by his wife Rosalind. The Libra Playwright Arthur Miller is famous for his plays, like *Death of a Salesman* and *A View from a Bridge,* but he's even better known for his marriage to Marilyn Monroe. Mention the name of another Libra, Mickey Rooney, and if people don't recall his films, they'll remember his achievement of having been married more times than Elizabeth Taylor . . . so far, at least. And if you have any doubt of the importance of relationships to the sign of Libra, what about the literary Libran F. Scott Fitzgerald, whose courtship and marriage to the southern belle Zelda looked for a while to be the epitome of the Great American Romance?

As Scott and Zelda proved to the world, marriage is quite a business. So are relationships. And they provide many Libras with a worthwhile career. Libra people enjoy matchmaking, something they could capitalize on by setting up or working in a dating or marriage agency. Many Librans who have serious relating problems have been supported and helped by appropriate therapy and counselling to face marital difficulties, broken relationships and the pain of bereavement. With the insight of their personal experience and their talent for standing outside any situation, Libras could make first-rate marriage guidance counsellors, family therapists, or psychologists. The psychiatrist R. D. Laing, a Scots-born Libra, has contributed through his work to a deeper understanding of ourselves and how our families influence us.

If you prefer the sound of something at the lighter end of the scale, how about a career that's more entertaining? Libras in the entertainment industry have left us with an image of what love is all about. Some of the great sex symbols of all time were born in the sign of

Libra. For example, Brigitte Bardot, the fifties French sex kitten who has now given herself to campaigning on behalf of the fair treatment and protection of animals; Bruce Springsteen, the all-American boy frequently in an all-American sweat; Charlton Heston, who played Moses with muscles; Christopher Reeve, everybody's superman; the gentlemanly Trevor Howard, who made a memorable brief encounter in 1940; Carole Lombard, the brazen blonde who was also Mrs Clark Gable; Sigourney Weaver... Rita Hayworth... George Peppard... Yves Montand... Linda Darnell... Montgomery Clift... Marcel Mastroianni, etc.

Not content with being seen simply as a pretty face, many Libras find that playing a convincing role also comes as second nature. Sarah Bernhardt, the most celebrated actress of all time, was born in Libra. It's said that she continued to play the role of Hamlet when she was over eighty, and wearing an artificial leg. That's quite a feat (or do we mean 'foot'?). Her great contemporary rival was Italian Libra, Eleonora Duse. Another Libra in the limelight during that period was the Jersey-born actress Lillie Langtry, who drew ecstatic audiences during the Edwardian age. She even managed to draw the attention of Edward himself. Being mistress to a king—now there's an occupation some Libran women would happily aspire to. (Of course, Libra leading lady Deborah Kerr said no to the King of Siam's offer in *The King and I*.) And while we're listing talented Libra ladies, we mustn't leave out Helen Hayes, once the queen of the American stage and still going strong in films and television, or the lovely Libra Carrie Fisher, Princess Leia of *Star Wars*, who with her recent best-seller *Postcards from the Edge* has shown the world she can not only act but write as well.

Like the other air signs, Libras have their way with words. Those with a literary flair could emulate other writers born under their sign. Besides Scott Fitzgerald and Arthur Miller, there's also Truman Capote, William Faulkner, Eugene O'Neill, Harold Pinter, Graham Greene and T. S. Elliot—Libras who have written about both the humour and the tragedy of human relationships. Some of the most memorable quotes, particularly on society and the institution of marriage are left to us by the eminent Victorian Libra, Oscar Wilde.

In married life three is company and two is none.

Never speak disrespectfully of society, Algernon. Only people who can't get into it do that.

There is only one thing worse than being talked about, and that is not being talked about.

All art is quite useless.

Whether or not you agree with Oscar Wilde's last comment on art, it hasn't stopped many Librans entering the art world and becoming painters, sculptors, designers, art dealers and agents, encouraging, managing and selling others. Libras have the right touch for setting up exhibitions and encouraging the influential to attend them. Their proven critical ability can be well applied in writing or speaking about the arts to the uninformed or the unappreciative.

And if you have a good musical ear, you may be interested to know that John Lennon wasn't the only Libra to tell the world that all you need is love. Only a Libra, Giuseppe Verdi, could have written the tragic romance *La Traviata*, and it takes a modern Libra like Luciano Pavarotti (who obviously enjoys the good things of life) to perform it. The powerful romantic music of Franz Liszt was made popular in his own time by his many recitals. Apparently, he was so attractive that women used to swoon during his concerts. A more modern Libra composer is the late great George Gershwin, famous for his romantic melodies and the touching love story of *Porgy and Bess*. And though he may be short, let's not overlook a contemporary singer-songwriter of considerable stature, Libran Paul Simon.

When it comes to sport, Libras will give anyone a run for their money—at least, that's how Librans Steve Ovett, Seb Coe and Steve Cram would see it. Jayne Torvill, the ice skater, is another limber Libra, who's graceful movements in the rink would make any dancer envious. But just in case you imagine it's all art in Libra, meet John L. Sullivan, the Libra bare-knuckle boxer who left an impression on the face of American culture.

With the goddess of beauty as your patroness, you Libras hate things to look a mess. Statistically, Libras come out very high in all professions concerned with style and beauty. You're a born matchmaker, and this applies to your choice of colours, shades and textures as well. You couldn't go far wrong as a fashion designer or interior decorator—but do be careful about your tendency to overdo the ruffles, frills and curls. Speaking of curls, you'd also make a good beautician, hairdresser, stylist or even wigmaker. (Wherever possible, Librans are quite happy to improve on nature!) Libras who like to dress well often have a flair for selling clothes—they manage to find just the thing for the most awkward customer. Libras are excellent salespeople in any field. They particularly like to advise on intimate details like perfume or exotic underclothes and nightwear for not-so-quiet evenings at home. Librans entertain with a style that is professional in standard. Whatever their line, many a Libra promotion is due to their talent for impressive home entertainment.

Librans show all their colours in any occupation where they are able to represent others. Many people born under this sign could find success in a legal career, firmly but graciously settling messy divorces and unpleasant misunderstandings. What better thing for a Libran to balance than the scales of justice itself!

Libra compatibilities

Libra/Aries *(Air/Fire)* Opposites attract, but they sometimes repel. You'll either love each other at first sight, or hate each other immediately. If you do get on, you're bound to continue your friendship outside work. But be careful—Aries can be a bossy Ram, so be sure you get your own way sometimes.

Libra/Taurus *(Air/Earth)* With this earth sign, everything takes time to grow. Your appreciation for Taurus people will blossom when you see how patient and easy-going the Bull can be. Of course, they can be so slow and set in their ways that sometimes you'll find it hard to be patient and easy-going with them. Never mind, when it comes to indulging your appetites, your Taurus colleague will be very happy to join you for a leisurely lunch at the best place in town.

Libra/Gemini *(Air/Air)* You needn't worry about running out of things to talk about when there's a Gemini around. Working together will always be stimulating, even if you do spend hours debating your different points of view. And should you get bored with the humdrum of daily living, don't wait a minute longer; team up with your Gemini friend for a vigorous intellectual workout, a night on the town, or just a quick juicy gossip.

Libra/Cancer *(Air/Water)* This could be a little difficult. You enjoy Cancers' taste and sensitivity, but their moodiness will probably drive you crazy. You'll never be quite sure where you are with a Crab—one day they're open and warm, the next they'll cut you off if you try to get near them. Before you talk sense into them or reform their ways, remember that they belong to a feeling sign, not a thinking one like yours.

Libra/Leo *(Air/Fire)* Leos love a good audience, and they couldn't have a more attentive one than you. You'll win their favour in no time, and when you do, they'll shower you with golden compliments and make you feel the most important person in the world. This combination is unbeatable; they could do with your kind of insight into other people, and you'll learn a lot from the Lion's confident approach to life.

Libra/Virgo *(Air/Earth)* Okay, they're fussy and a bit prissy at times, but so are you. When it comes to doing a job well, you're a perfect match. You like to do things with style and taste, and they'll gladly keep at you till you get it right. But when the day's work is done and you want to let it all hang out, you may find them a little too serious for your liking.

Libra/Libra *(Air/Air)* How charming! You're both considerate, kind and thoughtful – and so pleasing to other people. But this is work, not a gavotte! You can spend so much time deferring to one another that nothing ever gets done. And as for making joint decisions, forget it. Long after the cows come home, you'll still be debating the pros and cons of every possibility.

Libra/Scorpio *(Air/Water)* A tricky match. You like people to lay their cards on the table, but Scorpio doesn't give much away. They don't always play fair, and that's one thing you can't tolerate. So unless you're prepared to compromise your ideals, you might be wiser to keep your distance from this sign. Sooner or later, you'll get stung.

Libra/Sagittarius *(Air/Fire)* If you're looking for a playmate, this is the sign for you. You're both enthusiasts, interested in life, and the conversation is sure to be lively, stimulating ... and never-ending. But be warned—Sagittarius people are very direct, They won't pay you compliments just to be nice. If they don't like your new haircut, they'll be the first to say so. Horrors!

Libra/Capricorn *(Air/Earth)* You're both snobs at heart, so that's one thing you have in common. But you're much more flexible than the Goat, and their stubbornness is bound to get on your nerves. They've got their principles, you've got yours—and chances are they're not the same. That's not to say you won't respect their disciplined, hard-working nature, even if they do bore you to tears.

Libra/Aquarius *(Air/Air)* Aquarius people can be a little strange for your taste, but you can't help appreciating their friendliness and their concern for humanity at large. There'll be lots of lively conversation and an endless supply of interesting ideas to share. And even when you don't have a clue what they're talking about, you'll still find them fascinating.

Libra/Pisces *(Air/Water)* Of all the water signs, Pisces is the best one for you. Fishes are even more sympathetic and willing to go out of their way for others than you are. And you'll love how they agree with everything you say, until you discover that's how they are with everyone. Need sympathy and a shoulder to cry on? Pisces will be right there to comfort you. Of course, there's a price—you'll have to listen to all their problems as well.

The Libra boss

If you want one example of a Libra boss, look no further than the Boss herself, Margaret Thatcher—the last person in the world to be undecided about anything. Did you know that Libra has long been referred to as the sign with the iron hand in the velvet glove? It seems that some Libras in charge are so intent on having their own perfect way, they simply refuse to listen to anything or anyone who disagrees. Their strategy for achieving a unity of opinion is to get rid of anyone who doesn't agree with them. Simple but effective, and just how a Libran likes it.

However, Libra bosses of the Mrs Thatcher kind are few and far between. The typical Libran boss is usually much more flexible. They're always aware of every employee in the building, and they'll encourage you to bring your problems or complaints to them—especially if you think you're being treated unfairly. When you have a grievance with a colleague or if a customer has treated you badly, rely upon your Libra boss to intercede on your behalf. When Libra Delia Jones (she asked us not to use her real name) opened her charm school on the south coast some years ago, she had a typical Venus approach: 'I always treated my girls as if they were a part of the family.' Delia is happily retired now, and she lives in Mallorca with her three poodles.

You can rely on a Libra to look after your interests. They won't have forgotten the time when they themselves were on the receiving end as employees, and they'll do whatever possible to ensure you have everything they were denied. So you'll probably get luncheon vouchers, time off without question when you're sick, and a pay rise when you want it. Of course, it won't be necessary to tell a Libra boss what you need, because they'll already have it all very carefully worked out for you. And if you don't get it straightaway, just be patient. It doesn't do to complain or push them, because if there's one thing a Libra boss won't tolerate, it's ingratitude!

The Libra employee

If someone comes along and offers you three wishes, be sure to ask for a Libra employee. Aladdin never had a better service! If you're lucky, the Libra working for you will do anything you command. But beware if you find them staring at you a lot with a glazed look in their eyes. The curse accompanying this kind of Libra is that they usually expect something back in return. The game is to guess whether it's a pay rise, a promotion or a love affair. And if you're wrong, there are no second chances. Your time starts now!

A Libra employee wants to be one in a million, rather than one of the crowd. So they never aim to give less than the very best at work. But the very best by a Libra's standard may not necessarily coincide with what you want. When you decide to air your views as boss on how a job really ought to be done, it may not make any real difference to what the Libra employee will actually do. Librans who know their own views are really right will say one thing to your face, and do something completely different when your back is turned. Frankly, you could find your Libra employee just a little bit big for his (or her) boots. Naturally, if you're the boss, you're entitled to have your say. But if you make your observations on their work in a tone that suggests they really could be doing better, don't be surprised if you have to spend all night trying to persuade them to come out of the washroom. You really must appreciate that your Libra will take every criticism you make very much to heart.

Maybe you just don't appreciate that a Libra employee has the potential to be your right arm. If you require someone to act as intermediary between you and a difficult staff group, you can trust a Libra to find words to cool a difficult situation. Librans like to be the doves of peace at work, hovering and cooing around anyone in the office whose feathers are ruffled. Wherever there's an ugly clash of temperament, whenever there's a conflict of opinion, a Libran will appear like magic, leaving concord where there was discord. However, if Libra workers are the slighted ones, they're capable of dividing the workforce as effectively as Moses parted the Red Sea. So if you don't want a disaster on your hands, treat them with the kind of love and respect they're working so hard to get.

The Libra colleague

You may notice that your Libra colleague likes to use the word 'we', as in the phrase 'Shall we dance?' The first person plural is the sound of music to their ears. It suggests that Librans aren't just speaking selfishly on their own behalf, they're speaking for others too. Libra-speak isn't an easy language to master, so here's a first lesson. When a Libra says to a client, 'We so much enjoyed your visit', it really means, 'I personally found you long-winded and boring, but some of the others looked very interested.' And when a Libra colleague sweetly enquires across the office, 'Can we have this window closed?', he or she is asking in other words 'Are you trying to freeze me to death? I wasn't born in a field!'

If you're very nice to them, Librans make perfect friends and co-workers. They always smile radiantly when you take them out to lunch, and especially when you buy them a present at Christmas or on their birthday. They're always there for you when you need to talk and you want someone to listen, or when they have something to say that they think you ought to hear. When you have a problem, they're more than happy to tell you what they think you really ought to do. Unpleasantness is the thing that infuriates them, so if you're in a foul mood and feel like dumping it on somebody at work, don't choose a Libra unless you're willing to pay the consequences—which won't be cheap.

Trust your Libra colleague to notice your new hat, your new tie and your new lover. So wear your hat or your tie to work, but better leave your lover at home. Treat a Libran with fairness and respect, praise them two or three times an hour, and they'll never let you down. Whatever else they might not do, they're bound to bring a touch of class to any establishment where they work.

Scorpio

Element:	Water
Symbol:	The Scorpion
Ruler:	Pluto/Mars

The Sign of the Scorpion

One day a frog met a scorpion by the edge of a lake. 'Hello, Frog,' said the scorpion, 'where are you heading?' 'I'm just off to my lily pad over on the other side,' answered the frog. 'Great,' the scorpion told him. 'That's what I was hoping you'd say. Do you mind giving me a ride on your back to the other side of the lake?'

The frog had heard all about scorpions. 'I don't trust you,' he croaked very nervously. 'How do I know you won't sting me?' The scorpion looked straight into the frog's eyes: 'Frog,' he said earnestly, 'Trust me. I won't do anything to hurt you.' The frog, finding it hard to say No, reluctantly responded, 'Well, okay, but you must promise not to sting me,' 'Of course not,' said the scorpion. 'Why would I do a thing like that?'

The frog got into the water. He let the scorpion climb onto his back and began to swim to the other side. Halfway across, the scorpion suddenly curled his tail and stung the frog in the neck. The frog felt himself getting weak as the poison entered his body. 'But, Scorpion,' he gasped as they both began to sink helplessly in the water, 'why did you do it? You promised you wouldn't hurt me.' To which the drowning scorpion replied, 'Why did I do it? Because I felt like it!'

Thanks to the commercial cinema, we all know the scorpion as a dangerous tropical creature that just loves to crawl up bedclothes and sting people. The scorpion has a bad public image. Actually, there are over eight hundred different types of scorpion. They can all hurt in a way you'll never forget, but only some have the famous lethal sting. Basically, they're peace-loving. Leave them alone, and they won't bother you . . . probably. That's the story with most of the people born in Scorpio—it's only when they're crossed or in a bad mood that you have to look out. But there are some Scorpio types who can be treacherous even at the best of times. The trouble is that you can't always tell the difference between the nice Scorpios and the dangerous ones. And you can never be sure when a nice one will suddenly turn nasty.

Scorpio isn't all dark and deadly. Besides the treacherous scorpion, the high-flying eagle is another symbol which traditionally has a strong influence on many of the people born under this sign. So you're also going to encounter very proud-spirited Scorpios with noble minds and high ideals. But, of course, when you threaten what's near and dear to an eagle, they're liable to swoop down and kill you, so they need watching too. Why is it that when we're talking about Scorpio, we always end up talking about death?

Pluto, the god of the Underworld

Nobody went out of his way to meet the god of the Underworld. Pluto's kingdom was the realm of the dead, and you normally only travelled there on a one-way ticket. Everbody who did meet Pluto had one thing in common . . . their lives were never the same again. And that's the effect a Scorpio person might have on you. Let a Scorpion in your life, and you'll be reborn a different person. You'll change so much you won't even know yourself!

That's exactly what happened to Persephone. Before she met Pluto, she was as innocent as a rosebud and sweet as a new potato. Her mother, Demeter, who was very loving but a little overprotective, raised her in a sheltered valley away from temptation or harm. But one beautiful afternoon when Persephone was in a meadow playing with her equally virginal friends, the goddess Aphrodite caught a glimpse of her. Aphrodite's life was always in a mess, and she hated clean-cut Persephone on sight. In the eyes of the goddess who promoted sensual love, this kid was too naive and childlike for her own good. Aphrodite decided to teach Persephone a lesson, something to wipe that Shirley Temple smile right off her cute little face.

Without further ado, Aphrodite instructed her son Cupid to aim one of his passion darts at Pluto, the god of the Underworld. At that same moment Persephone plucked a narcissus (a flower sacred to Pluto), and the earth suddenly opened up. Pluto appeared in his black chariot, snatched Persephone and drove her back with him into the dark Underworld.

Life can be a little rough for all of us at times. But if we aren't totally crushed or destroyed by something devastating, in time we become stronger through it. Persephone lost the innocence of childhood, but she was reborn a woman. Through her ordeal, she gained power, wisdom and a deeper understanding of life. Sometimes we have to go through a struggle before our real strength can be found. If you're a Scorpio, you probably know what that means.

The Scorpio temperament

Libra men and women like things to look good. Scorpio people aren't that bothered about how things look on the outside—they're more concerned with what's happening under the surface. Flash a Scorpio your most reassuring smile, and they'll know immediately if you're only doing it to hide something. It's hard to put one over on a sharp-eyed Scorpion. Even if they can't see exactly what's going on, they can smell when something is up. The eighth sign is a water sign, and like the people born in Cancer and Pisces, Scorpios operate from their feelings. They are deeply sensitive people. On the outside, they give nothing away; inside, they're reacting strongly to everything that happens. Beneath the determined, affable assurance of a Scorpio, there's a volcanic sea of emotion.

Scorpios take very little at face value. Unlike other people, they can't just accept a gift, thank you for it and enjoy it, because they're too busy wondering why you gave them that *particular* gift, and what you're going to expect in return. With this sign, you'll often feel you're guilty until proved innocent. Make a remark that bothers a Scorpio, and for a week afterwards you may get the feeling that two interrogating eyes are boring holes in the back of your skull. When they're upset, the atmosphere around them can be as thick and dark as molasses. Of course, there are Scorpios who insist that their lives are as uncomplicated as tea with Mary Poppins. The reality is probably more like breakfast with the Borgias (the scheming Italian family who made so many enemies, all their food had to be tasted for poison). Anybody who loves a good thriller could get more dramatic intrigue and suspense in half an hour with a Scorpio than they'll see in twenty Hitchcock movies.

Mention that you're a Scorpio, and some people back away as if you were carrying a king cobra or a hand grenade. Okay, it's true that Charles Manson, the power-crazed murderer, was a Scorpion, but all people born under this sign aren't like him. In fact, many Scorpions are truly caring souls. They feel things deeply, and if they love you, they'll do *anything* for you. But Scorpions are also private people, who allow only a chosen few to get really close to them. Personal privacy is absolutely sacred to a Scorpio. You'll only be invited into their homes if you are really welcome. Their front doors frequently have more security locks than Fort Knox.

But curiously enough, Scorpio's mysterious, inaccessible manner also makes them very alluring. Many Scorpios are so devilishly attractive that other people find themselves unable to resist (even the little scorpions that don't kill with their sting use it to paralyse their victims before they devour them!). Of course, not every charismatic Scorpio goes in for the kind of sizzling sexual hanky-panky that keeps Sunday tabloids in business, with whips, skintight leather or the dance of the seven veils. Remember that the list of famous Scorpios includes names like St Augustine, Martin Luther, Billy Graham and gospel singer Mahalia Jackson. Many Scorpions would insist (passionately, of course) that a powerful thing like sex should be kept firmly under lock and key—and they don't mean bondage.

Scorpios feel things intensely—that's why they try to keep themselves in control all the time. They're afraid of what they would be like if they took the lid off their feelings and let it all hang out. Maybe you've heard of Pandora—she was given a special box and told not to open it. But she did, and all hell broke loose. When Scorpios get a strong feeling, it completely takes them over. Sometimes that can be very positive; when something or somebody matters to them, no act of devotion, no effort, no sacrifice is too great. But at the other end of the scale, Scorpios know they could turn very nasty—and some of them do. If really provoked, they'll exhibit reactions we all like to pretend we haven't got.

When we see people raging in a riot, battling with police or screaming and fighting out in the street, we are usually aghast and fairly certain that we would never act that way ourselves. But maybe we're not really quite as civilized and superior as we like to make out. We don't go out and hack people to death, but, on the other hand, we do pay taxes so we can have an army that's ready to do any killing on our behalf. On the outside, we all like to believe we're really civilized, sane, reasonable people . . . but on the inside, we get mad as hell. We're raised believing that we shouldn't be *negative* about anything. But life is a mixture of black and white, and where there's positive, there's got to be negative too. So where do all our negative feelings come from, and what do we do with them when we know they're there?

Let's start at the beginning. We are all born into this world helpless; unless there's somebody around to feed and take care of us we won't survive. We feel great love for others when we're looked after. But when our basic needs for warmth, food and comfort are not being met, we feel a lot of rage and fear—because we know that if we are not cared for properly we will die. When we're babies and we are ignored or kept waiting, the only thing we're certain about is what we feel—hungry, lonely, wet, cold, etc. We don't know that mother is busy and she'll be coming back to us as soon as she can. We think we've been abandoned forever, and this makes us incredibly scared and angry. Babies can get really worked up about life at times. You don't see adults in that kind of temper very often, but there is still a raging, frightened infant lurking somewhere inside all of us.

Let's take another look at Pluto, Scorpio's ruler and the god of the Underworld—the place where things are buried. Anything that's buried in a Scorpio, sooner or later has to come up to the surface. Some Scorpios have a violent streak—most of the time they can be super-calm and under control; but offend them or try separating them from something that matters to them, and you're liable to lose your arm! It's not surprising that these Scorpios are sometimes too frightened to expose what they really feel. But anger has to go somewhere, and if it's not expressed it turns back in on itself—and that's when Scorpios can get self-destructive. Some Scorpios use so much of their energy holding back their difficult feelings that they have very little energy left over with which to lead a full life. Rather than getting angry, they become depressed and broody—which is really the root cause of the legendary moods that Scorpios are so famous for.

Of course, you can't just unleash all your bad feelings every time they come up; but it's important at least to realize that these kinds of emotions are there, and that it's quite human to have them. Otherwise, you might spend your whole life constantly blaming and condemning other people for what you don't want to face about yourself. You can't change anything in yourself until you have accepted it's there. Once you admit you have negative emotions like anger or jealousy, then you can begin to take the tremendous energy contained within those feelings and begin to use it more constructively. All that buried power that felt so dark and negative can give you a whole new driving force in your career and your private life. Pluto was also the god of buried treasure: when Scorpions begin to look inside themselves, they usually unearth a great many talents and resources they never even knew were there.

What the ancients called the Underworld, modern psychology terms the unconscious mind. We all have drives and urges which compel us to act in certain ways, even when we don't wish to. However much we want to be in charge and responsible for what happens to us, many of the big decisions in our lives are made unconsciously without our being aware of them. That's why we can suddenly find ourselves in marvellous or tricky situations, having no idea how we got there.

Like Pluto, many Scorpions are at home in the Underworld, probing the hidden dimensions of the mind or exploring the secrets of nature and the cosmos. Some Scorpios can become fascinated (even obsessed) with finding out what makes them or other people tick. True detectives at heart, most people born under this sign never lose their curiosity about life. Mark a door KEEP

OUT, and you're inviting a Scorpio to pick the lock. Give these people the smallest whiff of a secret, and it's like teasing a cat with the smell of fresh herring. Scorpio children can be quite a handful for their parents because they always ask awkward questions. While other kids get into dolls, soldiers and jigsaws, the consuming interests in the life of a little Scorpio are sex, death, family skeletons and anything else that nobody wants to talk about. Their ears prick up when an adult conversation drops into a whisper. What whispering adults fail to appreciate is that Scorpios are more than a little psychic—they can see round corners and hear an interesting conversation through a concrete partition.

If you're a searching Scorpio, you've probably noticed that you've a real talent for finding trouble. Mark, a Scorpion social worker, explained how he felt about it:

Now and again I'd just like to get on with my life. I go out into the street to get away from work, and what happens? I see a traffic accident. A minute later I'm back in the middle of a crisis.

At first, Mark looked disappointed with life. Then he looked up and smiled. 'I don't know. I suppose I must like it that way!'

Scorpio types

Scorpios born between 24 October and 2 November There aren't many people around who have your kind of drive and determination. When something matters to you, you'll put all your energy into it. You're not only the most intense, but you're also the most secretive of all the Scorpio types. Even your best friends won't be able to figure you out.

Scorpios born between 3 November and 12

November You have a deeply passionate nature, easily moved by people who are suffering pain, neglect or ill-treatment. At times you may give so much, you could end up feeling undervalued or taken advantage of by others. You may not think so, but you've a tendency to overdramatize life. The more you can learn to relax and laugh at yourself, the better you'll feel.

Scorpios born between 13 November and 22 November There's nothing you wouldn't do for a good friend. In return, you can usually get other people to do just about anything you want them to. Under your genuine care and concern, however, you're a shrewd operator, looking out for Number One. And when you're in a bad mood, Attila the Hun could be Snow White in comparison.

Scorpio and work

Pluto, the god of death and destruction, isn't the only ruler of Scorpio. Mars, the god of war, also rules the sign. That means a double dose of trouble when a Scorpio shows up at work. Beware especially of sociable Scorpions who apparently want to get along with everyone—they're potentially more trouble than a keg of dynamite with a very long fuse. If they blow up, they'll take the whole building with them.

Whatever Scorpios take on, they do it with a passion, or they don't do it at all. They offer a refreshing challenge to the people they work with. Unlike their opposite sign, Taurus, if Scorpios are not happy about something, they won't quietly put up with it. Whatever the problem is—a fractious colleague, an outdated or unfair work procedure, or a toilet that doesn't flush properly—a Scorpio won't sit on it for very long. Scorpio is a secretive sign, but when a bee gets into their bonnet, everybody will know there's something astir, even if

Scorpio doesn't choose to reveal right away what that is.

Nothing is sadder than a Scorpio without an adversary. Most people prefer peace and quiet at work, but for Scorpios, strife is a many-splendoured thing. They thrive on conflict. Give them the challenge of an enemy, and their eyes take on a new sparkle—suddenly they discover a reason for being alive. Scorpios may moan about how they always seem to be at loggerheads with somebody, but they can't resist the theatre of war. Don't let their often aloof exterior fool you: Scorpios are drama queens at heart.

Scorpio is a water sign that pours itself into everything it does, and every Scorpio needs a work which challenges them, something to get their teeth into. When they're absorbed in a task or project, nothing else exists. Come hell or high water, they won't stop till they're finished. But if they aren't careful, they're liable to burn out and exhaust themselves physically, mentally and emotionally. Traditionally, Scorpios suffer high blood pressure and back trouble, probably due to all the stress they carry. Yet, like the phoenix, a mythical bird that is consumed by fire and rises reborn out of the ashes, after a brief holiday or a change of scene, Scorpios can bounce back feeling a thousand years younger and ready for the fray all over again.

Scorpios may act or look tough, but underneath they are one of the most sensitive signs of the zodiac. They're easily hurt, and a wounded Scorpio takes a long time to heal. If they've been treated badly in the past, they will be on their guard to make sure it never happens again. A Scorpio never forgets.

Over the years, Scorpios store up a lot of resentments, and this is not a healthy situation for anyone. If you're a Scorpio, and a really angry mood takes over, here's an exercise which will help you to channel some of that energy more constructively:

1. Think of a project or task that you want or have to do, but haven't yet put as much energy into as you would like.
2. Now, putting aside the idea of your project for a moment, take some time to get in touch with what you feel angry about. (It may be something in the present or the past, something from work or from your personal life.) Really get in touch with your angry feelings. Don't act on them, but let yourself feel their vibrancy, their power, and what they do to your body. Don't judge these feelings, just be with them.
3. Now, consider this fact: these angry feelings contain within them a lot of energy. Even though the anger might seem negative and destructive, the energy contained in that anger can be redirected and used to fuel some project or task that you would like to undertake.
4. Come back now and think again about the project you thought about in the first step of this exercise. Picture yourself taking the energy contained in your anger and using it to attack that task. Imagine what it would be like to work on that project with the same amount of energy your anger has kindled.
5. Now go and do something to get your project moving.

Scorpio careers

You Scorpios are well advised to choose a career you feel passionate about. With Pluto, the god of death, ruling your sign, there's always the slight risk that your job could cost you your life, so it makes sense to get into something which you're willing to make a few sacrifices for. That has happened to a few famous Scorpios. One of them was Bobby Kennedy, the American senator and brother of the assassinated president. He pronounced the definitive Scorpio creed: 'Always forgive your enemies . . . but never forget their names!' Indira Gandhi, Charles I, Leon Trotsky and Marie Antoinette are other well-known Scorpios who got the chop, one way or another. But usually if there's anybody going to swing an axe, it's a Scorpio who'll be doing it. When Scorpio Martin Luther attacked the Catholic

Church, he pronounced a death sentence on the power and corruption of the popes of his time. Other Scorpios who have left a political mark include French Presidents Charles de Gaulle and François Mitterand (the first socialist in the Fifth Republic) and American Senator Joseph McCarthy who in true Scorpio fashion set up the infamous anti-Communist witch-hunts of the 1950s.

You'll probably be relieved to read that there are less extreme Scorpios who also succeed. Many of them are very happy living a quiet life amassing loads of money. Money! That's something they can get excited about. They love their own, and they're pretty good at handling other people's resources as well. (Remember, the opposite sign here is Taurus the Bull, old moneybags himself!) And don't forget shrewd Scorpio's obsession with security: you couldn't make a wiser investment than in a Scopio-run business. Those of you born under this sign have a natural business head and could make successful careers in the world of finance, banking or insurance (but don't expect to get money for nothing if you run across a Scorpio claims investigator.)

Scorpio is the sign of spies and detectives—the sort of people who prowl around after hours (after all, the scorpion is a nocturnal creature). One of the most notorious spies of them all, Mata Hari, was born under this sign. You too may fancy your chances working in the secret services (sorry, we can't tell you where to apply) or as a private detective, uncovering the full details of who, what, why and when—legitimately, for a change! (Alternatively, you could rake up a little muck as a journalist, like the Scorpio columnist Nigel Dempster.)

But perhaps your probing mind is more academic or scientific, in which case you may want to use your investigative powers to do some kind of research work into something that matters to you. Michel Gauquelin, the statistician and psychologist we mentioned in the introduction, is a Scorpio. Years ago he set out to prove to the world that there was no concrete evidence to support astrology. He examined the birthcharts of thousands of people in every walk of life with all the thoroughness you would expect from a meticulous French Scorpio. And, in the end, he found to his surprise that there was something in astrology after all! Another Scorpion, Marie Curie, famous for her research into the use of radium, was one of the many pioneers born under this sign. South Africa's Professor Christian Barnard was the first surgeon to perform a heart transplant, offering the Scorpionic possibility of renewed life to thousands. Transforming the lives of others is something a Scorpio can do very well. They can usually manage to do that in whatever field of work they go into. Often they're cashiers at the bank, assistants and clerks, choosing to be inconspicuous but in a position to meet other people and touch their lives. There are many committed Scorpio doctors, nurses, radiographers, community, prison and social workers, all driven by their sensitivity to other people and inspired by the need to help those less fortunate improve their lot.

Some Scorpios turn to religion to find their true mission. Evangelist Billy Graham is among the more famous inspired speakers born in the sign. However, if you think you're a Scorpio with a powerful pulpit manner, you will have to be prepared to encounter some opposition to your views. Joseph Goebbels, Hitler's infamous propagandist, used his Scorpion powers of persuasion to brainwash millions, and gained just as many enemies in return.

There are many ways to alter other people, and some Scorpios have achieved it through the arts. You may like to add your name to the long list of Scorpios who have taken up the pen to probe beneath the surface of life. Passionate Scorpio poets like the vulnerable American Sylvia Plath and Welshman Dylan Thomas (*Do not go gentle into that dark night/Rage, rage against the dying of the light*) have been a strong influence on generations of readers and writers. For greater insight into the undercurrents and misunderstandings in human relationships, read the works of Russian Scorpio Ivan Turgenev, or Scorpio Frenchmen André Gide, André Malraux and Albert Camus. Or, if you're one of the Scorpios for whom life is basically absurd, you'll probably enjoy reading the plays of Scorpio Eugene Ionesco. For a Plutonic tale of buried riches, how about *Treasure Island*, written by a Scottish Scorpio, Robert Louis Stevenson (and if you're really curious about what lies beneath the surface in all of us, you might want to take a look at his tale of *Dr Jekyll and Mr Hyde*). For one of the most popular books of all time, read the passionate life of Scarlett O'Hara, heroine of *Gone With The Wind* by Scorpio Margaret Mitchell. (Interestingly, the part in the film was played by another powerful Scorpio, Vivien Leigh). Other Scorpio writers include John Keats (La Belle Dame Sans Merci was surely a Scorpio beauty); George Eliot ('*It was a pity he couldna be hatched o'er again, and hatched different*'— *Adam Bede*); and the playwright Richard Brinsley Sheridan, whose plays include, appropriately for a Scorpio, *The Critic*, *The Rivals* and *School for Scandal*!

Scorpios who paint can draw enormous encouragement from the successes of artists born in their sign. The best-known is twentieth-century Spanish Scorpio Pablo Picasso. Other Scorpio artists include the English aesthete Aubrey Beardsley; Claude Monet, the Impressionist innovator; the French Pointillist, Paul Signac; and the very talented, disturbing genius Francis Bacon. Even if you've never heard of the Italian Scorpio sculptor Benvenuto Cellini, you'll probably have seen pictures of his work. And there's no mistaking the figure of '*The Thinker*' created by the sensual French Scorpio Auguste Rodin, or his other famous statue '*The Kiss*'.

Sporting Scorpios include boxing superstar Frank Bruno, who proves that Scorpios can be knock-out nice guys. So if your blood starts to rise when you think about a sporting career, why not tackle it? Scorpio Diego Maradona did, and look at him. So did Scorpio tennis star Billie Jean King, and she netted twenty Wimbledon titles. Remember you're a water sign, so you might want to take on the sea. Scorpio-born Ted Turner did his battle with the elements and won the Americas Cup yacht race.

Scorpions are still leaving tracks in the field of music. The French Scorpio composer Georges Bizet wrote one of the best known arias in the world, *'Habanera'*, in his opera *Carmen*, the passionate story of the gypsy girl eventually murdered by her lover. Although Noel Coward (a typically witty and outspoken Sagittarius) once cruelly commented that the opera *Carmen* is 'as Spanish as the Champs Elysées', its music takes a Scorpion hold on those who hear it. Johann Strauss is another example of the spell-binding Scorpio effect—he kept the world turning in three-four time for half a century.

With Scorpio's magnetic ability to hold people's attention, it's no surprise they have what it takes to succeed on stage and screen. The fascinating Katharine Hepburn is a tireless Scorpio actress who's collected four Oscars in her time. The energetic and dedicated actress Sally Field is another Scorpio, with two Oscars under her belt. Some Scorpio actors and actresses have made their impact as much for their sex appeal as their ability to perform, like the steamy newcomer Demi Moore *(About last Night)*, the fantasy-inducing Bo Derek, and veteran heart-throb Burt Lancaster, who went—in Scorpion style—through a host of different professions before making it as an actor. Scorpios often have distinct and dramatic changes in their lives and careers: when Hollywood lost one of its biggest Scorpio attractions, Monaco gained a princess in Grace Kelly, the star of such suspense-filled classics as *High Noon*, *Dial M for Murder* and *Rear Window*. Scorpio Linda Evans is another American beauty who for several years has weekly risked life and limb as Krystle at the Carrington mansion in *Dynasty*. Rock Hudson was a Scorpio whose sex appeal kept him top of the American box office for two decades. And like a true Scorpio, he had a secret life most of his fans knew nothing about. The revelation in 1985 that he was dying from AIDS finally helped bring home to the American government the imminence of a huge international health crisis. Other Scorpios who've made an impact on audiences around the world include Henry Winkler (the Fonz), Richard Dreyfus, Goldie Hawn, Bill Wyman, Simon LeBon, Petula Clark, Lulu, Tatum O'Neal (it took a Scorpio to tame John McEnroe), and the late Richard Burton, the talented Welsh actor whose private life was characterized by an intensity not uncommon in this sign.

If you still haven't seen the line that suits you, consider the following careers which traditionally are considered to fit the Scorpio temperament: plumbing, drainage and sewage maintenance (Scorpios go where others fear to tread); any work in morgues, cemeteries or funeral parlours (don't forget Pluto was the god of the dead); mining and archaeology (Scorpios like to dig deep into things); demolition work or the nuclear-power industry (a literal chance to tear down and transform); seismology, the study of earth movements and earth-quakes, appropriate for the people who often start them; a career involving ballistic fire-arms (one way to let out that Scorpion aggression); and of course there's always room for more Scorpio psychologists and sex therapists (can you think of a more fitting way to legi-timize your desire to get all the dirt on people?). Don't worry if the career of your dreams doesn't appear here. You probably know very well what you want to do already, and you won't be stopped by anybody!

Scorpio compatibilities

Scorpio/Aries *(Water/Fire)* Watch out! You're both ruled by Mars, and without a little diplomacy, that could mean war. When you fall out at work, it'll be a fight to the death. But if you're on the same side, no opponent will have a chance. A combustible combination, to say the least. Give each other miles of space, and it may work out.

Scorpio/Taurus *(Water/Earth)* One thing about Taurus people, they have the patience to put up with anything. And they'll need all they can muster with you around. They like security; you crave excitement and intrigue. They take life at face value; you're constantly probing and questioning. But opposites do attract, and even with all your differences, you'll still probably gravitate to one another.

Scorpio/Gemini *(Water/Air)* Geminis won't be able to resist your power and charisma, and you'll be fascinated by their insights into life. But there's one big problem here: you're intense, possessive and jealous, and light-footed Geminis aren't about to get caught in that trap. You two could spend all your working time together trying to out-smart one another.

Scorpio/Cancer *(Water/Water)* Now here's a sign that can cope with all your moods and feelings. If you're looking for an ally, Cancer is your best bet. Loyal and sensitive, they'll stand by you, even when everyone else has had enough. Show the Crab how deeply you appreciate their friendship, and you'll have it for life.

Scorpio/Leo *(Water/Fire)* Pluto is the planet farthest from the sun, which just about sums up your chances with this sign. Leo is as sunny and outgoing as you are dark and brooding. Their grand gestures are bound to rub you the wrong way, which isn't going to make them appreciate you all that much. Unless you're willing to get along with Lions on their terms, you had better keep a polite distance.

Scorpio/Virgo *(Water/Earth)* A good combination, both in and out of work. There's something about a Virgo you know you can trust—maybe it's because they're as critical, precise, and as good at picking people apart as you are. And when you put your heads together, there's nothing you two couldn't scheme and no one you couldn't figure out.

Scorpio/Libra *(Water/Air)* There's bound to be some mutual attraction here, but how far it can go is a moot point. At some stage, Libra has to pull back—especially when they twig that you won't always play by their rules. No big loss for you—in the end, you're likely to find them a bit too sweet and lightweight for your complex tastes.

Scorpio/Scorpio *(Water/Water)* All in all, this isn't a bad match. No one understands a Scorpio better than another Scorpio. You'll like the way they instinctively know when to come close and when to stay clear. And when you feel like a good gossip, your Scorpio colleague will have enough dirt on others to fill the Albert Hall. Some people would say that two Scorpios deserve each other. Just don't turn your back, that's all.

Scorpio/Sagittarius *(Water/Fire)* Your mysterious aloofness is a real challenge to an Archer, and they'll be determined to find out what you're all about. In turn, you'll be intrigued by some of their daring exploits. It's true, Sagittarius people are natural teachers, but you were never one to take kindly to a know-it-all. Others may delight in the fact that Sagittarius is an open book, but it's probably one you won't feel like reading very often.

Scorpio/Capricorn *(Water/Earth)* You could do worse than teaming up with a Goat. With your imagination and insight, and their reliable, practical approach to life, there's no mountain you two couldn't climb. But the Goat is not one to be easily led, and a few power struggles are unavoidable. Once you've settled who's in charge, this combination could bring you both success—even if it's not a barrel of laughs.

Scorpio/Aquarius *(Water/Air)* Sorry, Scorpio, you're in for trouble here. Nobody, not even you, can control an Aquarius—so why even try? They have minds of their own, and certainly don't need yours. Emotionally, it's a non-starter: you pretend to be aloof and cool, but an Aquarius really is that way. You might as well live on different planets.

Scorpio/Pisces *(Water/Water)* Ah! You think—two water signs must get along. The Fish will be sensitive to your moods, tolerant of your tantrums, and forgiving of your foibles. You don't normally find people as easygoing as that. But there are no sparks without a little friction, and you won't get much of that with the Fish—unless, of course, you're the one who makes it.

The Scorpio boss

Scorpio bosses are famous for an ability to work in a pressure-cooker situation, and they're usually the ones applying the heat. They'll do anything to make a job more exciting, even if it means creating a crisis now and then. But one thing is sure, Scorpio bosses are devoted to their work—they wouldn't be there if they weren't. A job they really love is almost as appealing for them as a passionate relationship. Speaking of sex, let's be honest. It's possible your Scorpio boss may try to come on to you. (After all, they have the reputation of being the sexiest sign in the zodiac.) A few words of caution, though: Scorpios don't just have affairs. It's all or nothing with them. So take our advice—decide which of these two options you want, and stick to it!

There is one rule you must always remember when there's a Scorpio running the show: Never threaten their position of power. Scorpios don't like the taste of their own medicine. And they especially don't appreciate other people trying to change them. They'll dig their heels in and make you pay dearly for even attempting such a thing. They'll change when they're good and ready, not when you want them to.

Your Scorpio boss is not the most open person that you could hope to meet. There's bound to be important information at work to which you will never be privy, because that's how a Scorpio likes things. You may be dealing with a deeply secretive person who slams down the telephone or stuffs everything on the desk into a drawer if you happen to enter the room without knocking. Scorpio bosses don't give a lot away, but they'll do what they can to find out everything about you. Don't be too surprised if they accidently overhear you making a personal phone call at work, or they just happen to be hiding behind the vending machine when you're gossiping with a colleague about them.

Bosses born in Scorpio will reassure you one minute and then make you feel insecure the next. They'll praise and congratulate you warmly when you do something well; but before you have time to get carried away with your success, you may find yourself brought down a peg or two. When they're dealing with other people's lives, Scorpios don't mind imposing upheaval and change. They'll confront you with challenges and stretch you to your limits; but in doing so, they bring out all your hidden talents and abilities—even ones you didn't know you had.

The Scorpio employee

If Scorpio employees are in a job they like and if they respect the people they're working for, they'll work harder than almost any other sign. Like Virgo and Capricorn, Scorpio is one of those signs that does everything as thoroughly as possible. They don't miss a trick, and they'll stay up all night if there's a deadline to be met. Hire a Scorpio to do the job, and you could strike gold. Pluto, Scorpio's ruler, governs everything that's hidden underground—and that includes buried treasure. But that could also mean worms, rats or sewage. A Scorpion employee, especially if he or she doesn't think much of those in charge, could turn out to be a real snake in the grass. So how can you make sure you're getting a valuable Scorpio employee and not a rotten one? The answer is you can't be sure, but it helps if you treat them with the respect and consideration they think they deserve.

Scorpios often imagine themselves to be simple, straightforward people. But without a doubt this is the most complicated sign of them all. A mask of deferential smiles could conceal a loathing that would turn your blood to ice if you knew about it. But you won't. Scorpios keep their thoughts to themselves. Even if you use pliers to pull out their toe-nails, Scorpio employees will never tell you anything they don't want you to hear.

One way to win over a Scorpio employee is to stamp everything you give her or him CONFIDENTIAL or TOP SECRET (of course, this may not be very convincing if you operate a dry-cleaning business). Scorpios might appreciate you more if you established a generous bonus system . . . but then again, they might equally despise you for resorting to bribery. When it comes right down to it, you may never be sure where you really stand with a Scorpio under you. One day you'll think the employee is your best friend, and the next day you'll be given the cold shoulder and left wondering what it is you've done wrong. And if you think Lady Macbéth had a thing about usurping power, you haven't seen your Scorpio employee in action yet. But wait. Before you leap from the tenth-floor window, there's one thing you haven't thought of. You could always fire the Scorpio.

Be careful, though. Bosses who fall foul of a Scorpio worker may end up regretting the day they were born. Never underestimate a Scorpio's capacity for revenge. A vindictive Scorpio is not to be messed with, unless you really are a sucker for punishment. Scorpios will find a way of turning everyone else in the company or firm against you. So don't be astonished if, when you serve notice on your Scorpio employee, an army of people are there awaiting to attack you with their bare hands and throw you from that tenth-floor window. Perhaps you'd better jump, after all. Just make sure you do a proper job of it—there are plenty of Scorpios in the nursing profession!

The Scorpio colleague

This sign loves tearing down what's served its purpose. So be very careful, because if you get in the way of a Scorpio colleague, that could mean *you!* Scorpio co-workers should always be approached with the respect that you might accord an ancient Indian burial ground. If you commit the heresy of disagreeing with them or the sacrilege of ignoring their presence, from that day on your working life will take a turn for the worse. But if you manage to keep out of their bad books, you'll find yourself with the staunchest of all allies (the term friend is somehow too mild to apply to a Scorpio). Your enemies are their enemies, your war is their war, your victory is their victory. Should you get in any kind of trouble, they'll fight alongside you to the death—probably your death (a Scorpio has more lives than a litter of cats).

But don't forget that Scorpios have their own peculiar logic. However much your Scorpio colleague appears to be on your side, if you talk together long enough, you'll always find a point where his or her personal opinions start travelling in a completely different direction. Scorpios present their views in such a way they seem to invite debate, but don't get into that hole—you may never get out again. If a Scorpio is against you, you may as well wait for hell to freeze over, because he or she will oppose you all the way. This sign does nothing by halves.

Some Scorpios have bad tempers. They may lash out suddenly, and when they do, they go straight for the jugular. Or they may hold in their anger for a while and just smoulder quietly like Mt Vesuvius. You might not even guess they're upset, except for the fact that every time they pass your desk, you feel a cold shudder up your spine, as if a poltergeist had just passed through the room.

There are many Scorpios born with the gift of second sight. So if a colleague can tell just by looking into your eyes what you had for breakfast on your fourth birthday, you may be right in assuming they were born under this sign. Before making any major decision, ask their advice—and ignore it at your peril. When the weather's bad and your normally quiet Scorpio workmate says 'Mind how you drive home tonight', don't push your luck; leave your car keys in the office and take a bus home—or, better still, get yourself a room in the hotel across the street. And if your Scorpio co-worker declines to take the lift and decides to walk to the tenth floor instead, that'll be the day the cable snaps and the elevator ends up as a sardine can in the basement.

Team up with a Scorpio, and your working life may start to resemble an ongoing episode of *Cagney and Lacey*. One thing is for sure, it won't be boring. Considering how het up Scorpions can get on the inside, it's amazing how cool they manage to appear in even the most tricky situations. When the armed raider who bursts into your place of work is brought to the ground by a quick karate chop to the back of the neck, you can bet that the person who delivers the blow and then carries on as though nothing has happened is your typical peace-loving Scorpio colleague.

Sagittarius

Element: Fire
Symbol: The Archer
Ruler: Jupiter

The Sign of the Archer

The symbol of Sagittarius is a centaur (half man, half horse) shooting a bow and arrow—not a character you'd expect to meet on your way round to the corner shop. Like the archer, Sagittarius people are always aiming their arrows at something. More than any other sign, they set goals and targets for themselves, things they would like to have or achieve. Sometimes they are so focused on a goal that they miss everything else along the way. They also suffer from a tendency to aim their arrows far too high, and inevitably fall short of the mark. Of course, there are some people born under the sign of the Archer who have the hardest time deciding in which direction to shoot: they start aiming for one thing, change their minds and go after something else, then change their minds again, etc, etc. In the end, they wind up just scattering their arrows and their energy all over the place.

Chiron was one of the most famous of the centaurs, and his story gives us insight into the deeper meaning of Sagittarius. The god Saturn and the sea nymph Philyra were having an affair. One day Saturn's wife caught the two of them in the act. To get out of a very awkward position, Saturn changed himself into a horse and galloped away, leaving poor Philyra pregnant. When her term was full, she gave birth to Chiron—the first centaur, part god and part beast. Philyra couldn't quite believe what had come out of her. In dismay, she pleaded with the gods: 'I'll do anything only please take away this monster I've produced!' Obligingly, the gods removed Chiron and turned her into a lemon tree.

Half divine, half animal, rejected by his bitter mother—little Chiron certainly had a hard start in life. Fortunately, the gods took good care of him and he grew up full of their divine wisdom. He also had real horse sense, the wisdom of the earth, which gave him the power to heal. Chiron became a teacher to Asclepius, the god of health, and to great heroes like Hercules. But one night when Hercules was a bit drunk and more boisterous than usual, he accidentally scratched Chiron with an arrowhead dipped in the poisonous blood of the Hydra. Although Chiron could cure any ailment, his skill as a healer was useless on his own painful wound.

Like Chiron, people born in Sagittarius sometimes feel a little out of place in the world. Their lofty aspirations and noble ideals are often in conflict with their more human or animal side. They preach 'the truth' to others, and then they turn around and do the very opposite. It isn't easy for them to apply all their marvellous innate wisdom and insight in their own lives. Archers are a bit like Chiron—they're the first people you turn to when you have problems, but when it comes to dealing with their own troubles they really haven't a clue.

Jupiter, the bringer of light

Of all the deities of ancient Rome, Jupiter (known to the Greeks as Zeus) was the most prolific—he truly was the father of the gods. But he was the kind of father who doles out the cigars, poses for the pictures with the baby, and then disappears to find another adventure. Archers have a lot of Jupiter in them. They're great at sowing new ideas and getting something started, but they're not so good at hanging around long enough to watch what they planted grow. Before you know it, they're on their way somewhere else, looking for fresh fields to conquer.

Jupiter was a talented actor, a man of many parts who loved dressing up. Sagittarius people are never averse to a quick transformation when the occasion demands, or simply because they feel like it. When Jupiter saw a female he fancied, he usually first appeared to her in disguise. At different times, with various women, he turned himself into a swan, a bull, and even a shower of gold. He used to get so carried away with his performance, he'd forget all about his shrewish wife, Hera—but she wasn't the sort who took kindly to his little adventures. She was forever catching him with his pants down, and hounding him home to face the music. There's a playful and potentially irresponsible side to Sagittarius, delightful to some, but infuriating to others.

He might have been a womanizer, but Jupiter was still highly respected as the protector of humanity. When people were in trouble, any kind of trouble, they prayed to him—just like people today, ringing up their Sagittarius friends for some help. Archers can't resist stepping in to make things better—if they're available, that is! Jupiter was also considered the guardian of law and religion. When somebody—a mortal or a god—was offended or insulted, they went to Jupiter for a judgement on the situation. And when Jupiter acted, he did so impulsively. If somebody was doing something he shouldn't be, Jupiter would hurl one of his great thunderbolts and stop the culprit dead in his tracks—permanently. Sagittarius people are prone to take things too far and go over the top. They're not famous for tact, and their comments often hit you like a thunderbolt. Those arrows of truth they are so fond of firing may well be full of wisdom and insight, but they're occasionally a little off target. Even when they're accurate, they hurt if they happen to strike you where you're most sensitive.

Whatever Sagittarians do, they like to do it on a grand

scale. They're the kind of people capable of marrying on impulse, taking off on a trip around the world at a moment's notice, or giving away all their money to some downtrodden soul they happen to meet on the street. Their optimism is both their curse and their salvation. They believe that no matter how hard life gets, eventually things will get better. And, like the god Jupiter, many of them are extremely lucky. When they say, 'I just know it will all work out somehow', the extraordinary thing is that very often it does. But Sagittarius people need to remember that they aren't Jupiter. After all, he was the king of the gods, and they're only human. And whether we like it or not, being human has its limitations.

The Sagittarius temperament

If Scorpio's dark intensity was a bit much for you, there's no better antidote than a great big dose of the Sagittarius elixir of youth. Now you'll find the energy and enthusiasm to leap around and enjoy a land of wide open spaces, big ideas and exciting possibilities. (If that sounds too much like Disneyland, don't forget that Walt himself was born under this sign.) The motto is 'Nothing ventured, nothing gained'. Sagittarians approach every new experience with a travel bag full of expectations. Their optimism is naive, but it carries them over all the problems that defeat the dreary fainthearts in this world. If the grass in the next field looks green and inviting, they will be off like a shot to get there, leaping over any hurdles in the way. Of course they do sometimes trip up and fall face down in a cowpat . . . but they probably wouldn't want us to talk about that!

Sagittarius is the exclamation mark that tells you you've reached the last word in fire signs. They're warm, generous and friendly, and incredibly hard to pin down. A very fiery Archer can magically appear in your life

and sweeten a sad moment; but they can disappear
again faster than a chocolate mousse if they think you're
starting to depend on them. All in all, there's something
theatrically splendid about Sagittarius people. They
rarely resist the romantic flourish, the gallant gesture,
the dramatic overture or the grand entrance ... but
they've usually cleared out long before the finale. For
free-spirited Sagittarius, life is one long adventure
story—and you never know what's going to happen in
the next chapter. Naturally, they hate rigid plans and
tight schedules; like a child at play, they prefer to impro-
vise their way through life. You're likely to see an
Archer adventurer saying or doing something just to see
what will happen next—that's how they often wind up
biting off more than they can chew.

When you hear Sagittarians talking about their lives,
they make it sound as though they aren't troubled by
the same humdrum problems that get the rest of us
down. Of course, they're bluffing (Archers often make
great poker players). More than anything, they hate to
sound old and boring. Some Archers won't even talk
about tedious subjects like money and housekeeping
unless there's a lively anecdote or a dramatic story to
liven it up. They love to spin a good yarn, full of their
extraordinary, fantastic, amazing (not to mention exag-
gerated) experiences and brilliant insights. You'll rarely
hear them talking about problems—mind-blowing catas-
trophes and life-shattering disasters, perhaps—but never
problems.

Even Centaurs who insist they have all four feet on
the ground often keep their heads somewhere up above
the clouds. Cruising along at the height of twenty thousand feet, Sagittarius people see life through a very wide
lens. The bigger picture is always very clear, but they
don't seem to notice the tiny details. They're masters
of the sweeping statement (which is a pretty sweeping
statement in itself). Leave all the particulars to a fussy
sign like Gemini or Virgo! Irrelevant information only

muddles a Sagittarius's thinking. Worse than that, it ruins a good story.

Just think about the story of the Ten Commandments in the Bible. A great saga so full of magic and excitement a Sagittarius could have written it (and probably did). What does it matter if Moses had a big boil on his nose, or if he burned the toast or kicked the cat on the day when he went up into the mountain? These details won't help you to understand the Great Plan, and that is the most important thing for an Archer—knowing what life is all about. Surely life's not just about work, earning money and dying! If you're close to a Sagittarius, you're with somebody who occasionally lives in another world. But don't dismiss the value of a seeker, a person sincerely searching for the meaning of life.

If you haven't worked out the meaning of life yet, don't worry. You may depend on a Sagittarius somewhere to tell you the answer. They're natural philosophers. Most of them have a strong faith in life—they really believe there's a light at the end of even the darkest tunnel. Somewhere deep inside, they feel the positive influence of benevolent Jupiter (he was, after all, the king of the gods, and you won't find many aces that can top that one). And, like Jupiter, Sagittarians love guiding other people. They'll direct you to the best places to go, the best films to see, the best new restaurant in town. If your Sagittarius friend is excited about something, you're sure to know all about it. And if they think you should change your hairstyle or way of dressing, you're sure to know about that as well. Archers may be born travellers, but they don't beat about the bush.

Jupiter people see life as a journey. They're always aiming for something, or seeking broader horizons. And some Sagittarians take that quite literally; they couldn't be happier humping a rucksack across a new frontier, ready to begin drinking in the wisdom of a different culture. So when you bump into a traveller at the airport or the railway station who jolts you out of your doldrums with a broad friendly smile and a clever observation, you're very likely facing one of the many Sagittarius guides to life. They'll remind you that your time down here is brief, the world's a very small place and this is the first day of the rest of your life. These words may sound corny, and yet we all need to hear them now and again (even though they would have been scant consolation to Marie Antoinette on Bastille Day). Sagittarius people can be wonderfully inspiring and take your breath away with their expansive ideas and insights. Too bad they're not always so adept at paying the rent or dealing with the everyday practicalities of life.

Jupiter had a few serious handicaps, and facing up to responsibility was one of them. He liked being in charge, swaggering in front of an audience, being big, bold and dazzling. But he wasn't so keen on picking up the mess after his escapades. Sagittarians don't like to feel tied down. You might even say that they really don't ever want to grow up. It's understandable. When you're young, everything seems possible. Facing reality means facing what we can't be and accepting what we can't have. Choosing one path means kissing 'goodbye' to another—and such choices are often hard for Sagittarians to make. If there's one thing they hate it's limits.

The Sagittarius types

Sagittarians born between 23 November and 2 December Naturally restless and curious, you'll try anything once. No enterprise is too big or too mad, no obstacle too great. The empire you're planning to build may crash tomorrow, but you've enough resilience to build another by Friday—from scratch. And your many friends and associates will always be around to help you.

Sagittarians born between 3 December and 12 December Once you get going, nobody can stop you. You'll stand up for your beliefs to the end, and take on causes like there's no tomorrow. What's your hurry? Excitement and adventure is what it's all about, but if you don't learn to control your naturally rash and impetuous nature, it could get you into trouble.

Sagittarians born between 13 December and 21 December You love attention and you don't mind who knows it. One way or another, you need to make your mark in the world—but it would help if you were a bit more practical and down-to-earth. And be careful you don't take advantage of others when you're making your way to the top. It's great to be a success, but having people's love and respect is even better.

Sagittarius and work

Let the story of Icarus be a lesson to every Sagittarius who doesn't want to face some of the harder facts of working life. Icarus was locked up in a tower with his father Daedelus, a famous craftsman who unfortunately had offended Minos, King of Crete. To make their escape, Daedelus fashioned two pairs of wings from bird feathers held together by wax. He warned Icarus of the dangers of flying too near the sun. But Icarus was young and headstrong and wouldn't listen. Naturally, when he flew up too high, the wax started to melt and Icarus fell to his death in the sea. Sagittarius people who go too far are always coming down to earth with a wallop. They usually think they've heard it all before and they rush into things before they know enough about it. Whoever coined the maxim 'A little knowledge can be a dangerous thing' must have been thinking of a Sagittarius at the time.

Superior Sagittarians have one main problem at work—they rarely listen to anybody. When you try telling them things they ought to hear, you'll realise from the way they stare out of the window while you're talking that they think they know it all already. Of course, every rule has its exceptions. From time to time, a Sagittarius will come across another person he or she really thinks is worth listening to. It may be an older person, or someone from a different cultural background. Sagittarius people go for gurus—men or women whose wise perceptions place them well above the ordinary. At their command, an Archer would jump into any lake.

Although they hide it well, deep down inside Sagittarius people are very sensitive to criticism. They hate anybody to think they're anything less than marvellous. The idea that we all start from a point of imperfection and strive towards something better runs contrary to their thinking. In most cases, it's their pride that makes them as resistant to advice and help as a duck's back is to water. And yet, in spite of their own sensitivity, when it comes to dealing with other people, they can have all the subtlety of a sledgehammer.

A high-flying Sagittarius would be far happier jetting to Acapulco every morning than going to work. In order to get the greatest possible mileage out of each day, they'll find a way to turn even the most routine task into some kind of challenge or adventure. While they can be quite happy working on their own (especially outdoors or in nature), they thrive in an environment where there are other interesting people around to talk to. If there's one thing they hate, it's someone dull or unimaginative, the kind of person who wouldn't recognize a joke if it fell out of a Christmas cracker. They like working with people who are young in spirit, colleagues who'll be impressed with their élan and their savoir faire. And, of course, work is always more fun when it presents them with an opportunity to step in and take over, so they can show others how it's really done.

Sagittarius people need a job they believe in—something worthwhile or exciting they can throw themselves into. If your present work is boring and uninspiring, or if you're still looking for that thing which is right for you, try this exercise. It may give you a clearer sense of what direction you should take.

1. Make a list of those things in life that you really find interesting or worthwhile.
2. Go through this list and pick out the three things which hold the most fascination for you.
3. Consider these three choices and see if there is any way you can turn these interests into a career. For instance, if travel is on your list, it might be possible to get a job which would bring more travel into your life. If helping others is on your list, then you could look for work which would give you a chance to be of service to people in need.
4. Decide on one of your three choices, and do what you can to follow through finding work in that field.

Sagittarius careers

The English word *travel* is a close relative of the French word *travail*, meaning work, and you can see the translation in action with Sagittarius. There are many voracious voyagers in this sign who have made travel their business—and a very lucrative business it is too. The world's pleasure seekers are always waiting to be served up a different holiday platter, and Archers are the very people to dream up colourful things for them to do and fascinating new places to do them in. Sagittarius travel agents or tour operators will be able to recommend (from experience) trendy beach resorts where you can sip your pina colada and watch a dazzling sunset reflected in a thousand pairs of designer sun glasses. But most Sagittarius people also recognize the Real Thing when they see it. Expose any Archer to ten minutes of a lamasary in full chant, introduce them to a local medicine man or take them slumming anywhere that only local people go, and you'll see them transported to paradise. Real ethnic 'finds' are harder to get hold of these days. A Sagittarius can get pretty disheartened to discover, after a thousand miles on horseback, that in the primitive village once untouched by Western culture the locals are now going loopy over Kentucky Fried Chicken. Sagittarius stewards or stewardesses would really be in their element, zipping off from one place to another and enjoying the perk of cheap air fares for their own holidays.

But the travel business isn't the only way to see the world. The army gets just about everywhere, and there are legions of military commanders born in Jupiter's own sign. Long-distance couriers, pilots (always above the clouds), international lawyers (Jupiter was the great lawmaker), diplomats and public relations people all manage to get around the globe. Representatives in every business line (especially clothing and sportswear manufacturers) get the opportunity—or create it—to go all over the place, buying, selling and exploring the market (incidentally, footwear—making it or selling it—is another Archer speciality). Then there are thousands of permanent travellers born in this sign who use their talents and their gift of the gab to pick up work wherever they go. One survey showed a high proportion of Sagittarius barmen and barmaids—now there's a career you can take almost anywhere. But do be careful: Jupiter governs the liver, so don't let your spirits get the better of you! Sagittarius journalists (especially sports or travel correspondents) can write their way around the world. And don't forget avid academic Archers who travel on research grants, following in the footsteps of the famous—like Sagittarius anthropologist Margaret Mead, who spent many years in the Samoa Islands, living among the people and writing about their customs, their beliefs and their everyday lives.

But when you have a typically expansive Sagittarius imagination, it isn't even necessary to go farther than the shop on the corner to expand your horizons. If everyone were as stay-at-home as the Sagittarius poetess Emily Dickinson, travel firms would quickly run out of business:

'*I never saw a moor,*
I never saw the sea;
Yet I know how the heather looks,
And what a wave must be'.

And the decline in trade would be even greater if all tourists received the same bizarre hospitality as Gulliver, the voyager in Sagittarius Jonathan Swift's book *Gulliver's Travels*; or suffered the same fate as the hapless hero of *Candide* by the Sagittarius French philosopher Voltaire, a tale which descibes the exploits of a naive young man thrown against hardship who discovers ultimately that the only true pleasure lies in cultivating your own garden.

Staying at home is no protection against catastrophe. Sagittarius Russian author Alexander Solzhenitsyn's life was altered by an enforced journey to a Siberian labour camp. The female Archer Jane Austen revealed that the savageries of the English drawing room are no less terrifying than the horrors which descended on poor Gulliver or Candide. The galloping pace of Jane Austen's own eventful social life shines through in her most famous novel *Pride and Prejudice*. Mark Twain was another Sagittarius writer who captured the popular imagination with his lovable boy heroes Tom Sawyer and Huckleberry Finn. And in the same period in America, Louisa May Alcott was describing the adventures, the loves and the growing pains of a family of girls in her famous book *Little Women*. But for the definitive exposé of the Sagittarius in love, read Gustave Flaubert's classic *Madame Bovary*, the tale of a provincial doctor's wife who escapes the misery of bourgeois life by having a series of passionate affairs. Emma

Bovary, like many a Sagittarius, believed that salvation and real happiness always lay somewhere else. Seekers after inner truth shouldn't miss a visit to the inner world of the metaphysical Sagittarius artist and writer William Blake or the lost paradise of Sagittarius poet John Milton. If you're an Archer who dwells in fantasy, you may recognize your foible in fellow Sagittarius James Thurber's book *The Secret Life of Walter Mitty*. And if you're weary of this world, try an intergalactic cruise with the great sci-fi adventure writer Arthur C. Clarke, another illustrious writer born under this sign.

Skilful Sagittarius people find outlets for their expansive imaginations through different disciplines. Diego Rivera, for instance, was a Mexican-born Sagittarius painter who created murals which are now part of the folklore of his country. And engineer Gustave Eiffel was the French Archer responsible for the bold metal tower that has become an international symbol for the city of Paris.

The big screen is a perfect medium to give form to the Sagittarius imagination. Maybe you'd like to write or direct films like Steven Spielberg, an Archer who has aroused the adventurous child hiding in even the most sober grown-up with his great fantasy films like *E.T.* and *Raiders of the Lost Ark*. Fifty years ago, another magician of the movie industry sank all his money in true Sagittarius form on a project that eventually grossed millions. His name was Walt Disney, and the film was *Snow White and the Seven Dwarfs*. His Sagittarius talent was to access all the magic and awe of childhood. The creation of Disneyland and Disney World show what is possible if you keep dreaming the impossible.

Are you good at entertaining? That's another Sagittarius talent. (Studies have shown that a high number of them become quality bakers and pastry cooks. Why not? You can go everywhere if you know how to cook.) But there's no business like show business, and there are no people like Sagittarius people to get a show on the road. Here's a profession full of legends: 'the long road to the top', 'the show must go on', 'the lucky break', etc. Many Sagittarius performers have found fame and fortune; while others acquire at the very least enough stories to see them through every dinner party for the rest of their lives—although no after dinner raconteur will ever compare with the late great Sagittarius actor, playwright and wit Noel Coward.

Who else but a Sagittarius could have made the song 'Come Fly with Me' so famous? Frank Sinatra is far too rich and famous to be typical, but he exemplifies a Sagittarius performing style: easy, cruisy and fun. Married almost as many times as Jupiter, with alleged Mafia connections and a personal fortune as big as Mount Olympus, his private life is even more dramatic than many of his big films. There's a long list of entertaining Sagittarius people past and present, including the diverse talents of outrageous Bette Midler and the outspoken Jane Fonda, as well as Harpo Marx, Jeff Bridges, Liv Ullmann, Billy Idol, Don Johnson, Richard Pryor, Ralph Richardson, Billy Connolly, Pamela Stephenson, Boris Karloff, Kirk Douglas, Arthur Rubenstein, Brenda Lee, Edward G. Robinson, Sammy Davis Jr., Connie Francis, Dionne Warwick, Andy Williams, and the indefatigable Tina Turner. And there are other Sagittarius stars like Edith Piaf and the great Maria Callas—who will be remembered perhaps as much for the ups and downs of their lives as for their great talent. Like the wounded centaur Chiron, they had a rare gift which their audiences found healing, but personally suffered great torment. Sagittarius Woody Allen is someone very much under the influence of Chiron. His films take us on a journey into the labyrinth of his neuroses, revealing the work of a brilliant humorist and a serious philosophical thinker. Through the medium of comedy, Allen's audiences are brought face to face both with the joys and the tragedies of life.

Another Sagittarius touched by Chiron was Henri de Toulouse-Lautrec, the Post-Impressionist painter crippled in childhood, who through his pictures chronicled the twilight world of Montmartre. Fellow French Archer, Jean Genet, became against all odds one of the biggest influences on twentieth century literature. A reject of society, at times a thief and a male prostitute, he wrote of the true dignity of spirit he found among people who have nothing left in the world to lose. (Speaking of outlaws, don't forget that gangster Lucky Luciano and the rootin' tootin' Billy the Kid were also born in this sign . . . but let's not get too carried away in this direction.) The torment of deafness drove Sagittarius Ludwig van Beethoven to an inner world, where he heard his most inspiring music. (There's a tenuous connection with another famous Sagittarius here. Beethoven's Fifth Symphony became Britain's signature tune during World War II and always preceded the rallying speeches of that very Sagittarian Prime Minister, Winston Churchill).

Sagittarius people are born scholars, tireless learners who love to meet others on the road to self-improvement. The secret of their great talent for teaching is their ability to take people on a mental journey, breathing life into material that other teachers manage to make as invigorating as suet dumpling. Great minds born in Sagittarius include the Swiss alchemist and physician Paracelsus; Nostradamus, the sixteenth century French astrologer; Spinoza, the Dutch philosphical anthropologist; and the socialist thinker Friedrich Engels. Not every Sagittarius who reads and thinks is necesarily a genius, although many aspire to be so, but many have reason to thank Andrew Carnegie. Born in Dunfermline, Scotland, he went to America as a boy and made a huge fortune wisely investing the income he earned working as a telegrapher. In true Sagittarius spirit, he believed his privileged life gave him a responsibility to the less fortunate, a philosophy he wrote about in his book entitled *The Gospel of Wealth*. (One can only imagine that fellow Sagittarius J. Paul Getty must have read it from cover to cover.)

Archers frequently concern themselves with gospels of one sort or another. They're natural philosophers, religious teachers and spiritual guides. Many will be drawn to preaching—if you live with a Sagittarius you won't need us to develop that idea any further! The famous guru Bhagwan Shree Rajneesh, now living God knows where, was born in the sign of the centaur. But even less spiritually minded Sagittarius people are not short of things to share. People born under this sign are more than happy to tell the rest of the world what turns them on. Provided they believe in who or what they're pushing, they make superior book publishers, literary or theatrical agents extolling the virtues of the new talent they have just discovered, and managers or coaches who will give their team a pep talk they'll never forget.

Which finally brings us to sports—a field where the Archer has a real chance of hitting the mark. Baseball player Joe DiMaggio is just one of many athletes born under this sign who have made it to the Hall of Fame. Tennis champ Chris Lloyd, footballer Gary Lineker and cricketer Imran Khan are all good Sagittarius sports. Ian Botham is another Sagittarius cricket player as famous for his exploits off the pitch as on. Indoors or out, Sagittarius people are renowned for their love of wildlife. Zoo parks, game reserves or any place where they can work in the great outdoors and have an opportunity to explore nature suit this sign superbly well. The worst thing you can do to Archers is to fence them in.

Sagittarius compatibilities

Sagittarius/Aries *(Fire/Fire)* Team up with a Ram, and every day will feel like the office Christmas party.

You'll spark one another off, come up with all sorts of new ideas about how things should be run, periodically hate each other with a vengeance, and keep everyone else amused in the process. And after working hours, the fun will really begin.

Sagittarius/Taurus *(Fire/Earth)* The down-to-earth Bull just doesn't have the same perspective on life as the high-flying Archer. They move so slowly and you move so fast, it's hard to imagine you two ever being in the same place at the same time. It sounds impossible, but provided you're both willing to adapt now and then, you could learn a lot from one another.

Sagittarius/Gemini *(Fire/Air)* Geminis are gregarious, intelligent, and they love to gossip. Sounds just right for you. You'll never run out of things to talk about, even if you do argue for days over some minute detail that wouldn't even bother most people. And when you start making sweeping generalities, your Gemini colleague will be there to point out all the exceptions to your rules. Yes, they're infuriating—but so are you sometimes.

Sagittarius/Cancer *(Fire/Water)* You're both warm, kind-hearted and affectionate. If either of you needs help or understanding, you'd be there for each other in a flash. Seems like you could work well together, but let's face facts, when it comes to getting along on a regular basis you're much too fiery and direct for a typically sensitive and touchy Cancer. Unless you slow down and soften your approach, you'll drive most Crabs you meet right back into their shells.

Sagittarius/Leo *(Fire/Fire)* A playful combination that's likely to work if your egos don't get in the way. You'll generate a lot of energy together, and come up with truly creative ways to attack any work situation.

Leos will love your cheek, and you'll like their generosity and warmth. The only problem is that your arrows of truth could easily bruise the Lion's pride. And a wounded Lion will turn on you, so take care!

Sagittarius/Virgo *(Fire/Earth)* Contrary to popular belief, this combination could prove mutually beneficial. Virgos can help you direct your abundant energy more constructively and show you practical ways to develop your potential talents and skills. In return, you'll give them the confidence to do things they would be afraid to try on their own. But after work, you'll both be better off going your separate ways.

Sagittarius/Libra *(Fire/Air)* The blunt side to your nature could do with some refining, and Libra is the sign to do it. They'll like your warmth and enthusiasm, and you'll appreciate the insight they have into people and life. When you go over the top, the sign of the Balance will get you straight again. This is a good combination, and a friendship could develop which is well worth exploring outside working hours.

Sagittarius/Scorpio *(Fire/Water)* Of all the signs, you are the most straightforward. Not so with Scorpions, who play their cards close to the chest. They're bound to intrigue you, but be careful how you tread. They don't forgive easily. Sooner or later you'll inadvertently say something that offends them, and they'll retaliate by teaching you a lesson you'll never forget.

Sagittarius/Sagittarius *(Fire/Fire)* Put two Archers together, and you'll soon be competing against one another for first place. This combination can bring out the best and worst in both of you. You're bound to egg each other on, and together you'll generate enough ideas and schemes to keep you busy for the rest of your lives. But be careful when your Sagittarius co-worker suggests a night out on the town. You're both so extravagant, you'll be broke till next pay day.

Sagittarius/Capricorn *(Fire/Earth)* This one will take time. Capricorn has a natural detachment and reserve that even your friendly and outgoing nature will have difficulty penetrating. But if you can settle down to work with them, they'll show you how to follow through your ideas to a profitable conclusion, and in return you'll give them the added insight and encouragement they need to make their own lives more successful. Be patient, and you'll be glad you got to know the Goat.

Sagittarius/Aquarius *(Fire/Air)* With your mutual originality and creativity, anything is possible. The Water Bearer is always willing to try something new, and you're never short of suggestions. Whatever working situation you share, you'll both fight to the end against any injustice or unfairness. This is a meeting of two minds, and one that can benefit not only yourselves but everyone else around you.

Sagittarius/Pisces *(Fire/Water)* On the surface at least, you're a lot stronger and more assertive than a typical Pisces. You're bold and daring, they're more shy and reticent. But with you as their guide, they'll soon learn to open up. And you're going to be shocked when they do, because underneath they're as idealistic and eager for new experience as you are. It won't be long before they're taking *you* places you never even knew existed.

The Sagittarius boss

A Sagittarius boss, male or female, may be the nearest thing you'll meet to Father Christmas. They almost always turn up with a bright cheery face, they like to look after you, and you may only see them about once every year! An Archer in charge will rarely pass up the smallest pretext for dining out on the company's money, dashing off to the coast for the afternoon, or flying over to Paris or New York on business for the weekend.

Jupiter, the king of the Gods, ruled from pretty lofty heights, so it's not surprising you may sometimes feel that your Sagittarius boss is looking down on you. Still, no one appreciates freedom and space more than a Sagittarius. They're not the type to stand over you with a stopwatch or keep a padlock on the telephone. And they'll usually give you the chance to approach your job in your own way before they tell you how it really should be done. If they are despots, they're likely to be benevolent ones, a bit like loving parents who are sure they know what's best for their children. Your Sagittarius boss could even turn out to be the favourite uncle you longed for or the kind of sister you never had. If you've led a rather dull and sheltered life, these Jupiter-ruled chiefs will find it impossible to resist corrupting you—in the nicest possible way, of course. When Sagittarius bosses are having fun, they'll invite you to come along for the ride.

Some Sagittarius people at the top cultivate the 'I'm-so-laid-back-nobody-would-ever-take-me-for-the-boss' look. Whatever image they go for, they're terribly concerned with getting it right. They approach every role in work with all the dedication of a professional actor. When it comes to being boss, even if they're only guaranteed a daily audience of one, they pull out all the stops. A lot of research goes into the part. The male Archer who is head of the English department, for instance, is bound to go for the gold-rimmed intellectual look. The female Sagittarius lawyer might opt for something more classy: a measure of Meryl Streep, a hint of Margaret Thatcher and more than a suspicion of Jane Fonda.

Sagittarius bosses move with the times. In any career, they like to be up to date with the newest equipment and gadgets, even if they haven't a clue how to use them. And if one day over breakfast they should happen to read the latest report on how to improve efficiency and output, you can expect a flood of memos on everybody's desk by eleven that morning. They may be cranks, but be careful not to wind them up too much.

The Sagittarius employee

You couldn't ask for better workers than Sagittarius people in jobs they like. They'll whistle while they work, put their all into it, come up with loads of fresh ideas and keep everyone around them happy. But the unhappy Sagittarius employee who feels trapped in a dreary job is another story altogether. Ask them to do something they don't like, and they're liable to be very insulted. And when a Sagittarius is offended, one way or another you'll know it.

Some Sagittarius employees have the cheek of the devil. They'll spend half the morning typing up their personal letters on the word processor, and the rest of it playing games on the computer. They can decide to take the afternoon off, and delight in the fact that nobody noticed they were gone. If given the opportunity, they'll fill up their cars with petrol on the firm's account and ring their friends around the world on the office phone. Should an irate employer come down on them too hard, you can count on Archer employees to find some way of getting their own back—like ordering kinky underwear brochures to be sent to the boss's home address.

Some Sagittarius workers can get away with doing so little that people underestimate their ability to work at all. And yet when it comes to the crunch, a Sagittarius who doesn't clear out always manages to pull it off. Miraculously, when they really have to, they'll go at it hell for leather and complete a month's work in less than a week. Doing it this way is much more exciting for them than just plodding along conscientiously day by day, as a boring old Taurus or Capricorn would do. No, there's nothing like a little drama to really get a Sagittarius worker moving.

But bosses aren't really blind or stupid. Eventually they get the full picture of what is going on. Finally they've had enough. One day after lunch, Sagittarius is summoned to the office. Everybody knows what's about to happen. The entire floor is seen to be working more diligently than usual, but all eyes are fixed on the manager's door, ready for the showdown. Two o'clock passes. Then three o'clock. Finally, at four-thirty, the door opens. The boss is laughing. 'Yes, I'll have to think about that idea, Sagittarius! Oh, going home, are you? No, that's fine by me! See you tomorrow.' Yet again, that natural Sagittarius insight, charm and humour have got them out of a sticky situation.

The Sagittarius colleague

Have faith in your Sagittarius colleague. She or he can be very understanding and sympathetic. If they see you arriving at work looking like Wigan on a wet afternoon, they won't stand back and let you suffer. Turn to a Sagittarius and you'll see your oldest problem in a whole new light. A cheerful Archer will lift you out of your despondency and put you back on the road to recovery. It's true that sometimes their overly direct manner can be a little offensive. In fact, a Sagittarius pep talk may be as sensitive and reassuring as a slap across the face with a wet fish. So what if they list all the things you've been doing wrong with your life? So what if they tell you that the dress or the jacket you're wearing makes you look fatter than you really are? It's very hard to be angry with someone who means so well.

Most Sagittarius co-workers are generous and helpful to a fault. Do you need somebody to cover for you at work while you run out to do something you aren't supposed to? A Sagittarius will take on the task with all the artfulness of an army supply sergeant. You'll get enough cover to let you run all the way to Budapest and back before anybody even suspects that you left the building. Confidentially, if you're ever stuck for a place to meet somebody you're seeing on the sly, a Sagittarius could be the person to help you out there too. But beware on that score—Archers who aren't into side orders themselves have possibly been cheated on in the past. And if that's the case, they'll take a pretty dim view of your clandestine liaisons.

If you've got problems in your personal life, don't worry about a Sagittarius colleague getting involved—it's the kind of thing they love doing! When you're really down on luck, they'll talk to you for hours on the telephone, and give you plenty of wise advice on how to deal with your troubles. If necessary, they'll put you up in their home, feed you and lend you money till your crisis is over. But watch out if they offer to intervene on your behalf with your husband, wife, father, mother or lover. When Archers feel you've something to beef about, they never mince their words!

Capricorn

Element: Earth
Symbol: The Goat
Ruler: Saturn

The Sign of the Goat

The goat isn't essentially what you'd call exciting or dashing. He doesn't strike terror in men's hearts like the lion. And he won't bring you out in a cold sweat like a sneaky old scorpion. He may be unusual in his own way, but he likes the steady, predictable life. He climbs, he eats, he has sex—and that's enough to be getting on with. Climbing takes most of his time—it's his work, his hobby, his relaxation. Like the average person born in Capricorn, the goat is only concerned with moving up in the world.

If you want to see a goat in his element, get yourself a pair of good boots with a solid grip, and find a suitable mountain. When you've grappled your way to the top, having managed to keep a hold on the slippery rock face thanks only to a prayer and a fingernail, it's hard not to feel a possessive pride in your achievement. The mountain has become *your* personal conquest! That's probably how the goat feels about it too, and that's why you'll feel like an awkward trespasser when you finally encounter some bearded old billy fixing you with his ancient gaze as you shuffle awkwardly towards him. He might very well remind you of the stone-faced old primary school teacher who caught you reaching into the cookie jar, sharing a stolen cigarette behind the garage, or playing doctors and nurses with the kids across the street.

In days of old the goat's great enemy was the big,

bad wolf who, in the best fairy tale tradition, lay and waited in hiding for his next kid cutlet. Wolves are in short supply these days, but in the psyche of every Capricorn the wolf is very much alive and prowling around not far from the back door. Capricorns easily feel insecure. Perhaps the seven little goats in the story were naive enough to let themselves be caught unawares and eaten, but you won't find Capricorn people so easily taken in.

If you want a fuller understanding of the Capricorn temperament, the goat is only half the story. Originally, this sign was associated with a strange mythological creature called a goat-fish, a goat with a curly fish tale. Fish, as you'll know when you read the chapter on Pisces, are at home in water; and in astrology, the element of water is associated with the realm of feeling and emotion. The symbol of the goat-fish tells us something very important about Capricorns: they may look tough on the outside, but that exterior is just cover for a very sensitive and feeling person. In fact, it's probably true to say that the reason they develop that tough exterior in the first place is to hide how vulnerable they are underneath. Goats want to have as little as possible to do with water—they hate getting wet, they're never sure how deep it is, and they don't trust what's going on under the surface. Like all earth signs, Capricorns prefer to be on land, the drier and firmer the better.

Saturn, the god of restriction

To the Greeks, Saturn was known as Cronos. Cronos fathered a number of children, but he wasn't what you would call an ideal parent. He was uncomfortable with the thought that his off-spring were growing up. It's only a matter of time, he thought, till they overthrow me and take away my kingdon. He didn't much relish the idea of giving up his power so, as they were about to reach maturity, he ate them all. Gobble, munch, burp . . . no more problem! Cronos' wife quickly got tired of her husband's constant snacks. It's nice to see a father enjoying his children, but couldn't he do it more conventionally? When the time drew nigh for him to eat young Zeus, she drew the line. She served up a boulder instead of her favourite son, and Cronos swallowed it. And in the end things turned out exactly as Cronos had feared. When Zeus came of age, he took over his father's kingdom and Cronos was banished forever.

Capricorn people, as a rule, don't devour their children. But they aren't comfortable losing control of them, or anything else for that matter. Even the least inhibited Capricorns always have things pretty well under control. They're capable of enjoying a wild good time, but they don't always choose to. The tenth sign in the zodiac knows everything there is to know about restraint.

Saturn doesn't need an introduction. You've known him all you life. He's the little man on your shoulder who nags you and never leaves you alone when there's something left undone. He's the voice in you which reminds you of all the 'oughts' and 'shoulds' of life. With Saturn around, you never get the chance to sit on your laurels and enjoy your achievement. He's there in the background, moaning and groaning worse than any Capricorn about what you haven't done yet. He might be reminding you about the tax form you should be completing, the tacky paintwork in the bathroom, or the bigger place you need to buy. If you can't hear him, you're either not a Capricorn or you're dead from the neck up.

But he has another face too. In mythology he appears not only as a cruel tyrant who devours his children, but also as a very wise old man—someone who has lived a full life and has the solid wisdom of experience behind him. Saturn will never let us forget our duties, responsibilities and human limitations, but he also symbolizes our capacity to enjoy a rich, full and productive life. In Roman myth, the age of Saturn was a golden age when the earth yielded its crops freely and life was abundant. Capricorns who learn the lessons of Saturn know that life is brief, but the fruits of the earth are all the sweeter because they don't last forever. Saturn's yearly festival, the Romans' Saturnalia—now replaced by Christmas—was a time of unrestrained merry-making. So if you think of Capricorn as a boring sign, think again!

The Capricorn temperament

Sagittarius people are always looking up for inspiration and better weather. But Capricorn people know that if you don't look where you're going, sooner or later you'll trip over the carpet. Capricorns are practical. They're deep thinkers, but they aren't interested in airy-fairy theories that come to nothing. Don't talk to the sign of the Goat about all your promise and potential—big ideas are all very well, but what have you achieved that's solid and real? Don't forget, this is the real world and the rent won't pay for itself, will it? And we all need to eat two or three times a day don't we? When you're a Capricorn, you never take these things for granted. What's guaranteed today could be gone by tomorrow. Now and again, Capricorns have to let go and enjoy themselves, but for many of them the greatest pleasure in life is work. Even the most frivolous people born under this sign treat life as a very serious business.

Achievement means everything to Capricorns. They are the natural builders of the zodiac, working with their ideas, putting theory into practice, always learning lessons as they go. They're miserable if a day goes by when they haven't somehow been productive. They like to see concrete and tangible results for their efforts. Capricorns love solid structures. Without them, life would fall apart. Can you imagine, without our bone structure (ruled by Capricorn), the human body would be like a big bag of skin and jelly. What a Capricorn nightmare! These people hate the thought of collapsing and being dependent on anybody else. That might be alright for a clinging sign like Cancer, but if you're a Capricorn, *you* like to be firmly in control of the situation.

From Day One in life, Goat people have a highly developed sense of responsibility. (One Capricorn woman who came for an astrological consultation had started running her family's business when she wasn't much more than twelve years old.) Nagging consciences won't let Capricorns wriggle out of something they know they really ought to be doing. No matter how much they have accomplished, they're always whipping themselves until they're well into their thirties. This sign does everything back to front. Newborn Capricorn babies have an expression that says 'I've been here before!'—a wisdom as ancient as Methuselah's older brother. Later on in life, when the rest of us are starting to show the ravages of care and woe, Capricorns begin to look a little younger and more attractive with the passing of each year.

Capricorn is the third sign in the element of earth. Like all the earth signs, Capricorns feel a strong need for security. A quick look across the zodiac to the water sign of the Crab is enough warning for any Goat that if you don't control your whims and emotions, they can easily drown you. Like the mountain goat, Capricorns learn that they get on better by taking life cautiously, one thing at a time: one day, one goal, one step. In this way, they gradually arrive where they really want to go.

Earth signs, whether they admit it or not, are concerned with material well-being. In this sense, Capricorn is a very traditional and conventional sign. Young Goats often rebel and kick against the values of their parents or society. But as they get older, they usually get more and more into old-fashioned values and old-fashioned things—like money and property. There are greedy Goats who gravitate towards money as compulsively as iron filings are pulled to a magnet—if it's true that you can't take it with you, there's a pretty good case for grabbing it while you can! But your average Capricorn is more restrained and steady-going, making each day of life a wise investment for the future.

Home life with a Capricorn is basically a very civilized affair. They aren't riotously affectionate. In fact when it comes to their feelings, Goats are notoriously awkward and reticent. But don't believe that they're short on passion. Beneath their dignified and often reserved appearance, Capricorns have a deeply sensual, earthly nature, reminiscent of the Greek god Pan (born with the legs, horns and beard of a goat), who spent most of his spare time in pursuit of wild young wood nymphs.

With the sign of Capricorn, there is clearly a time and a place for everything. Saturn, the god of restrictions, was also the god of boundaries. The body has its limits: we're stuck with being tall or short, and there's no way of getting around the fact we have to eat, drink or sleep. We're held back and controlled by other people—our parents, our teachers, our employers. We're restricted by our society—its laws, its social rules and its morality. And, whatever we make of our lives, we have a limited time to carry out all that we can achieve.

But we do have a choice about how we deal with life's limitations. It's frustrating to feel restricted, especially when we're young. But gradually, as we give up struggling against life's boundaries and begin accepting them as inevitable, we discover that we achieve much more within them. As we learn to work in harmony with Saturn, we not only learn discipline, but we also find out that even within limits, we have the freedom to develop and grow into our full potential, to become what we alone are capable of becoming.

Time is an important factor in developing your full

Capricorn potential. We're talking now in years rather than week or months. All you Capricorn people have to learn patience. Whatever you want, don't expect to get there tomorrow. You'll arrive where you're going by perseverance and sheer hard graft. Short cuts never satisfy you—you're a Capricorn, not a high-flying Aries or Sagittarius. When Sagittarius people see a mountain they want to climb, they get so excited about it, they're immediately off on their way to the top. It makes no difference if it's snowing and they've never climbed a mountain before—they'll pull through somehow. It's different for Capricorns. When they see a mountain they'd like to climb, they know they have to do their groundwork. First they'll take a comprehensive course in mountain climbing, then they'll start saving money to buy the best equipment, and finally—but only after they've checked and re-checked the weather report for the region—they're prepared to begin the trek. If you're a Goat, don't fret because you're only moving one centimetre at a time. If you listen to your common sense, your earthy instincts will tell you that for your sign real growth and change happen inside and in their own time. Think of the earth in the northern hemisphere when the sun is in Capricorn. On the surface, everything's cold and nothing's happening; underneath there's a power-house of activity just waiting to be released.

Other human beings matter a lot to Capricorns. Goats are strong family people, even if they rebelled as children against their own parents. And they have a marked social conscience. When Capricorns reach the top, they frequently turn round to help all those behind them who are still struggling to get on. Looking back on life, as Capricorns frequently do, they see the value of discipline, perseverance and hard work. With that outlook, many Goats become pillars of their communities, upholding society's standards and beliefs. (Of course, the high wall that protects also excludes. Other people can suffer from a rigid Capricorn's narrow-mindedness, and the Goat's unshakable conviction that his or her way is the only right way, and that nothing counts unless you've earned it yourself.)

Perhaps Capricorn's biggest problem is not knowing what to do when there's nothing to do. Goats are happiest when they're making order in their own life or organizing other people's. They get so accustomed to applying themselves to endless little duties and responsibilities, they don't know what to do with their free time. Never ask a Capricorn to relax, lie back and do nothing—that's the biggest effort of all.

The Capricorn types

Capricorns born between 22 December and 1 January You were born when Father Christmas was around, but that doesn't mean you have to imitate him all the time. You're great at helping others to sort out their lives. Why don't you take the time to do the same with your own problems? You're right to be a little wary, but too much caution could be what's standing in the way of the happiness and fulfilment you're looking for.

Capricorns born between 2 January and 10 January You're the most sensual and creative of all the Capricorn types. On the surface you may appear stern and rigid, but underneath you're softer than you look. People will like your dependability, but don't be afraid to let your hair down and live it up now and then. You'll surprise yourself and others in the process.

Capricorns born between 11 January and 20 January You're the most outgoing of the Capricorn types. You're also the most analytical. When you do assert yourself, it will only be after careful consideration and reflection. So don't let others stand in your way—you've got too much to say and teach to the world to allow yourself to go unnoticed.

Capricorn and work

It's hard for Capricorn people to sit still and let life go by. In fact, they don't. Even when they seem relaxed, they're usually thinking ahead, looking back, planning or checking. Even their social lives are frequently work-related, but don't feel sorry for them—they like things that way. They tend to make friends with people they meet through work, which is very convenient for a sign that likes to get on in the world. Capricorns find it easy to rub shoulders with people who are likely to be useful to them. Company presidents and multi-millionaires usually have more Capricorn friends than a camel has fleas. Does that make Capricorn people seem very cold and calculating? Well, they're very often quite *warm* and calculating.

Work is as necessary for a Capricorn person as eating, sleeping and breathing. Even so, the goat doesn't look like an animal who put a lot of effort into life and that's true for many Capricorns as well. Don't let yourself be fooled by appearances: people born under this sign are more determined and persistent than any other in the zodiac. The main reason they get so much done is that they simply never stop. But they pace themselves well, which is why they still appear fresh and lively even after a long working day.

You'll rarely see Capricorns letting life get the better of them for very long. A Goat without a job on Monday will have visited every agency and scoured every newspaper by Tuesday. By Wednesday there's a letter written off to every prospective employer. By Thursday there's at least one interview somewhere, and if the Capricorn isn't working by Friday, then it must be a bank holiday!

Capricorns who reach the top of the mountain are not happy just to stay there and bask in the sun. It's then that they look around for a new mountain to climb, preferably a higher one. Even when their contemporaries have settled into a cosy retirement villa in some sunny clime, Capricorns are still challenging themselves to achieve more. In many respects this is a noble way to live, but you can't help wondering why they feel the need to push themselves so hard. Perhaps it's because they don't give themselves enough credit for what they have already accomplished. Compliment a Capricorn on his or her successes, and the reply will go something like 'Oh, that! Anyone could have done it. And really, I didn't do it that well. I should have. . . .' If you're a Capricorn who's worried about not having achieved enough, then try this exercise. Besides giving you a chance to validate what you have done, it will help clarify your next step or course of action.

1. List all the things you have accomplished so far in your working life.
2. Take some time to pat yourself on the back for what you have done. Really let yourself feel good about what you have managed to make of your life.
3. If you still feel you haven't done enough and there is farther to go, now is the time to make a plan for the coming year. Close your eyes and see if you can come up with a picture in your mind of what you would like to achieve next. Don't judge or force it, just let a picture emerge in its own good time.
4. Now ask yourself if this picture is something valid or at all possible. If it isn't, close your eyes again until you get an image of something feasible.
5. Once you have a realistic picture of where you would like to go, ask yourself what is the first step you need to take to get there. Within the next week, do something towards making that step. Repeat this exercise once a month for the next year.

Capricorn careers

Occasionally you get Capricorns, like David Bowie or Rod Stewart, who look unconventional. But don't be fooled by outrageous appearances, Capricorns are empire builders at heart. The way some successful Goats behave is reminiscent of all the soap opera clichés about tough tycoons (maybe criticisms and complaints from people farther down the ladder don't trouble you very much when you've reached the top of the pile, and you're looking out over the world from the 125th floor of your own building.) You couldn't ask for a better example of this sign than Greek shipping magnate Aristotle Onassis, who made himself more money than Midas, and then set himself the task of ascending the social ladder through his relationship with Maria Callas and his marriage to Jacqueline Kennedy.

For the goat's taste, the sweetest herbs grow in the highest altitudes. Who cares if the air up there is a little sparse—there aren't that many people around to share it with, anyway. One Goat who built a very impressive and tall empire was Conrad Hilton, a man who made his millions providing the standard of hotel entertainment many Capricorns aspire to. Then there was the Capricorn cosmetics empress Helena Rubenstein, who capitalized on an earth sign taste for style and worldly sophistication. Unfortunately, life at the top can be lonesome. If they're not careful, Goats can end up living in very secluded private towers. Witness the sad example of the eccentric multi-millionaire Howard Hughes, whose wealth didn't do much to assuage his feelings of isolation and loneliness. While many Capricorns are upright pillars of the establishment, some are not so scrupulous. Al Capone is an example of a Goat who was prepared to get rid of anyone who got in his way. And who can forget the cliff-hanging trial which raised questions about the executive style of Capricorn businessman John DeLorean?

If you get into the building trade, you can hardly fail to move up in the world. There's always a call for competent Capricorn technicians—engineers, architects, surveyors, carpenters or masons—to build or supervise construction. Capricorns aren't afraid to get their hands dirty, but they know they get far more done when they've learned how to delegate. It's difficult to imagine something that could bring more satisfaction to Capricorn people than owning their own building company and feeling an office block or luxury mansion slowly rising beneath them. And if you're a Capricorn who *really* likes to see things grow, then farming or horticulture could be the field for you.

Capricorn climbers are also very much at home in the money market. A penny saved is a penny earned, and clever Capricorns rarely kiss a penny goodbye without first making an investment for the future. Cautious and calculating, Goats are sensitive to danger but still very quick off the mark when they need to be—indispensable qualities in the financial world, where the mere mention of sums involved is sufficient to give most people a bad attack of vertigo. Security is important to most Capricorns. They worry about things like health insurance and what will happen to their loved ones when they're gone. So you'll meet plenty of Capricorn bankers, cashiers, tellers, insurance sales people, accountants and private secretaries. For many, these jobs are the first important rung on the ladder. Like the best mountaineers, shrewd Capricorns in business are prepared to learn every inch of the way, right from the bottom to the top.

There's many a Capricorn career built on rocks—and when we're talking Capricorn, we don't mean rhinestones! Precious and semi-precious stones are always big business, and a clever Capricorn could make mountains of money looking for them, setting them or selling them. If your interest in rocks is more academic, you might want to consider a career in geology or minerology. (Incidentally, at the top of the list of famous Capricorn scientists is Sir Isaac Newton—you can't be surprised that it was a Goat who first formulated the laws of *gravity*!) Other Capricorns simply climb, which is never as simple as it appears, although the experience of skilled Capricorn mountaineers can make it look so easy. For professionals in this field, their natural Capricorn talents come in handy; before one step is taken, the Goat's ingenuity will be needed to find the sponsorship to finance a big climb. And that Capricorn penchant for organizing people is necessary in any team effort, whether it's a climbing expedition, a ball game, a construction crew or a department of government.

With their concern for others and their strong sense of social responsibility, Capricorns often gravitate to professions in the public services. Studies have shown that many firefighters and ambulance drivers are born under this sign. A Capricorn social worker or doctor would be very glad to help you sort out your life and look after yourself. But it's in the field of education that a Goat's true colours really show. We teach best what has been hardest for us to learn, and there are no better teachers than those who have struggled with a subject from the bottom up. Of course, a Capricorn teacher might be rather strict—after all, this is the sign of law and order. Which explains why so many Capricorns enter the police force, or join the ranks of civil servants helping to keep society on the rails. A Capricorn barrister or solicitor has enough patience to deal with the most tedious cases and clients. And what better sign for a sombre-faced judge than one ruled by Saturn, the original rule-maker himself. Capricorns love to put people and things in their proper place, and a career as an archivist, statistician or historian would give plenty of opportunity to exercise this prerogative.

History has shown that many Capricorns are more than happy holding the reins of power in their hands. If you're born under this sign, you might consider a career in politics, where you can keep a sharp eye on what's going on around you, and make a name for yourself into the bargain. But power isn't the only thing driving a Goat into the political arena. More than any other sign, Capricorns relish the chance of taking an abstract philosophy or political system and putting it into practice. Chairman Mao Tse-Tung was a Chinese Capricorn leader who wasn't afraid to put his thoughts and theories to the test. Nor was Capricorn Clement Attlee, the Labour Prime Minister who headed the post-war government that instituted large scale nationaliz-ation and an unparalleled welfare state. And Egyptian President Anwar Sadat was a truly stalwart Capricorn, willing to risk his life to further his vision of peace between Israel and the Arab world. The roll call of Capricorn political figures also includes such famous names as Gladstone, Lloyd George, Disraeli, Helmut Schmidt of West Germany, trade unionist Arthur Scar-gill and P. W. Botha, State President of the Republic of South Africa, whose Capricorn view of society couldn't be more black and white.

Unfortunately, nothing corrupts like power, and the absolute power of Capricorn Joseph Stalin brought absolute terror and misery to millions of Russians, in the same way that Uganda suffered at the hands of Capricorn President Idi Amin. Ambitious Capricorns who end up in high office should heed the lesson of Richard Milhous Nixon, a Goat who must have felt like kicking himself for not applying typical Capricorn thoroughness when it came to the destruction of tapes that cost him the presidency.

Making a political vision a reality isn't easy, but bringing a spiritual vision down to earth is even harder. It's surprising how many Capricorns are willing to take up that challenge. Maybe it isn't so surprising when you consider that the biggest religious festival of them all—the celebration of the birth of Christ—comes in the early days of this sign. In the Lord's prayer, 'Thy

Kingdom come, thy will be done on Earth, as it is in Heaven', is a line many Capricorns of various denominations would take very seriously. And reflect a moment on the poignant words spoken by a black Capricorn preacher the Rev. Martin Luther King on the evening before his assassination:

> . . . I just want to do God's Will. And He's allowed me to go up to the mountain. And I've looked over, and I've seen the Promised Land. I may not get there with you but I want you to know tonight that we as a people will get to the Promised Land. . . .

St Teresa of Lisieux, whose tender love for Christ inspired profound religious experience in others, was born under this sign. So too was the stoic Bernadette, whose rapturous visions of the Virgin Mary brought her scorn in her short life and later sainthood. According to some sources, we can add to this list the names of St Ignatius Loyola and St Joan of Arc–the maid of Orleans whose Capricorn spirit and determination lives on as an example to millions fighting off oppression. There's also the Nobel Prize-winning doctor and theologian Albert Schweitzer, whose selfless devotion to the sick is a testament to the humanitarian spirit of a Christian Capricorn. From the East came two hardworking Carpricorn gurus, Maharishi Mahesh Yogi and Paramhansa Yogananda, whose spititual ambitions helped make meditation a household word in the West. If this catalogue of names doesn't inspire you to make the most of yourself, nothing will.

If you're a literary Goat, you would be following in some pretty worthwhile footsteps. Capricorn writers often concern themselves with the problems we all encounter adjusting to the demands and expectations of the society in which we live. In his play *Le Bourgeois Gentilhomme*, the French Capricorn playwright Molière described the ridiculous posturing of an inept social climber. E. M. Forster wrote about the unbearable pressure of conformity in *A Passage to India* and *A Room with a View*. Some of the poems of Rudyard Kipling, another famous Capricorn, became touchstones of a patriotic society during the heyday of the British Empire. In very sharp contrast, female Goat Simone de Beauvoir in her book *The Second Sex* pointed out how patriarchal society has traditionally excluded women. Capricorn Jacob Grimm with his brother Wilhelm gathered the unconscious wisdom of the people in folk and fairy tales. And A. A. Milne left us the sage observations of a Capricorn bear called Pooh. Other Capricorn story-tellers include Henry Miller (one of his books is actually called *Tropic of Capricorn*), J. D. Salinger, John Dos Passos and (a typically morbid Capricorn) Edgar Allan Poe.

Show business is a profession you might not at first associate with Goats, but there are some who've ascended to the heights in this field as well. A Capricorn immortal, referred to by one and all as The King, was Elvis Presley, born on 8 January 1935. The rise to fame of many Capricorn stars like Elvis is classic 'rags to riches' stuff. One outstanding example is country singer Dolly Parton (it would be thoroughly bad taste to indulge here in crude jokes about 'career peaks' and 'bustin' into show business). Singer John Denver is a Goat who sold over a million records with his hit song 'Rocky Mountain High'. Mary Tyler Moore, a talented actress who started her own highly profitable televison company, and Regine, the French songstress who became one of the most successful nightclub owners in the world, are two hard-working Goats with a nose for money. Other top entertainers born under this sign include Marlene Dietrich, Maggie Smith, Faye Dunaway, Anthony Hopkins, Joan Baez, Shirley Bassey, Janis Joplin, Jack Jones, Ethel Merman, Danny Kaye, Diane Keaton, George Burns, Sissy Spacek, Oliver Hardy,

Victoria Principal, Tracy Ullman, David Bowie, Cary Grant, Rod Stewart and Paul Young—to name a few.

The actress Patricia Neal deserves special mention as another classic example of Capricorn strength and fortitude. At the top of her career, she suffered a massive stroke which left her physically paralysed and incapable of speech. In true Capricorn style, she used every ounce of her will to learn to walk and talk again. Three years later she was well enough not only to resume acting, but also to travel around America helping others who had been similarly afflicted. Leave it to a Capricorn to turn a crisis into an opportunity.

Natural determination and application are assets that can help any athlete get to the top, which probably explains why there are so many Capricorns in professional athletics. But Capricorns don't just rely on their feet, they can use their fists too—something boxers Joe Frazier and Muhammad Ali showed the world. In any sport—or any career going, come to that—nobody should expect to lock horns with a Goat and win.

Capricorn compatibilities

Capricorn/Aries *(Earth/Fire)* The Ram will call to the fore all your talents for organizing, sorting out and calming others down. Hot-headed Aries people get the best ideas in the world, but they aren't always so clever at carrying them through to the end. That's where you come in—providing they give you the chance.

Capricorn/Taurus *(Earth/Earth)* There's something about a Taurus you'll immediately trust. Maybe it's because they're as cautious about things and people as you are. More than any other sign, you need to learn how to relax—and a Taurus is the one to show you how. Once you break the ice, you'll be the best of friends.

Capricorn/Gemini *(Earth/Air)* Not everyone takes

life as seriously as you do, and Geminis will never let you forget that fact. It's a chalk and cheese match, but it could be a good one if you begin by accepting your enormous differences: you're into work, Geminis like to play; Capricorns are determined and single-track, Geminis are more the stereo types. If you aren't both prepared to make an effort, it's better to call it a day before you ever get going.

Capricorn/Cancer *(Earth/Water)* Cancer is shy and you aren't exactly the most forthcoming of people, so there's bound to be difficulty making contact at first. Learn to appreciate one another as opposite signs should, and you'll both have a friend and ally. You can offer a crestfallen Crab encouragement and some practical advice. And even when you're trying you're hardest not to show it, Cancers will instinctively know when you're in need of some homespun sympathy and understanding.

Capricorn/Leo *(Earth/Fire)* Give the Lion a chance. Okay, you aren't impressed by extroverted, outgoing types, but don't imagine that they've nothing to offer. Under all the show, Leos are warm, caring and often misunderstood—a bit like yourself. You both go for class, you both like to be on top, so learn to respect one another and you'll both gain a lot.

Capricorn/Virgo *(Earth/Earth)* You understand one another so easily, you'll sometimes wonder if you aren't related. You're both reliable, thoughtful, thorough and hard-working. And when it comes to criticizing things, you'll never be short of conversation. No problems here. You two go together well—like bread and butter, but not quite so exciting.

Capricorn/Libra *(Earth/Air)* You're both snobs at heart, and Libra's style and good taste is bound to appeal to you. It's a good working combination. If a job requires tact and diplomacy, the two of you are the ones to pull it off. In fact, whatever you do together will be done to perfection, even if you're months over the deadline.

Capricorn/Scorpio *(Earth/Water)* A Scorpio enemy you don't need. You're not the most flexible person around, but it's worth bending over backwards to win the support of this sign. If you do, you've got an ally who'll stand by you, come hell or highwater. You're an unbeatable combination, especially in any situation where you have to hold out for a long time under fire.

Capricorn/Sagittarius *(Earth/Fire)* There's no use telling Archers to hold their horses, so you might as well save your breath. Barricade yourself behind brick walls and they'll still find a way to tell you all about their brilliant new schemes and notions. But don't close your ears to everything a Sagittarius has to say. That crazy idea they're talking about today may be the conclusion you'll reach in five years' time.

Capricorn/Capricorn *(Earth/Earth)* Provided you don't encroach too much into each other's territory, you two Goats could get along surprisingly well. Who said Capricorns don't have a sense of humour? Think of all the fun the two of you will have working overtime together and continuously moaning about it to each other. Things take time for Capricorns, but given a chance, the bonds between the two of you can be deep and lasting.

Capricorn/Aquarius *(Earth/Air)* Capricorn is the sign of restraint, and Aquarius is the sign of freedom. The right ingredients for war, and yet there are times these two signs can work well together. Inventive Water Bearers are never short of ingenious new ideas, and it could be a Capricorn who turns one of them into a real moneyspinner. Stay clear of talking politics, and you two might have a chance.

Capricorn/Pisces *(Earth/Water)* Pisces people do things you wouldn't even dream of doing. They forget appointments, walk off with other people's pens and leave their desks in a mess. Still, there's something about the easy-going Fish which calms and relaxes you. And you can't help appreciating the uncanny way they get around other people—especially when it helps you clinch a deal you'd probably bungle on your own.

The Capricorn boss

Capricorn people can make the sweetest old-fashioned boss types—attentive, considerate, concerned and supportive. Leaving a Capricorn boss for another employment could be like leaving home. In fact, you may simply never leave.

Do bear in mind, however, the other side of the picture (remember, Al Capone was born under this sign). The Capricorn exterior is often deceptively low-key—a bit like the calm at the centre of the whirlwind. But an ambitious Capricorn is as powerful as they come. No matter how agreeable, pleasing and accommodating a Capricorn boss may appear, if it comes to the pinch, the Goat can be ruthless. If you've ever travelled to a place where goats live wild, you might have seen a horned skeleton lying at the bottom of a deep ravine. Don't imagine that the deceased was stricken down with old age, or tripped over something and accidentally fell to its death. More likely than not, there was only enough room on the mountain ledge up there for one animal, and a goat's priorities are clear when it comes to the push. If you try to infringe on a Capricorn's territory, you're in for a fight.

But relax. A Capricorn has an exact and undeviating

sense of justice. If you work hard for your Capricorn boss, he or she will be glad to reward you for your loyalty and effort. After all, you're part of one big family. Be nice to a Capricorn in charge, and (male or female) they'll treat you as only a loving father would. Do them harm, however, and they may start behaving more as a godfather would—especially if you're the person who has been taking things from the stationery cupboard. To you it may be just two pencils and a notebook. To your Capricorn boss it's as if you spat on their mother's grave. So if you get the impression that you're being followed home each evening, or if your telephone clicks strangely when you've finished a call, maybe you should own up and confess your sins. If you are contrite enough, your Capricorn boss will probably forgive you this time. But once your copybook is stained, a Capricorn isn't very likely to forget.

The Capricorn employee

Bosses could do a lot worse than hiring a Goat. Capricorn employees are slavishly devoted to the execution of their duty, and usually as reliable as a micro-chip alarm. They don't mind being told precisely what to do and how to do it, and they'll always deliver what they promise, more or less on time. All that's missing is a tattoo on their foreheads saying 'Promotion this way please'.

Are you a Capricorn employee who really wants to get ahead? Why not marry the boss? Too old? Wrong gender? Well, don't give up, keep thinking. Does your boss have any children? You wouldn't be the first Capricorn employee to marry well. Of course, some people will say you didn't do it for love. How wrong they would be! Don't they know how much you love money and respectability?

If marrying into better prospects is definitely out, you'll just have to do it the hard way. Licking the boss's boots is a bit obvious, so try these tactics instead. First of all, you should always wear an expression on your face that says 'I'm devoted to my work, and I seek no reward beyond the satisfaction of doing it well'. Second, you should take on the work of at least three other people, and then make sure (in the most unassuming way possible) that your boss knows about it. With your natural shrewdness, you won't have too much trouble pulling these things off.

The other thing that usually does the trick is a bit of home entertaining. Invite the boss to dinner, and really lay it on thick. Find out his or her favourite foods and what kind of music they like. The only problem is that you're going to have to take your purse out of mothballs on such an occasion. Some Capricorn home entertainers have been known to save up expensive wine bottles and fill them with cheap plonk, thinking nobody will ever be any wiser. When it comes to advancing your career, we suggest you avoid those little Capricorn money-saving devices.

The Capricorn colleague

To understand your Capricorn co-workers, you have to appreciate the fact that they are perfectionists at heart. When there's a job to be done, they're not happy unless they've done it well. They'll persevere at something long after you've given up. Of course, these qualities are bound to irritate some people who just aren't prepared to put that much effort into things. In fact, a Capricorn worker could become the office scapegoat—the one everybody else likes to complain about or make fun of. But Capricorns can't help their fastidious approach to work, or their natural inclination to please the boss. That's the way they are. These traits are so deeply ingrained, Capricorns probably couldn't change them even if they wanted to.

What really goes on in that Capricorn head? It isn't

easy to know. They're pleasant but diplomatically tight-lipped with strangers. They're normally charming in a distant sort of way, but their intimate revelations are as closely guarded as government policy statements. They certainly aren't people who will burden you with their emotional problems, although they'll gladly listen to yours and offer advice. Beneath their often cool and aloof facade, Capricorns are one of the most sensitive signs in the zodiac. And even though they believe that showing too much emotion is a sign of weakness, they couldn't be more touched or moved by the pain and suffering of those around them. In the end, the only way to find out what Capricorns are really thinking or feeling is to get them drunk.

Some people really can't resist trying to corrupt a Capricorn. They're prime targets for the office Romeo or the Mata Hari at the corner café, who'll be determined to find out if they're as innocent, humdrum and unadventurous as they appear. But remember, this is the sign of the goat-fish. Still waters run very deep where Capricorn is concerned. A supposedly boring or naive Capricorn colleague who lets his or her hair down could probably show you a thing or two you've never seen before.

Aquarius

Element: Air

Symbol: The Water Bearer

Rulers: Uranus/Saturn

The Sign of the Water Bearer

You already know that each sign belongs to one of the four elements—fire, earth, air or water. So isn't there something funny here: Aquarius, the Water Bearer, in the element of air? Well, Aquarius people are full of contradictions, and they aren't ashamed of the fact. As the element of air has to do with thinking (which is what Aquarius types do best) let's think about water for a minute. Water isn't just something you wash in or drink when you're thirsty. It also provides a way of getting around. Most of the important towns in the world were originally built by the sea or near a river for easy access. Until not so long ago, people travelled a lot in boats, picking up languages, ideas, products and customs from one culture and passing them on to others as they travel. You might say that kind of global sharing and communication is what the sign of Aquarius is all about. Nowadays the only real difference is that we're doing it in jets and spaceships. We're no longer held back by natural borders and we've expanded our frontiers well into outer space. Aquarius is definitely a sign that keeps up with the times.

It wasn't unusual for early travellers to change the lives of local residents in the countries they visited. For instance, when William the Conqueror took a trip over to Hastings in 1066, he had quite an impact on the English way of life. He wasn't the only sea traveller who brought change. There were the Greeks, the

Romans, the Vikings, the Pilgrim Fathers and all the hundreds of unknown tribes and cultures who migrated across the globe, by land and sea, before history was recorded. Even the most patriotic Water Bearers also feel themselves to be citizens of the world who like to distribute new ideas, shake things up and make changes. Their innovations may be positive and genuinely progressive, although sometimes they don't turn out so well. Whatever happens, you'll never find out if you don't give it a try!

According to most astrologers, we're now in the Age of Aquarius. To the Aquarian mind, the people on the planet earth are essentially one big family in which we're all brothers and sisters. The Water Bearer's jug contains the water of life and he distributes it freely to one and all. The glyph for Aquarius is two little waves, one on top of the other, and they don't just represent waves of water. They're also the airwaves that carry communications all over the world, and the electrical waves that lighten up the darkness and carry powerful energy. We have never before been so linked up and inter-connected with the rest of the people on the planet as we are now. Dial a few digits in London, and within seconds you can be talking to a friend in New Guinea. Turn on a television in Aberdeen, and you can see what's happening live in Adelaide. We're no longer isolated individuals in isolated communities—we are now part of a rapidly accelerating global network. The planet has shrunk, and with it comes the possibility of getting to understand one another better, putting our heads together and making the world a better place for everybody. Of course, there are people who might argue that some of the progress we've made isn't all that positive, but they aren't likely to be born under the sign of Aquarius. It's true, all this talk about everyone getting together and the world becoming a better place sounds terribly idealistic—but that's how most Aquarius people think.

Uranus, the sky god

Uranus was the first sky god—the god of the starry heavens—who ruled vast and limitless space (Aquarius people need a lot of room). He was married to Gaea, mother earth. Every night, the god of the sky came down and lay on the earth, and Gaea kept producing children. She hatched the strangest brood imaginable: first there were the Titans, a race of giants; then the Cyclopses, hideous beasts each with one eye in the middle of its forehead; and then a whole string of miscellaneous monstrosities with arms, ears and heads where you wouldn't expect to find them. Uranus was disgusted at the sight of his offspring—they weren't what he had in mind at all! Just as soon as his children were born, he promptly shoved each one of them in turn back into poor Gaea's womb (with all their wisdom and understanding, Aquarius people can be terribly insensitive to the feelings of others). Uranus was nonetheless persistent. Every night without fail he came and lay on Gaea once again, hoping that this time the results might prove more satisfactory.

What does this myth tell us about people born under the Uranus-ruled sign of Aquarius? Like Uranus, in their minds Water Bearers often have a vision of how things should be—they have a picture of the perfect job, the perfect relationship or the perfect political system. But when they attempt to turn that wonderful vision into reality, the end result is often very different from what they imagined. Aquarius relationships don't always turn out so hot; the jobs they hope will give them everything can be very disappointing; and supposedly ideal political systems can result in mayhem and disaster. So what next? Almost inevitably, they get rid of the offending relationship, job or government, and they try all over again. Aquarius people keep searching and searching until they find those things that live up to their ideals.

Consider the French Revolution, for example, which occurred in the 1780s—curiously enough, the time when the planet Uranus was first dicovered. There was something very Uranian about this historical event: the revolutionaries were intent upon establishing a state based on the typically Aquarian ideals of liberty, equality and fraternity. Unfortunately, they over-estimated the capacity of most individual people to live up to such noble notions. What was meant to be wonderful turned into a bloodbath instead. Lofty Aquarian ideals, beautiful as they are, can be extremely difficult to put into practice. Very often, other people just aren't ready for them; sometimes Water Bearers themselves find their own high ideals and expectations hard to live with. But what can you expect from a sign that's so ahead of its time?

The Aquarius temperament

If you felt a cramp coming on in the last sign, you'll be glad to rip off the tight Capricorn corset now we've reached Aquarius. This is the place to meet lively, friendly people with an unusual perspective on living. Water Bearers enjoy good company, although in their terms that may mean you sitting listening while an Aquarius does all the talking. But you'll be surprised at how well they do understand you, even when they don't seem very interested in what you have to say. Aquarians are truly original, almost impossible to classify or pigeonhole. You'll probably get along with them like a house on fire—until you start getting too close, that is. People born in the eleventh sign need to have plenty of space to themselves. They love to share their time and thoughts with other people, but they value above all things the freedom to come and go as they please. Normally they're very reasonable people, but just try taking away their liberty, and they'll retaliate with a force that would burst the bars of a dungeon window.

Of course, they're not selfish about it. They may demand freedom for themselves, but they want it for other people too. And equality as well. Who else but an Aquarius like Abraham Lincoln would have the guts to proclaim equality between blacks and whites at a time when slavery held up the economy? Water Bearers will give their all—even their lives—for a cause they truly believe in. All over the world Aquarius people climb up on soap-boxes and talk themselves hoarse campaigning for free speech, real democracy and the equitable distribution of wealth. They're intelligent, well-informed, genuinely concerned about the welfare of other people . . . and they would gladly lock up anybody who thinks otherwise.

Undeniably, Aquarius people are the toughest in the world to argue with, because they're always right—or so they generally think. They can be so adamant about their beliefs, they even make a Taurus look flexible. They hold on to their principles like you'd hold on to a jug of water in the desert, and they'd sooner leave a lover in the lurch than abandon a firmly held opinion. Of course, you're entitled to contest their views if you insist, but you'll never win. When it comes to defending a point of view, an Aquarian citizen of the world will talk you off the face of the earth.

Although they love to participate in groups and causes, at heart Water Bearers enjoy being individuals. Those swayed by the Saturn co-rulership of their sign may be more held back and restrained, but most are true Uranus rebels who wouldn't bat an eyelid at the thought of overturning the existing structure of society to make way for their idea of something better. Invite a rebellious Aquarius to a cosy family gathering with the words 'Come as you are', and you're really asking for trouble. In most situations, Aquarius people aren't afraid of being unconventional. (Confidentially, 'unconventional' is something of a euphemism in the case of a few born under this sign—they're often a little weird, and they know it!) Not all of them are extreme but even the more conventional Saturnine Water Bearers will support changes that make life more fair and just for everyone involved.

You can really see Aquarius' originality shining through in the sphere of personal relationships. The most peace-loving Water Bearers have a knack of ending up in unpredictable, disruptive or unusual living situations. They're innovators, always ready to try an experiment—social, intellectual, scientific or sexual. And they're terribly curious about things; they'll do almost anything once, just for the experience. Some of them freely admit to taking their pleasures every night in a different room, in a different outfit, and occasionally with a different partner. And yet Aquarius people are very loyal—in their own way. But like all air signs, Aquarius needs plenty of space to spread his or her wings.

There's also a self-centred streak in the Water Bearer. Each sign borrows from its opposite; look straight across from Aquarius and you'll see flamboyant, glittering Leo. Leos unashamedly head right for the centre stage. Aquarius people often do exactly the same thing, but they find a good reason to justify their need for attention. Water Bearers like to have their egos stroked as much as any lens-loving Lion. But they hate to admit it—maybe because as children they were told to put other people before themselves.

Aquarius children are unusually bright, as dazzling as the sky at night. But sometimes they feel like stangers in a very strange land, as topsy-turvy as Alice in the wonderland created by that wacky Aquarius Lewis Carroll. As time goes by, many little Water Bearers find that life gets 'curiouser and curiouser'. For some, it really feels as though they inhabit an entirely different world from the rest of us. An idea they pick up in a storybook or on television is enough to take their imaginative minds soaring far above the planet earth.

Aquarians live in their heads. They're always busy

analysing how things and people work. Like fellow air signs Gemini and Libra, they're not that at home with their feelings. Dramatic outbursts aren't an Aquarian speciality. They're uncomfortable with anybody who gets too emotional (like a typical Scorpio, for instance). Sometimes it's very difficult to know what's going on inside a Water Bearer's head. If you stand up an Aquarius friend, she'll probably tell you very coolly that it isn't fair to make an appointment you can't keep. That's the Aquarian way of saying 'You rat! Where the hell were you? If you do that to me again, I'll kill you!' You can't help being impressed with how reasonable Aquarius people can be, but sometimes you wish they would just get angry and throw a tantrum like the rest of us.

The Water Bearer likes things crystal clear, cut and dried. Feelings can get so soppy and messy—they start to take over, and before you know where you are, you're out of control. The trouble is, Aquarius, if you try to live your life without experiencing what you're feeling, your reality can become as cold and barren as an Arctic landscape. It's okay to be cool as a cucumber; it's not so good to be as frozen as an iceberg.

If you've never clapped eyes on a Water Bearer outside captivity, there are several natural Aquarius habitats where you may just be able to spot one. Begin your search in the fringe theatres—they're always full of the kind of people your mother warned you about (or maybe she never even mentioned them in case it only encouraged you). If you happen to be passing near a secluded laboratory late at night and you hear the cackle of manic laughter and the slow clank of mechanical limbs, don't hang around—there's probably a mad Aquarius scientist inside on the look-out for a fresh human guinea pig. Or, if you can live with the insects that creep out of the cargo, you'd probably run into an Aquarius on board a banana boat, travelling under heavy gunfire from one Central American republic to another.

Find a renegade, maverick or rebel, and you've probably found somebody born under the sign of the Water Bearer. Of course, there are many Aquarius people who don't choose to live on the outer fringes of life. The majority stay within the structure of society—even if they always seem to be at odds with it. A classic example is Aquarius writer Muriel Spark's heroine in *The Prime of Miss Jean Brodie*, a teacher at loggerheads with the rigid conventions of life at Marcia Blaine, an Edinburgh school for young ladies:

It has been suggested again that I should apply for a post at one of the more progressive schools, where my methods would be more suited to the system than they are at Blaine. But I shall not apply for a post at a crank school. I shall remain at this education factory. There needs must be a leaven in the lump. Give me a girl of impressionable years and she is mine for life.

Aquarius types

Aquarians born between 21 January and 29 January Don't compromise and conform more than you really want—it will only make you miserable. Be true to yourself, and you'll succeed. So what if your behaviour drives other people crazy and your interests are a bit unusual? There's nothing like a little controversy to make life more exciting.

Aquarians born between 30 January and 9 February Restless, insatiably curious and all over the place, you're not the easiest person to keep tabs on. Here one minute, gone the next—if there's something new, you've got to try it. Thank God for your irreverent sense of humour. How else could you get away with the kind of things you do and say?

Aquarians born between 10 February and 18

February You are the most creative of all the Aquarius types. More than anything, you need an outlet to give expression to your artistic or inventive side. How you manage to be so obstinate, dogmatic and charming all at the same time is quite a feat. Somebody with your charisma can't help getting a lot of attention. Too bad it makes you feel claustrophobic.

Aquarius and work

If there's something Aquarius people hate, it's the repetitious drudgery of a nine-to-five job. Save your breath trying to win them over to secure monotony. Water Bearers aren't to be bought with conventional perks like a good pension scheme or a two-week holiday once a year. You may be able to seduce people born under the sign of Taurus, Cancer, Virgo or Capricorn with those sort of things, but not an Aquarius. As a rule, Water Bearers aren't interested enough in a big bank balance or lots of security to waste their time with a boring job. Don't get us wrong. This doesn't mean Aquarius people aren't willing to work hard. They are capable of working as hard as anyone, but it has to be work they believe in, something they feel is worthwhile.

Aquarius is the most inventive and original sign in the zodiac. Whatever their line, Water Bearers need plenty of space and freedom to approach it in their own way. They don't work well with someone standing over them, shouting orders how to do things. An Aquarius probably invented the very first robot, and an Aquarius will undoubtedly be the first person in your area who owns a robot. It's true that they're at home with technology, machines, appliances and gadgets—but automatons they are *not*. Perish the thought! An Aquarius couldn't be more badly placed working in a big chain store, or slaving away as one of a thousand minions for an ogre bureaucrat.

Even in jobs they love, Water Bearers' approach to

work isn't very steady or consistent. They do things in spurts. They'll start something with a great rush of inspired and frenetic energy, but then that phase will taper off. It's at this point that their minds wander away from the job at hand and on to other things, like organizing a campaign to raise money for the latest charity they've become involved with. But this too will pass, and then they'll get back into the project they were first working on with more intensity than ever. Aquarius people can't force themselves to do anything; they have to wait for the inspiration to hit. You might suppose that they'll never complete any task that way, but don't be such an old fuddy-duddy about it. When it comes to the crunch and they can't delay a deadline any longer, they'll burn the midnight oil for a week to catch up on what's outstanding. Water Bearers avoid commitment and deadlines like the plague, but when they finally give their word to do something by a certain time, they'll keep it. Yes, they're erratic and unpredictable, but they're also incredibly honest. When they make you a promise, they honour it.

Outside activities often absorb a lot of their time. They'll organize little outings for everyone at work—group bookings at the theatre, trips to a sporting event, a picnic now and then. And if there's a union where they work, depending on their bias that year, they'll either be leading it or among its fiercest opponents.

You Aquarius people who are bored with your present job, or who don't feel you're using your mental potential to the fullest, should try this simple exercise. It will enliven your mind and show you just how inventive you can be.

1. Find a pencil and paper and then sit somewhere quiet. Now give yourself five minutes, and write down all the different ways you can think of using a paper clip.
2. When the time is up, review your list. Some of your ideas are probably incredibly original and inventive. It may seem

silly at first, but this exercise can really stretch and open up your mind.

3. Now that your imagination is active, get a new piece of paper, and take five minutes to think of ways you can make your current job more interesting. Don't censor your thoughts, just write down whatever occurs to you.

4. Pick out one of the things on your list, and on your next working day, do what you can to put it into practice.

Aquarian careers

If you want to make the most of your sign's extraordinary gifts, you have two choices: you can take up a very ordinary occupation and make of it something quite extraordinary; or you can take off in a new direction entirely and try something truly unusual.

Let's begin with some of the occupations traditionally associated with this sign. We've stressed the highly original nature of Aquarian thinking, and some could make a comfortable living as researchers and inventors, working privately or for industry. Water Bearers are obsessed with understanding how things work. What makes a machine run? What makes an engine tick? Why do some structures stand up and others fall down? If you're fascinated by engines, you could always get into the garage repair business (a very suitable Uranus profession—the prices they charge nowadays are out of this world!). Architecture and engineering are other good professions which would give Aquarius people a chance to combine their technical know-how with their ability to envision something before it exists.

Uranus rules electricity. Thomas Alva Edison was an Aquarian inventor full of bright ideas, not the least of which was the light bulb itself. Talk electricity to some Aquarius people, and they immediately light up, and with good cause. Your lightning-rod intelligence already will have registered that it's a field alive with job possibilities and a variety of occupations to plug. For the sake of slower readers, we'll point out some of the options. You might want to sell electrical goods—machines for industry or appliances for the home. Or, if your hands are as clever as your head, you might want to try making them, or thinking up and patenting something new. And if you're really quick off the mark, you could easily capitalize on the extraordinary growth of the computer industry. (Why not? Your mind works almost as fast as one.) And what about radio? Or televison? Aquarians love to distribute and pass on information. Whether you end up behind or in front of the camera, you'd never be at a loss for something to say, that's for sure.

Science is an ideal sphere to put your mind to work. Water Bearers are often pulled in the direction of astronomy, astro-physics and space research. However, you could easily find yourself drawn to theories that are far out, extreme or new-fangled. If you decide to teach science, learn a lesson from the case of fellow Aquarius Galileo, the Italian mathematician and astronomer who shocked the world by drilling his pupils in the Copernican theory, which stated that the earth revolves around the sun. Of course, now we know it's true, but in 1590 that was dangerous talk! (Leave it to an Aquarius to turn the world upside down.) As a punishment, Galileo was locked up in his home for eight years. That must have been torture for freedom-loving Aquarius, but it's the price you may have to pay when you can't keep your ideas to yourself. There were plenty of outraged people around who would gladly have gagged the Aquarian naturalist Charles Darwin, who put humanity firmly in its place with his doctrine on the evolution of species.

Most Water Bearers have their own views about what makes people tick. If you're interested in the human mind, you may be intrigued enough by psychology to turn it into a successful career, like Aquarius Alfred Adler, the Austrian psychologist who believed a person's value was determined by his or her ability to contribute to 'the higher development of the whole of humanity'. How Aquarian can you get? Which brings us to another point: every Water Bearer is at heart a philosopher—some armchair, some professional. Maybe you never heard of Emmanuel Swedenborg, a famous eighteenth century Aquarius Swedish philosopher and physicist. A religious visionary, he stirred things up, as only an Aquarius can, when he bluntly described in a famous paper on prayer some of his dreams which were explicitly sexual in nature. Aquarius Sir Thomas More was also a philosopher and man of God. In refusing to go all the way with King Henry VIII in his rejection of the Catholic Church, More demonstrated (in true Aquarius fashion) that he was prepared to give up his life before he would give up his beliefs. Another Water Bearer, the philosopher and theologian Martin Buber, took the highly original step of coupling Jewish mysticism with modern psychology. His statements 'All real living is meeting' and 'Man becomes an I through a You' are expressions of the Aquarius belief in the need for individuals to get together and learn from one another's differences.

You don't have to be a psychologist, theologian or philosopher to observe people; you could also be a writer. Water Bearers often love to put their thoughts on paper—it's certainly one channel for their over-active imaginations. The Russian playwright Chekhov is one of the best examples of the Aquarius talent of standing back and acutely observing social inter-actions. But he certainly isn't the only one. The list of successful Aquarius authors is impressive: August Strindberg, Somerset Maugham, Norman Mailer, John Ruskin, Gertrude Stein, Christopher Marlowe, Stendhal, Virginia Woolf, James Joyce (his book *Ulysses* was a real shocker in its time), Lord Byron (whose private life was a public scandal), Lewis Carroll (who but an Aquarius could write a whole book about a girl falling down a rabbit hole?), Sinclair Lewis (the American muck-raker who

exposed the shallowness of middle-class values), and
Jules Verne, the nineteenth century French Aquarius
who had some extraordinarily innovative thoughts on
travel—*Journey to the Centre of the Earth*, *Twenty
Thousand Leagues under the Sea*, and *Around the
World in Eighty Days* are just three of his most famous
books. Did you ever read anything by the daring French
Aquarius who performed at the Folies Bergère and went
on to win the *Légion d'Honneur* for her outstanding
contribution to French literature? Her name was
Colette—creator of such fabulous characters as Clau-
dine, Chéri and Gigi. Speaking of liberated ladies, two
more writers deserve special mention for their role in
ushering in the woman's movement on a mass scale:
Australian Water Bearer Germaine Greer, author of *The
Female Eunuch*, and the outspoken American Aquarius
Betty Friedan, who wrote *The Feminine Mystique*.
Another revolution spearheaded by Aquarius writers is
the sexual one: Havelock Ellis *(Studies in the
Psychology of Sex)*, Helen Gurley Brown *(Sex and the
Single Girl)* and Dr Alex Comfort *(The Joy of Sex)* are
three Aquarius authors who weren't afraid to tackle a
few taboos. (By the way, you can also expect to see
the rules challenged and a few records broken when
Aquarius people turn up on the sports field. Tennis
terror John McEnroe, golf giant Jack Nicklaus, hockey
hitman Wayne Gretzky and swimming star Mark Spitz
are among many Water Bearers who have kept ahead
of the rest.)

But we can't leave the topic of Aquarius writers who
have had an impact on social awareness without
mentioning Charles Dickens, a superb teller of tales
who brought to life the multi-faceted world he knew in
Victorian England. Possibly the most Aquarian of them
all is the Scots poet Robert Burns, whose song '*Auld
Lang Syne*' is sung everywhere people gather together.
The words of this ploughman-poet echo the hope of

every Aquarius, 'That man to man, the warld o'er, Shall brothers be for a' that.'

Burns led an unusual, convention-defying life, yet his sentiments have become a pillar of establishment thinking. Many Aquarius people wear the label of odd-ball rather well. Like rabbits popping out of hats, they show up in the most unpredictable places. Naturally, many of them are drawn to the hectic and erratic world of show business, where they stamp their individuality on all they do. Nobody who has seen the famous film version of Oscar Wilde's *The Importance of Being Earnest* can possibly forget the magnificent, over-the-top portrayal of Lady Bracknell by the immortal Aquarius actress Dame Edith Evans. Eartha Kitt is the lynx-eyed, cosmopolitan star with a wild look and a confrontational performing style that's unmistakably Aquarian. Female Water Bearer Lana Turner, famous for the way she wore sweaters, became infamous when her gangster lover was stabbed to death by her teenage daughter. In later years Miss Turner took on the role of a self-styled guru, and in true Aquarian fashion, she used televison and lecture tours to share her philiosophy of life with millions. Aquarius Vanessa Redgrave has bowled over film and theatre audiences everywhere with her brilliant acting performances and then knocked them for six with her radical political views. Other Aquarius performers who have sent out shock waves in different directions include Tallulah Bankhead, Gypsy Rose Lee, John Hurt, Mia Farrow, Tony Blackburn, Zsa Zsa Gabor and Barry Humphries (alias Dame Edna Everage). Aquarius people are famous for creating ripples of laughter too, for instance Jack Benny, Les Dawson, Carol Channing, Jack Lemmon and Jimmy Durante. Durante certainly was no beauty, but there's often a cool quality to Aquarius men that is irresistibly attractive. Water Bearer heart-throbs Clark Gable, Humphrey Bogart, John Barrymore, Ceser Romero, actor/dancer Mikhail Baryshnikov, John Travolta, Tom

Selleck, Paul Newman (another Aquarius who isn't afraid to air his political opinions), are just a few examples. And let's add one more to the list—James Dean, the most famous rebel of his day, whose good looks and defiant Aquarian behaviour made him an idol for teenagers the world over. Water Bearers show up well in front of the camera, but they also work wonders behind it. D. W. Griffith, Joseph Mankiewicz, Sergei Eisenstein, John Schlesinger, Franco Zeffirelli, François Truffaut, and the outrageous Ken Russell have all impressed the world with their innovative Aquarius style of directing.

Aquarius inspiration has influenced the arts over the centuries. Wolfgang Amadeus Mozart was a precocious Aquarius child who was composing his first symphonies at an age when most of us are still trying to compose our first sentences. Aquarius artist Edouard Manet, considered one of the fathers of modern painting, broke all traditional restraints when he exhibited his famous picnicking nudes and launched the Impressionist Movement in France. In the twentieth century, Aquarius-born Jackson Pollock threw some paint on canvas and became one of the most famous exponents of free expression in modern art. Composers Franz Schubert and Felix Mendelssohn, the immortal Russian ballerina Anna Pavlova, the inspired cellist Jacqueline du Pré, and the acclaimed black opera singer Leontyne Price (honoured with the 1964 Presidential Medal of Freedom) are other Aquarius luminaries in the arts.

Aquarius people are famous for their social conscience, a quality which makes them ideal candidates for those organizations serving to promote a better world. If there's an injustice to be made right or an underdog to be saved, an Aquarius is the one for the job. Any charity, aid appeal or branch of social work would benefit from the kind of help and caring a typical Water Bearer has to give. Those determined to have a wider impact, could try politics, where Water Bearers from all sides of the political spectrum are doing their thing. On the left, there's black activist Angela Davis, one of the few women ever to grace the FBI's ten most wanted list. Move towards the middle and we have the great Aquarius democrat Franklin D. Roosevelt, who offered the American people a New Deal and gave them courage in the midst of war. Keep heading right, and you'll run headlong into Ronald Reagan, the Aquarius who tested his acting ability to its limits when he took on the role of President. He's not your typical Aquarius red activist, but he played a big part in revolutionizing American values by helping to bring conventionality back into fashion again.

If nothing so far has inspired you, it's hard to know what to suggest. Studies show that there are a huge number of Aquarius people working behind bars (saloon bars not prison bars, you understand). Think of all the advantages bartending has to offer: plenty of interesting people to meet, anti-social hours, and always the opportunity for a Water Bearer to serve up a life-saver that's a little stronger than H_2O.

If there's anything totally new under the sun, there's probably an Aquarius somewhere who is already doing it. This sign is well-known for its ability to see into the future. So if the tarot cards speak to you, or if you see messages in tea leaves, coffee grains and crystal balls, why not use your gift and help guide those in need of some direction? Or you could take up astrology, like breakfast-time Aquarian Russell Grant, a leading light among morning stars. True, it's not the newest of professions, but it is an ancient and honourable one.

Aquarius compatibilities

Aquarius/Aries (*Air/Fire*) You like observing people, and you'll never be short of things to look at when a frenetic Aries colleague charges into your life.

Impulsive Rams are full of new ideas, and you'll listen to anybody. Make sure you two sort out the sensible schemes from the crazy ones. Otherwise, there's no telling what the two of you might get up to.

Aquarius/Taurus *(Air/Earth)* Free-wheeling Water Bearers are heading for a collision when they run into the slow-moving Bull. Taurus' conservative and plodding ways can really rile you, but if you want constructive help to make your visions happen, this is the sign to turn to. And something else—when it comes to handling money, the Bull definitely has the lead on you.

Aquarius/Gemini *(Air/Air)* Twins are just as curious about other people as you are. So if it's stimulating conversation you want, or just juicy gossip, it's good to have a Gemini around. Whether a Twin is your colleague or your boss, you couldn't ask for a better friend during or after working hours.

Aquarius/Cancer *(Air/Water)* You'll be fascinated trying to figure out what goes on in a Cancer's mind, and the Crab will be glad to keep you guessing. Cancers feel more than they think, and understanding feelings is not your strong point. Keep working on it, though, and you'll learn more about human nature than any book on the subject can ever teach you.

Aquarius/Leo *(Air/Fire)* There's mutual attraction of opposites here, although the closer you get the trickier it becomes. Leos like to be in charge, but you're not the one to let others tell you what to do. If the Lion isn't willing to play fair, this match could be called off at any time.

Aquarius/Virgo *(Air/Earth)* Expanding other people's minds is your forte, but with a Virgo you'll have your work cut out. Getting Virgins to open up isn't always easy. You'll have plenty of interesting discussions, debates and intellectual skirmishes, and get on each other's nerves a lot—but in the end you'll both be a little wiser for the experience of having known one another.

Aquarius/Libra *(Air/Air)* Most people take a while to figure you out, and some never do. Not so with Libras, who'll know what you're trying to say even before you say it. How refreshing to find someone who actually understands you. You'll like their wit and poise, and the way they so easily appreciate your best qualities. What more could you ask?

Aquarius/Scorpio *(Air/Water)* You're both pretty demanding. The only trouble is that you demand entirely different things. You insist on space and freedom, and possessive Scorpio expects constant loyalty and devotion. There'll be a certain mutual fascination, but getting along is going to be difficult. The odds for this match aren't very good, and after a little while you'll probably give up even trying to make it work.

Aquarius/Sagittarius *(Air/Fire)* Never a dull moment when you two get together, and never a quiet one, either. Easy-going Sagittarius has that same come-what-may attitude to life you go on about so much. So watch out, they may take you up on some of your crazier schemes, and then you both might be headed for disaster. You two know-it-alls won't always see eye to eye, but you'll never remember a time when arguing has been so much fun.

Aquarius/Capricorn *(Air/Earth)* Different strokes for different folks. Conventional Capricorns are not going to be impressed with your eccentricity, so don't even try. The Goat might stifle and restrain you, but a little of that may be just what's needed to make your abstract ideas more practical. Go ahead, argue your point of view as brilliantly as you like—Goats don't budge unless they want to. With you and this sign, it's a case of live and let live.

Aquarius/Aquarius *(Air/Air)* There's a fine line between genius and madness, and deciding whether another Aquarius is one or the other may be a bit tricky. (Now you know what other people go through with you.) If the relationship takes off, the sky is no limit. But with your endless talking, it will be a miracle if any work ever gets done. On the other hand, when Water Bearers team up, the unexpected is always possible.

Aquarius/Pisces *(Air/Water)* One good thing about Pisces people—they won't put the brakes on you. Together, you two visionaries can come up with the wildest schemes of all. Others may laugh, but when has derision ever stopped either of you? Team up and keep dreaming, and one day you both could wake up with millions in the bank.

The Aquarius boss

Aquarius bosses frequently offer an exemplary consideration and respect totally lacking in the more traditional signs. They believe that everyone in this world should get a fair deal, and they'll try to live up to those fine standards. Aquarius bosses don't pull rank—so far as they're concerned, people are people. So whether you clean the office floors or run a multi-national company, you'll find an Aquarius treats everybody the same. If you think they sound too good to be true, just read on.

Aquarius employers are unpredictable, and that's not always the easiest thing to get used to. When they come across a new idea, they're like kids with a new toy. They've never seen anything like it before and they can't talk, think or see anything else. And then one day the toy is discarded. The new system, the dazzling theory or the revolutionary machine is out of favour, and your boss is either staring into space looking lost, or totally absorbed with something different. Aquarius bosses are at their best when things are at their craziest. Stability and too much consistency unnerves them. In the interests of peace and quiet, a wise employee should periodically set fire to the filing system or turn a gorilla loose in the office so that an Aquarius boss never gets too bored, for there's no saying what could happen then.

There are times when making any kind of contact with an Aquarius employer is out of the question—it's like trying to make radio contact with the planet Uranus on a bad reception day. Water Bearers often have a preoccupied look, as if there's something in another room that's more important. They're probably obsessed with what's going on out in the world, and they'll want you to be as well. You may be almost deafened by the quadraphonic blare of radio and televison tuned in to pick up all the news on the latest crisis situation. And before the newscaster has finished talking, you'll have to put up with your Aquarius boss's definitive view of how it ought to be resolved. Get them going on politics, and they might never shut up. Yes, of course this is work; but some things are far more important!

The Aquarius employee

Aquarius people guard their principles like dogs guard a bone. Water Bearers who don't approve of how things are run at work are not about to hang around and put up with it for very long. And if a job gets too monotonous, they don't generally stick in there just for the sake of security. Ross, a fairly typical Aquarius, said it all:

I like to try something different every now and then. I had

never done it before, so I took a job in the rag trade. But I couldn't stand how materialistic my boss was. One night after work I met Joe, who had a band that needed a roadie, so I decided to have a go at that. A few months later, the band broke up. I was on the look out for something else when Jim asked me to work for his travel firm, which organized trips for people with special interests—you know, film buffs to Hollywood, chess freaks to Moscow, Beatle fans to Liverpool, etc. The pay was great, but one day I realized I couldn't deal with trying to meet other people's demands all the time. And I just happened to be thinking, wouldn't it be nice to work with animals for a change, when the phone rang, and it was my friend Alex, who trains dogs. Well, he was at his wit's end because he desperately needed help and he'd decided to call me up out of the blue to ask if I knew anyone who. . . .'

Have you ever heard the word *synchronicity*? It describes those little coincidences that occur sometimes in life. You're sitting there wishing for something, and two minutes later it's there in front of you. It happens to Aquarius people all the time.

Water Bearers, in spite of the name, make lousy slaves. In their eyes, everybody should be treated equally—especially them! Try throwing your weight around with an Aquarius and you're liable to hear a recitation of the Bill of Rights or the Gettysburg Address. So look out if there's a union at work. Your typical Aquarius employee is sure to make use of it in some way. Even Ronald Reagan—not one of the most radical of Aquarius types—was an active union organizer in the days before he got more regular work.

So long as you respect Aquarius employees as people in their own right, and give them plenty of room to do their work in the way they think is best, you'll find them incredibly capable and trustworthy. But don't breathe down their necks. They have their own rhythm and pace of working, and if they promise something, they'll get it done in the end—and always in their own way, not yours.

If you're lucky, you might discover that your Aquarius worker is something of a whiz kid, with a laser-beam mind that can cut though the toughest problem. If you've spent weeks, even months, battling against some difficulty and getting nowhere, try asking an Aquarius employee to cast some new light on the subject. More likely than not, they'll come up with a brilliant solution so blatantly obvious that you kept looking past it. And if morale in the office drops dangerously low, leave it to an Aquarius worker to find the right words to get people motivated again. That's one role Water Bearers won't mind filling—after all, giving speeches is one of their favourite pastimes.

The Aquarius colleague

It won't be hard to recognize which of your co-workers are born under this sign. Just look for the people who are friendly with everyone. The bag lady on the street corner, the security guard on reception, or the vice president on the top floor—your Aquarius workmates are the ones who are on first-name terms with them all.

Being born in the sign that rules electricity makes Water Bearers unshockable. An Aquarius colleague won't give a damn if you come to work wearing eau de Cologne and nothing else. They won't balk if you're so prudish you never look at a table leg, and they can even cope with your allegiance to a different political persuasion to their own. BUT tell them a lie, snub them, insult them in public, or promise to meet them and let them down with no good reason, and you'll see their nasty side. Who turned off the heating? When an Aquarius gives you the cold shoulder, you'll know it—it feels as if an exterminating blast is blowing all the way from Siberia. Aquarius people never blow their tops and get angry. They sulk instead. And their way of sulking is to freeze you out. You may even get the feeling that you have ceased to exist at all.

The good news is that you can get away with doing almost anything to your Aquarius colleague, as long as you're willing to talk about it with them afterwards. So if one day you find you've seriously insulted or offended them, don't attempt to brush it aside or deny it. Talk to them about it. Analyse the situation—what led up to it, what it means to them, what kind of childhood you had and how this has affected the way you are now—and once they can see your point of view, and they have a chance to air their own reactions, they'll forgive and forget. In fact, they're so reasonable, it can drive you crazy.

The person who takes up the collection for needy children, refugees, seals or whales, or who asks you to sign a petition for a cause you're too embarrassed to say you've never even heard of, is your kind-hearted Aquarius colleague who hates to see unfair treatment. And when it comes to arranging little outings to make life more lively for everyone, your Aquarius colleague will be out organizing the block booking at the theatre (you know, the really avant-garde play with obscene language that everybody says should be banned), or the excursion to the tomb of Karl Marx, or even a holiday jaunt to that out-of-the-way spot in the Mojave Desert where a flying saucer was last reported.

You'll never be bored working with an Aquarius co-worker around. How could you, when you never know what to expect next? One day they're so involved in their work, they won't even notice you're alive. The next day they won't leave you alone. They'll want to talk for hours about everything under the sun—especially your private life. Along with Gemini and Scorpio, Aquarius people are the voyeurs of the zodiac. Their curiosity is boundless, and if they can't experience something first-hand, vicarious participation is the next best thing. They like people with imagination and wit. If you invite an Aquarius business colleague to lunch, you're skating on thin ice if you insist on talking about work, the weather or the stock market. You should always stick to thoroughly safe subjects—like sex, religion and politics.

Pisces

Element: Water
Symbol: The Fish
Rulers: Neptune/Jupiter

The Sign of the Fish

Getting to know a person born in any of the water signs isn't easy. Close in on a Cancer, and you'll soon feel the pinch! Snuggle up to a Scorpio, and you might get yourself stung! Fish seem harmless enough (if you ignore the fact that there are a few piranhas in the sign of Pisces). But try grasping what a Pisces person is all about, and you run into big problems. Just when you think you've got them figured out, they slip through your fingers before you can say *taramasalata*. How do Pisces people manage to be so confusing and occasionally infuriating? Don't forget, this sign's symbol is *two* fish swimming in opposite directions—which is very appropriate, considering that Pisces people often don't know whether they're coming or going!

The twelfth sign is a feeling sign. Whether they're aware of it or not, Pisceans are hypersensitive to atmosphere and to what other people are going through. Wherever they happen to be—at home, at work or on a crowded bus—they pick up vibrations like a vacuum cleaner picks up dust and cobwebs. Susceptible Fish have a hard time keeping the world at a distance, which is why they often find themselves in deep water, drowning in their own (or other people's) emotions. They can't say *no* to somebody who needs help, and they end up entangled in all sorts of dramas and messy situations. Ultimately, the main task for Pisces is to find ways to use their sensitivity constructively, rather than be overwhelmed by it. The two sides of the Pisces personality are symbolized by the two fish in the sign. One fish is a victim to life, tossed around on a sea of dilemmas, problems and passions. But the other fish is able to work positively with its strong feeling nature, and use it to make the world a better place.

During the past few decades we've been coming to the end of the Pisces Age, a two-thousand-year period during which the central figure has been Jesus Christ, who called to Peter and Andrew, 'Follow me, and I will make you fishers of men.' He loved the world so much, he sacrificed his own life for the sake of humanity. Many Pisces people are giving and deeply spiritual—they feel they are part of the great divine plan to which they have something to contribute. Equally, they are very theatrical. So when they talk about the many sacrifices in their lives, it can be hard to tell which part of them is speaking—the priest or the performer.

Neptune, the god of the sea

When you stand in front of the ocean, it's easy to be mesmerized by the rhythmic motion of the waves rushing towards you and drawing you away. In relationships, fluid Fish have that same hypnotic effect—their pattern is to come as close as they can and then pull back again. Don't try to figure out why. Just remember that their ruler is Neptune, the mysterious god of the sea.

Neptune's father was Saturn. When Saturn was defeated by his children, Jupiter took the rulership of the Heavens and dominion over the people on earth. Pluto was allotted the dark kingdom of the Underworld. Neptune became the god of all rivers, the seas and the vast oceans. You may have seen him in statues or in drawings on old maps. He's normally surrounded by nymphs and water sprites, holding his trident aloft as the symbol of his enormous power.

The sea god had an extensive kingdom, full of marvellous palaces decorated everywhere in shimmering colours and bright jewels. Neptune loved beautiful things. He accumulated so many he didn't know where to put them all. The floors of his mighty oceans were littered with the glittering treasures of ships he had dragged down to his level. But, like a few Pisces people you may know, Neptune was never satisfied. He always longed for more, for something other than he already had. All his possessions were never enough to make him happy. Likewise, even the richest Fish may find that material wealth and success are not enough to fulfil their deepest needs. The glistening gem or the gold coin beneath the water may turn out to be a worthless old bottletop when you finally take hold of it.

Now and then, the sea god would become so worked up about all the things on earth he wanted and couldn't have that he got completely of hand. When the mood took him, Neptune caused storms, created floods, dried up rivers, split mountains and lured sea travellers to their deaths. (If you've never seen it happen, a word of warning: when the chips are down, Pisces can be a real sea cow!) Fortunately, his brother Jupiter was usually on hand to put the frenzied Neptune back in his place. There are times when all you people born in Pisces feel Neptune's terrible dissatisfaction with life. But when you're thinking about what you really want, face the fact that dreams are dreams. If they're ever going to become a reality, you're the one who's got to make that happen—nobody else can do it for you. And even if you get what you hoped would bring you happiness, you might discover that it isn't quite as fulfilling as you thought it would be. Ultimately, the kind of peace and total fulfilment you might be seeking through a relationship, a job, or a big bank balance, can only be found within yourself. As the great master of the Pisces age himself reminded the world, the kingdom of heaven is in you.

For better or for worse, Jupiter shares the rulership of the sign. (He's much better known as the ruler of Sagittarius, but before Neptune was discovered last century, he had custody of Pisces as well.) When Jupiter, the consummate actor and role-player of the zodiac, joins forces with impressionable and romantic Neptune, melodrama often gets the upper hand. Many Pisces people have an impressive and natural acting talent, but unfortunately they don't all go on the stage. Instead, they use their acting abilities to play whatever role comes their way in life. Fish don't have a strong sense of their own identity, so they're often more than willing to take their cues from other people. Which may leave you wondering who they really are—a question most Pisces people are always asking themselves.

The Pisces temperament

When you reach the twelfth sign, the circle of the zodiac is complete. In the mystical domain of Pisces you discover that every human being, every animal, plant and object is somehow part of everything else. Like the sea, which gradually eats away at the land around it, the planet Neptune dissolves the boundaries between things. Watery Pisces is a sign where the differences between you and everything else around you become vague and fuzzy. Sounds and colours, feelings and faces, time and distance all merge and flow together in the inner world of a Fish. Good becomes bad, bad becomes good. Something that looks wonderful can turn out terrible, and the most awful prospect can be all right in the end. No wonder you Pisces people are often a bit confused—but not half as flummoxed as the rest of us who are trying to figure you out!

Emotionally, some Fish resemble chameleons—they change from red to blue to green, depending on where they are. A Pisces friend rings you up. Rummaging through the mess in her top drawer, she has just come across your photo and she had to ring you up to let you know how very much she cares for you. Of course, when you run into her three days later, she'll probably be so taken up with somebody else, she'll virtually have forgotten who you are. Pisces people have an uncanny ability to experience every known emotion in the human repertoire (and a few more besides) in less time than it takes to boil an egg. To muddle you even more, when they're uncertain about what to say next, they resort to their charming but maddening habit of telling you what they think you want to hear. Never mind what they really feel, it's what you need to hear that counts. With their remarkable gift for tuning into other people, they can read your mind from ten miles away. That's why your Pisces lover (with a little help from Oscar-winning Jupiter) may seem like the man or woman of your dreams—the perfect mate who knows you better than anyone else, the ideal lover you've always wished for.

Pisceans are often very seductive people. But when they go fishing for love or companionship, some of them lack discrimination. Unfortunately, it's far easier to throw back a wrong-sized fish than to reject a demanding friend or discard a difficult lover. That's the kind of awkward situation Pisces people frequently have to deal with. Even with their extraordinary understanding of others and their ability to sense trouble a mile ahead, they still end up in tight corners and terrible relationships—mainly because it's easier for them to say Yes to somebody than it is to say No. Born under a sign where everything is always changing into everything else, some Fish would say that whatever happens, it doesn't make much difference anyway.

Neptune blesses all Fish with vivid imaginations, and the first task for every Pisces is to learn to differentiate between fantasy and reality. Feelings are fine, but sometimes they can get in the way of seeing what is really going on. Gerry is a Pisces who came along to have an astrological consultation and find out why life had been treating him so badly:

Why are women so terrible? They always take advantage of me. I'm going out with somebody new at the moment. I've been so good to her—I even gave her a coat for Christmas that cost me nearly £1,000. But I know for a fact she's seeing somebody else, although she denies it when I ask her. What have I done to deserve that kind of treatment?

Gerry recited a catalogue of romantic misadventures that sounded worse than the plot of a day-time soap opera. And in each episode it was always a woman who was the villain. Helen, Gloria, Janice, or Eileen—they were all treacherous and cold. Rather like the motorist who said he couldn't take responsibility for hitting the other car because he was asleep at the wheel when the accident happened, Gerry was totally blind to the part he played in creating his own disasters. The real problem was that he only went for women who were unattainable. If a woman showed any affection or interest in him, he wasn't the least bit interested in her. But if she was otherwise engaged or impossible to get, then he was after her like a shot. Eventually, Gerry began to see that he brought about his own problems by acting this way. Acknowledging how his behaviour contributed to his trouble was the first step towards changing the very messy script he had been following. He could no longer get away with blaming women all the time.

Even though some Pisceans can be pretty masterful people, you'll frequently find them taking on the role of somebody's slave. In terms of human rights, that may sound like a somewhat negative statement. Nonetheless Pisces people seem happiest when they have a chance to give themselves wholeheartedly to a person or a cause. Without an object of devotion, the Fish is often adrift in a sea of self-pity and apathy. But when Pisces people discover a sense of purpose in life—it may be through a

relationship, a job, a religious calling or a philosophy—
they can achieve almost anything. Those who manage
to get their lives together are an entirely different kettle
of Fish to those who find it a challenge even to open
one eye in the morning! It's amazing how the same sign
can produce brilliant organizers and business people,
great artists and inspired visionaries on the one hand,
and victims, losers and dropouts on the other.

To understand why this is, you have to remember
that unless Pisceans find a way to use their sensitivity
constructively, it can cause them a lot of misery and
hardship. Most of them suffer from bouts of 'divine
homesickness'. They have a vague memory—an image
in their minds—of some place where everything was
beautiful and harmonious, where there wasn't all the
pain and suffering they see now in the world around
them. They take one look at the real world and wish
they didn't have to be here at all. Fish can become
escapists and dreamers, people who aren't able to cope
with the harsher realities of everyday life. Some can't
even walk down the street without feeling exposed and
vulnerable. They may be drawn to drugs and alcohol
as a way of quelling their sense of isolation and despair.

But there are other Pisces people who turn their divine
homesickness into a challenge. Rather than letting life
get them down, they take their vision of a better world
and try to make it happen right here on earth. They're
the ones who fight for justice, who want to ease the
plight of the underdog and the downtrodden, who set
out to make the world a happier and more beautiful
place. Even when they're children, Pisceans don't enjoy
cowboys and Indians half as much as a game of victims
and saviours. This early talent for rescuing others can
be a habit which stays with them for life. And when
they're not playing saviour, they'll take on the victim
role and look for somebody to rescue *them*.

Let's not deny that Pisceans often have a genuine
healing ability, and they're usually willing to go out of

their way to do favours for people in need. They'll travel across town in rush hour to water your plants when you're away; they'll take time off work to nurse you when you're sick; and they'll give you their last penny when you're really hard up. But the man who rips the shirt off his back to keep somebody else warm is going to wonder why *he* feels cold all of a sudden. None of us is so fulfilled that we don't have to think about ourselves now and again. Wanting to help other people has its merits, but don't forget that Pisces rules the feet. If you really want to save the world, keep yours firmly on the ground.

Pisces types

Pisceans born between 19 February and 29 February When it comes to caring for others, you'll do anything for those you love, even when it means putting yourself second. But you'll be lost if you can't find some way to put your artistic and sensitive nature to good use. Don't underestimate your own abilities—get out there and show the world what you can do.

Pisceans born between 1 March and 10 March Mothering people is fine, but smothering them is too close for comfort. Nobody could ask for a more loyal and considerate friend, even if you are a bit moody and irascible now and then. Overcome your shyness and try getting around more—it will do you good to spread your wings and broaden your perspective on life.

Pisceans born between 11 March and 20 March Intense and secretive, you're definitely not a Fish to toy with. Sometimes you're soft as cotton, other times you're hard as nails—even your closest friends won't be able to figure you out. It's true, there are times when life gets you down, but you'll always find a reason to bob up again.

Pisces and work

Come on, Pisces, stop putting yourself down. You'd get a lot farther in life if you had a little more confidence in your abilities. When it comes to work, one of your biggest problems is your lack of faith in yourself. With your innately sensitive and creative nature, there is so much you could achieve. So why do most of you Fish insist on devaluing yourselves?

Could it be that you're afraid of commitment? You keep going on about how you'd really like something to throw yourself into, but when it comes to taking action, you're always looking for the catch. Admit it, you're pretty good at finding ways to wriggle out of being pinned down. And isn't it true that one of your greatest fears is that of failure? By denying you have any real talents, you escape taking responsibility for them. How clever you are!

But why face reality, when you can spend all your life dreaming about how wonderful you could be? Yesterday you imagined what it will be like when your record makes it to number one; today you were rehearsing your acceptance speech at the Academy Awards ceremony; tomorrow who knows?—you might be the unstoppable player who scores the goal that wins the World Cup. Realism has never been your strong point. Stop fantasizing so much and put that energy into doing something practical to develop the skills and abilities you really have.

Some Fish lead charmed lives—almost by accident, they get where they would like to be. Paul is a good example. A school dropout, he took a job delivering pizzas. A few weeks later, he crashed his bike, and didn't have enough money to get it fixed. A friend offered him some part-time decorating work. One day Paul mentioned to a customer that he really wanted to paint pictures. The woman challenged him to try painting a mural in the hall, and he did it so well that it's now his full-time career. Paul used to walk around slouched over and apathetic about everything, but now he's successful, he stands tall and proud. Finding the right job can really give a Pisces a whole new outlook on life.

Cinderella must have been a Pisces. You'll often find Fish slaving away from dawn to dusk in order to support an ailing mother, or doing two jobs to keep an alcoholic partner who gambles away the mortgage. Many people feel flattened by heavy times, but it often takes a crisis to make a Pisces shape up. Ilse, a Danish Pisces woman, left home at eighteen to marry a man her parents disapproved of. She and her husband travelled to Africa, where he had inherited a derelict farm. A few years later, during a local war, they were completely burnt out; overnight they had lost everything they had worked so hard to build. They had to flee the country with their three small children and, on the way home, Ilse's husband became very ill and died. She was suddenly alone with the children, no money, no friends, and nowhere to live. Back in Denmark, she scraped together enough to rent a small house, and with the little money she earned from the chickens and goats she kept, she started her first small business. Within ten years she became a very wealthy woman. When their backs are up against the wall, that's when you see what Pisces people can really do. Never underestimate a Fish.

In the end, indecision and a lack of willpower and confidence are the main problems for most Pisces people in the sphere of work. If only they believed in themselves more and were better able to focus their energy, they could make a success of their lives. If you're an insecure Pisces baffled by choice, try the following exercise. It will help to clarify your goals and give you a boost in getting where you want to go.

1. Imagine you are the captain of a ship. You are at sea in the middle of a storm, but there is a lighthouse ahead of

you. The lighthouse is solid and unshakable, illuminating your way ahead. Concentrate on the lighthouse, and imagine yourself successfully steering your ship to it. No matter how rough the seas are, you safely reach your goal. If at first you don't succeed, keep repeating this scene in your head until you do.

2. Now decide on a realistic goal you would like to achieve in terms of work. Don't let indecision or hesitation get the better of you. Even if you feel confused or uncertain, decide *right now* one thing you would like to do or accomplish in the area of your career. It's time to be firm with yourself, Pisces.

3. Now imagine yourself manoeuvring towards your goal, and all the steps you might need to take to get there. Picture yourself overcoming any obstacles in your way, and achieving your goal.

4. Within the next two days, do something to begin to make your goal a reality. Every time uncertainty or lack of confidence takes over, repeat the part of this exercise where you imagine yourself successfully steering your ship to the lighthouse.

Pisces careers

If you're a Pisces, life is beautiful . . . and if it isn't, it's time you did something about it. You love things that are out of this world, so why not try seeing it from a different angle, like Russian Pisces Yuri Gagarin, the first man to orbit the earth. But until the first moon shuttle is operational, it might be more practical to make a career in astronomy like Copernicus, the Polish Pisces who advanced the theory that the earth moves round the sun. Keen to read more? Why not get yourself a copy of *De Revolutionibus Orbium Coelestium Libri VI*, published first in 1543? If you think that's baffling, what would you make of *Zur Elektrodynamik Bewegter Körper*? Better known as the Theory of Relativity, it's the work of a Nobel Prize-Winner, the Pisces physicist Albert Einstein. At the age of twelve he made the decision to devote his life to the riddle of the 'huge world' he saw about him. Maybe, like Einstein, you have an unconventional intelligence concealing not only true genius but also a deep Pisces concern with the welfare of humanity. He was not speaking just as a scientist when he wrote these words:

A human being is part of the whole, called by us 'Universe', a part limited in time and place. . . . Our task must be to free ourselves from this prison by widening our circle of compassion to embrace all living creatures and the world of nature in its beauty.

But if physics isn't your idea of heaven, you could always try painting something that is. Michelangelo was a Pisces who did just that. True, there aren't as many demands for chapel ceilings today as there were in 1500, but art does offer an infinite variety of commercial possibilities. Someone once said that art is one per cent inspiration and ninety-nine per cent perspiration—just as well you're a water sign. It's a tough field with very little remuneration until you get established, but we've never met a Pisces yet who didn't enjoy having to make some sacrifices now and then. At least, nowadays the world is more responsive to the talents of young artists than ever before. It's incredible to think that one hundred years ago the Impressionists were still being considered talentless and tasteless. Renoir was typical of great Pisces artists—selflessly dedicated to his art. When arthritis crippled his hands in old age, he asked that his brushes be taped to his fingers. What would he say now if he saw his pictures decorating chocolate boxes?

It only goes to prove that taste and beauty lie in the eye of the beholder. Adolf Eichmann's Pisces picture of an ideal world was one without any Jews. Known as the Executioner in Hitler's Third Reich, Eichmann was directly responsible for the transportation and extermination of millions of Jewish people. Which proves that a Pisces taken over by a strong vision will go to any lengths to see it come true. Mikhail Gorbachov is a Russian Pisces. During his time as leader of the Soviet Union, arms control has taken several steps forward, offering at least the illusion of a more secure future. His *glasnost*, the relaxation of the traditional Soviet rigidity, is helping to open up the Iron Curtain which has divided Europe for over forty years. But fifty years ago, when another Pisces tried a gesture of appeasement, it was a bad move. Neville Chamberlain was the British Prime Minister who thought he could make an honourable settlement with the Nazis.

Wouldn't it be wonderful if people all over the world could communicate better? You'll often hear it said, but few people do very much about it. A Pisces concerned with bringing young people together was Lord Baden-Powell, who inaugurated the Boy Scout movement. When we're talking about Pisces communicators, one name that rings out loud and clear is that of Alexander Graham Bell. Nobody ever said a more momentous 'hello' than he did in 1876, the year he invented the telephone. Bell started out as a teacher of the deaf. Rudolf Steiner was another compassionate Pisces who started out with the belief that people need to rise above their preoccupation with the world of matter by being more spiritually involved. He had many theories on the subject, but he was a man of action. He set up special education centres where drama, dance, music and eurythmics (the art of rhythmic movement) were taught to expand the consciousness of his students. He also encouraged the development of work with people who had profound learning difficulties.

Today this is very much a Pisces field, particularly at a time when more and more mentally and physically handicapped people are being released from incarceration in hospitals and encouraged to make a place for themselves in the world. You'll find Pisces people involved everywhere in the caring professions, as doctors and nurses, or as workers in psychiatric centres,

where their ability to relate to those who are confused
is second to none. They can also deal sensitively with
people in prison, or with those suffering from drug or
alcohol problems. And if you're a Pisces, you could be
of great service in community work programmes,
helping the cause of immigrant populations, the elderly,
the housebound, and anyone in need of sympathetic
representation and support.

A spiritual career is always a possibility for a Pisces
with a calling. David Livingstone heard his, and became
a missionary. He wanted to go to China, but finished
up in Africa, where, in spite of his zealous convictions,
he made only one known convert. Nonetheless, he did
everything in his power to fight the inhumane slave
trade of the Boers and the Portuguese, and in his explo-
rations he made an immense contribution to the
geographic, scientific and cultural knowledge of an area
uncharted and unseen by any white man. He died at
prayer. The influence of prayer and meditation on the
world's problems shouldn't be scorned or taken lightly.
Many Pisces people find fulfilment joining spiritual
organizations or taking holy orders. But if you don't
think you could get into the habit, you could always
design yourself something different. 'Poor little rich girl'
Gloria Vanderbilt used her Piscean talents to create a
line of jeans which sells over ten million pairs per
annum. Clever Fish with an eye for fashion design could
find their pockets bulging as well. Image-making is a
lucrative business—just ask any successful Pisces
photographer, model or public relations and advertising
wizard.

Money makes the world go round, but where would
it be without music? If you're rhythmic Fish who can
toot a flute, twiddle a fiddle, harp on forever, or whistle
a happy tune, why not make music your career? The
watery sign of Pisces is overflowing with famous
musicians and composers. There's Handel, a German-
born composer of Baroque music who found his fame

in England. (How fitting for a Pisces that one of his best-known works is his *Water Music*.) If you like a busy tune to set your feet tapping, you'll probably enjoy the spirited comic operas of Gioacchino Rossini, the Italian Pisces who set the very Fishy tale of Cinderella to music. For a quick trip into fantasy, allow Russian Pisces Rimsky-Korsakov to transport you with his mesmeric *Scheherazade*, or be entranced by the hypnotic rhythm of *Boléro*, created by *Poisson* composer Maurice Ravel. If you love the sad gentle ripple of a piano nocturne, you'll find it hard to resist the works of Polish-born Pisces Frédéric Chopin, famous almost as much for his tempestuous love affair with George Sand. And while you're in the mood, how about a boogie to the big-band sound of Glenn Miller, a musical Fish who got them going on both sides of the Atlantic? The world of popular music would be a whole lot poorer without the contributions of high-fidelity Pisces Nat King Cole, Quincy Jones, Fats Domino, Nina Simone and Harry Belafonte. And music lovers will always value the great golden arias of Enrico Caruso and the silvery sound of kiwi cantatrice Kiri Te Kanawa.

Even if you can't hit those high notes yourself, you could always be of service to people who do. Music is big business today. You could act as a musical agent, make musical instruments or work in a record shop selling the sound of music to the world. If you aren't up to performing, you might want to share your love of music through teaching it. And there are recording studios all over the place nowadays, where more technically minded Fish stand a good chance of landing on their Pisces-ruled feet.

How are you on your toes? Perhaps it's time you tidied up your entrechat, checked your fouetté and leapt into your leotard to practise all your ballet steps. Rudolf Nureyev and Vaslaw Nijinsky are two famous examples of Pisces dancers. Or kick your way around the football stadium like Scottish Pisces Kenny Dalglish. But if you

don't think your feet are up to it, you could do a lot
worse than step into the very lucrative shoe business—
unless you'd feel too much of a heel to enjoy all the
money you might make. Or, if you really care about
feet, your Pisces healing ability would serve you well
in a career in chiropody, foot massage or reflexology,
soothing away the pain and strain of living.

Pisces people know what it feels like to stand in
somebody else's shoes. Which not only makes them
great humanitarians, but great actors and actresses as
well. (Even if you don't want to be on stage or in front
of the camera, you still could find your niche as a
theatre, television, radio or film director or producer—
like David Puttnam, celebrated for *The Killing Fields*—or
as a set or costume designer, lighting expert or make-
up artist.) But if you're a budding Pisces thespian,
instead of acting shy, start acting ambitious and see
how quickly you can get into the business. One of the
most celebrated actors of all time, Edmund Kean, was
born in Pisces. (Kean was once described by a critic
as 'giving the illusion of *being* rather than *playing* a
character'.) Pisces people are everybody's notion of
what a star should be. The most classic example is the
unsinkable Elizabeth Taylor, whose numerous
marriages prove there are always plenty more fish in
the sea. And no cabaret act can ever compare with Sally
Bowles as played by ebullient Liza Minnelli, another
Pisces whose life has had its ups and downs. Other
famous fish include Jean Harlow, the screen's very first
platinum Pisces; the handsome black actor Sidney
Poitier, who helped to dissolve the race barrier in his
profession; frightfully Piscean Brits Michael Redgrave,
David Niven and Rex Harrison; Patrick Duffy (alias
Bobby Ewing) and Tyne Daly (Mary Beth of *Cagney
and Lacey*); Hollywood Cockney Michael Caine; the
extraordinary Miss Julie Walters; 'Moonlighting' Bruce
Willis; and Jennifer Jones, a star of Hollywood's
heyday, best remembered as the romantic heroine in a

very Piscean picture called *Love is a Many-Splendoured Thing*.

Love is also a favourite Pisces preoccupation. Many Pisceans are in love with love—a fatal illness indeed. You'd be following in honourable Pisces footsteps if you write of love like the Roman poet Ovid, or along the lines of Elizabeth Barratt Browning, whose life had every Pisces ingredient imaginable. Injured after a fall at the age of fifteen, she was forced to remain at home under the watchful eye of her tyrannical father. Her saviour was the poet Robert Browning, who took her away with him to Italy. Living up to Pisces' romantic image, she is most famous for her love poems. In later life she went in for spiritualism and the occult, something else which doesn't exactly make her unique among Pisces people. A Neptunian imagination is often the door to other worlds, and many Fish have a strongly psychic side to their natures. So if you keep hearing things go bump in the night, and you've checked the house for mice, maybe an exciting career is starting to manifest itself for you.

Love isn't the only thing literary Fish write about. Human suffering is also pretty high on their list of favourite topics. The French Pisces Victor Hugo wrote of wretched poverty and social injustice in two of his great novels, *The Hunchback of Notre Dame* and *Les Miserables*. And Nobel Prize-winning Pisces writer John Steinbeck scored his first great triumph with *The Grapes of Wrath*, a moving study of the misery of the Depression that could leave you in a flood of tears.

We can't talk about Pisces careers without mentioning water. If you don't want to sail the seas and rivers, you could choose to live nearby and cater for the millions of people who do. Cruise holidays are big business—you may not be able to afford to go on one, but you might want to work for a company that sets them up for those who can. And what about a career with boats—sailing them, selling them or, if you're really crafty, making them? Water is nice, but Fish often prefer something with a little more spirit. You will feel right at home behind a bar—what better place to develop your skills as a psychologist and counsellor? When you get fed up with other people's problems, you could always go fishing for the day or for a living. Or, should you prefer your fish dead on arrival, there's a fortune to be made in importing caviar. And if you discover that you're good at smelling something fishy, you might as well set up your own private detective agency while you're at it.

Pisces compatibilities

Pisces/Aries *(Water/Fire)* If you're looking for someone to take charge of your affairs, Aries will be glad to do the job. The only problem is that Rams don't just take charge, they take over—so make sure you really want to go where they're so intent on leading you. Fasten your seat belts, you're in for a bumpy ride, but one that could bring new sparkle to your working life.

Pisces/Taurus *(Water/Earth)* The Bull has a steadying and calming effect on you, and that's something a Fish needs more of. Yes, they may be slow to take up your new ideas, but if you bring up something worthwhile, they'll eventually come around. You've got the vision, they've got the common sense. Team up—you won't get rich quick, but when the rewards do come, you won't be sorry.

Pisces/Gemini *(Water/Air)* Geminis will give you plenty to think about, but when it's emotional understanding you need, we suggest you try elsewhere. Hold on, don't write this sign off entirely—especially when you feel like some interesting and lively conversation. Just make sure you listen carefully: when a Gemini and

Pisces start nattering away like there's no tomorrow, one of you is liable to get your wires crossed.

Pisces/Cancer *(Water/Water)* Birds of a feather flock together. Okay, so one of you is a Fish and the other's a Crab, but the saying still fits. There's a mutual attraction here, even though you'll have your ups and downs. What else can you expect when you link up with a sign that's as moody as you are? It's worth it, though—come hell or high water, you couldn't ask for a more devoted friend.

Pisces/Leo *(Water/Fire)* It's just as well you couldn't care less about being leader of the pack, because Lions are not the sort to ride pillion behind anyone—especially a Fish. Play by their rules, and a big-hearted Leo will never let you down. Just make sure you don't forget to tell them how much you appreciate them . . . every few hours, if possible.

Pisces/Virgo *(Water/Earth)* There's a lot in favour of joining forces with a Virgo. They'll find solutions to problems you wouldn't have a clue how to solve, and they're willing to take on even the most menial task. (How nice to have someone else do those for a change.) So what if they criticize you from time to time? You probably could do with it. In the end, you can always count on Virgos being realistic, steadfast and reliable—in fact, they're everything that you're not.

Pisces/Libra *(Water/Air)* Libras won't try to dominate you like an Aries or a Leo would, but they do have a way of coercing you into doing what they want. So long as you keep on your toes and pull your weight, this is a good combination—especially in careers involving the arts. And if after working hours you want to have a good time, the two of you are bound to come up with something.

Pisces/Scorpio *(Water/Water)* A lot of people have a hard time figuring you out, but an incisive Scorpio will see right through you. If you can bear the exposure and the occasional sting, there's a lot you can learn from this sign. Let's face it, you can be a bit wishy-washy at times. Scorpios are tough and single-minded—hang around with them a while, and maybe a little of their determination will rub off on you.

Pisces/Sagittarius *(Water/Fire)* Enjoy them when they're around, because tomorrow you may not see them for dust. Still it's worth the ride—what other sign can take you the kinds of places a Sagittarius can? And on those days when you feel as if you're drowning, the Archer's energy and optimism will always buoy you up. Just don't get too clingy, that's all.

Pisces/Capricorn *(Water/Earth)* Don't be fooled by the Goat's tough exterior and practical, determined nature. Underneath, they're as sensitive to things around them as you are. What's more, they can spot your potential a mile away. You could do with a good kick now and then. Listen to what the Goat has to say, and you'll achieve more in life than you ever thought you could.

Pisces/Aquarius *(Water/Air)* Fish can be influenced by anyone, but when it's by an Aquarius, the sky's the limit. The only real problem is that neither of you is very down-to-earth. You're the original space cadets, and without a more practical person to help you out, your schemes don't have much chance of getting off the ground.

Pisces/Pisces *(Water/Water)* Two Fish in the same tank isn't a bad thing, but unless you share some common interests, you could drift by one another and never really meet. If you want to break the ice, have lunch together. One drink, and you'll get along swimmingly; two or three more, and there's no telling where you'll end up.

The Pisces boss

Pisces, the last sign of the zodiac, contains a little of all the other signs in it. This doesn't make Pisces bosses the easiest of people to fathom: one day they're practical and cautious, like a typical Taurus or Capricorn; the next they're more zany and unconventional than even the most Uranian of Aquarius people. But underneath they're still a Pisces, which means they're sensitive, considerate, sometimes vague, and a bit forgetful.

Chaos might be the best word to describe what goes on in your Pisces boss's head. Although they try to hide it, some Fish are downright dizzy. Even the most methodical of the shoal still manage to draw confusion into their working lives by employing staff who are disorganized or somehow unsuitable for the job involved. It's not that Pisces bosses are stupid, it's just that they can't resist trying to help out a lame duck or ne'er-do'well.

Giving someone the sack can be a real heartache for them. They'll dance around the subject for years while an incompetent employee drains the business dry or makes the atmosphere at work impossible for the rest of the staff. Henry, a Pisces in charge of a small advertising agency, has a problem like that—he just can't bring himself to fire his secretary:

I don't even know why I hired Susan—she types badly and is a lousy speller. Everybody tells me I ought to get rid of her, but how can I? Somebody has got to give her a chance. Maybe she'll get better. Besides, she's had such a hard time in life, and I'm sure she won't be able to land a decent job anywhere else.

Of course, really shrewd Pisces bosses aren't nearly so

charitable. In big business, sometimes even feeling Fish can turn out to be sharks: Look at Pisces communications magnate Rupert Murdoch. Some people have hailed him as the saviour of an industry which was badly in need of an overhauling. Others see him as an artist who has brought new colour and sensation to the popular press. But there are others again who would point to the high toll in redundancies and the standards of reporting under his regime, and call him names not fit to print.

They don't talk about drinking like a Fish for nothing. Pisces bosses under a lot of pressure turn to alcohol as a way of alleviating tension. If they're not careful, they could end up like Ann, the head of an art firm. She worked around the corner from a friend, and every lunch hour they would head for the local wine bar. Ann wasn't used to being in charge at work, and couldn't get over the fact that nobody was standing by her with a stopwatch. Lunches got longer and longer, and she found herself drinking more and more. One day, having had one over the eight (or was it ten?), she fell over the carpet in front of her most important customer. That was the day she realized she had gone too far.

The Pisces employee

If they're happy in their work, Pisces people are dedicated and devoted employees who'll be an asset to all around. But in a job they don't like, they can be pretty miserable. Many Fish live a life of fantasy, helped in some cases by a steady diet of colourful fiction and romantic cinema. It's a blow for them to discover that their first boss looks more like Mickey Mouse than Mickey Rourke, or that their first big assignment offers as much excitement and challenge as opening a packet of cornflakes. To a Pisces with high expectations, after a few weeks even the most promising job in the world can seem just like all the rest. If only real life was like the movies, Pisces all over the world would be a much happier lot.

Of course, when the job is really boring, the Pisces employee is capable of finding imaginative ways to liven things up. Max, a March-born Fish, worked as a clothing salesman for nearly a year (not bad going for a fickle Fish). He very quickly hated the job—but that was when the enjoyment started. Sometimes, for a laugh, he would climb into the shop window and stick a price tag on his jacket, pretending to be one of the mannequins. Like many Pisces people, Max was such a convincing dummy, people passing by on the street didn't even notice he wasn't the real thing.

Maybe we're being a bit hard on Pisces, but they do have an amazing ability to blend in with their working surroundings. If the mood of the office is festive and lively, the Pisces employee will fit right in and be the life of the party. If their working environment is dull and dreary, they'll begin to look that way themselves—if they stick around long enough, that is.

It's true that Pisces employees are generally sincere (remember Pisces President George Washington, who never told a lie?), but what goes on deep inside the soul of a Pisces is always something of a mystery. When the situation or environment they're in changes, their whole personality is liable to change as well. They usually mean what they say, but it may only be true for as long as it takes them to get to the end of the sentence. One minute they're telling everyone how awful they feel, and then seconds later they're at the other end of the room laughing their heads off. For a Pisces, the distance between misery and ecstasy is a fraction of a centimetre. So when your Pisces employee insists he or she is happy, just count up to ten and watch to see what happens next.

The Pisces colleague

Remember Patricia Hearst? She's the American heiress who was kidnapped by the Symbionese Liberation Army, a terrorist organisation. Maybe she struggled at first to be free of her captors, but that didn't last for long. Within a short time she joined in the action and eventually was arrested taking part in a bank robbery to help swell their funds. Needless to say, Patty is a Pisces.

Your colleagues born under the sign of the Fish can be easily brainwashed. At the very least, they have to admit they're pretty impressionable—which isn't always such a bad thing. Having someone around who'll always agree with you is a lot of people's image of an ideal working partner. Pisces co-workers also make good scapegoats. When the coffee machine breaks down or the photocopier goes on the blink, the easiest thing to do is to blame the nearest Pisces. Some Fish are willing victims—they seem happy to spend their entire lives nailed to a cross. Observe Pisces people at work for a while, and you'll soon see they're full of contradictions. If somebody is being mistreated, a Pisces co-worker will do whatever he or she can to defend that person. They'll even risk losing their jobs to fight someone else's cause. But when it comes to standing up for themselves, that's where Fish really fall down.

Unless they're battling for other people's rights, Pisces men and women have a lot of trouble asserting themselves directly. They'll agree with everything you say, and then grumble away behind your back like a faulty water heater—although when they do muster up the courage to speak out, you may be surprised to find out just how scalding they can be! But no matter how badly anyone might have treated them, if someone's in a crisis, Pisces people are there to help out any way they can. And unlike a typical Leo or Cancer, they won't expect anything in return. If there's one thing they excel at, it's being a martyr.

It's a very rare Pisces who doesn't have time for fellow workers. When it comes to going out of their way for others, or healing a bad row between two feuding catfish in the office pool, they live up to everything their sensitive sign promises. A working crew could do a lot worse than having a Pisces on board.